ISSUES IN POLICING
New Perspectives

ISSUES IN POLICING
New Perspectives

Edited By

John W. Bizzack

ℋ autumn house publishing
Criminal Justice Series
Lexington, Kentucky

Published and Distributed Throughout the United States by

ℬ™ **autumn house publishing**
Post Office Box 1080
Lexington, Kentucky 40588-1080

Issues in Policing: New Perspectives

© autumn house publishing
ISBN 0-9630 878-9-4
Library of Congress Catalog Number: 91-078108

Manufactured in the United States of America

INTRODUCTION

As this century comes to a close, police leadership in this country will be made up largely from the ranks of those who took part in the renaissance of American policing that occurred in the late 1960s and in the 1970s. Policing has made incredible advances and remarkable transformations over the past two decades because it finally grasped the necessity of taking a long, hard, critical look at itself. The country was changing during that period, and policing was swept into the changes. Research, education and planning had at last found their way into the world of law enforcement.

A movement to professionalize policing that grew out of this period helped to seed and galvanize a field that is at best fragmented and segregated by varying community ideals, politics, geographics and life-styles. It's been an exciting period for policing. Ideas from those who led the renaissance as well as their students who are now leaders and spokespersons in the field are and will continue to be showcased in the 1990s.

Serious students of policing will recognize many of the authors who contributed chapters for this book. Works like these continue to serve as one of the cornerstones for progress in policing. They represent new perspectives that influence and provoke further thinking in this field and serve as literature upon which future students of policing may base views and positions. Each contributor has drawn on their unique insight and a multitude of experience about the subject and issues on which they have written.

The principal purpose of *Issues in Policing: New Perspectives* is to provide police executives, other command officers, practitioners, educators, researchers, writers, administrators in the field, students and public officials with a fresh view on new and some old issues. These issues will always be controversial and subject to debate. Hopefully this book will further contribute to the awakening of leadership and research in American policing.

John W. Bizzack
Lexington, Kentucky

PREFACE

The sixteen chapters in this book reflect perspectives from eighteen contributors whose views represent a breadth of range, experience and education. No central theme was selected for this work. Instead, various issues pertinent to American policing were singled out for exploration by these widely respected practitioners, researchers and educators.

Interestingly, one theme has emerged and each chapter is speckled with its undercurrent. The theme that binds this work may be described as a call for *effective leadership*.

In the first chapter, **Bizzack** calls for a philosophical autopsy of American policing in order to more accurately draw the necessary road maps for law enforcement to follow in its quest to professionalize. This chapter underscores the growing consensus that police leadership must become professional before police service stands a chance.

Dodenhoff follows up on this summons by firmly carving away layers of the hackneyed military models and metaphors of policing. He poignantly shores up the reasons why the quasi-military model cannot provide quality policing in the future.

The values and ethics elucidated by **Behan** in Chapter Three once again demonstrates the workability of his contention that leaders should not run their organizations by rules or procedures manuals, but by policies and philosophies.

In *The Blue Milieu*, **Thibault** reminds that while the police military bureaucracy *is* becoming more flexible, the police bureaucracy *is not*. His examination of the police subculture should put to rest any notion that in the future effective leaders will only need to deal with organizational mechanics.

How can we balance respect for truth and fairness with our powerful concern for public safety? **Skolnick** and **Leo** audit this crucial issue in their examination of deceptive interrogation practices.

Law enforcement accreditation has been embraced, but not too tightly, by American policing. **Oettmeier** asks the purpose of accreditation. He then supplies a reformulation of intent upon which a new platform for this worthy management tool might actually lend itself to the work of community-oriented police agencies.

Murphy emphasizes that police must understand their role in society in order to efficiently provide its services. He outlines a plan through which agencies can organize for community policing and encourages conventional wisdom to be challenged by leaders looking to yield the full potential of community policing.

With keen alertness, **Bouza** and **Sherman** persuasively profile arguments for reform. Their overview underpins the fact that police leaders can handle just so many issues at one time or during their short tenures, and the importance of selecting the right issue to handle.

Gallagher assembles a logical answer to a major problem in his systematic approach to managing liability. His views aptly conclude that leaders who continue to do business the way it has been done in the past will continue to pay the price of doing business that way.

Smith and **Alpert** delve into defensibility of police pursuit training. Their excavation of this issue identifies central problems and answers the questions of where pursuit training should be headed and who must translate policy into practice.

Eve and **Carl Buzawa** offer a full exhibition on the range of classic patterns of police behavior and attitudes toward domestic violence. They piece together the reason change has occurred on this issue and how the nature of policing today and this hotly debated topic will continue to evoke tensions.

Bouza's view on the police and the press is irradiating. He promptly makes the case that a chief at war with the media is, in reality, at war with the people he serves. **Kelly's** chapter firms up the constitutional correct role of the press. She espies the many values of cross-training through reviews of workable programs, and like **Bouza** makes a case that cross-education is a key to a comfortable co-existence.

Howard offers a contemporary view of the police family from a highly personal perspective -- her own. She posits the stand that genuine commitment is the most important ingredient in resolving problems in the family whose husband or wife is a police officer.

Policing a campus is unique and in many ways equal to the administrative and operational challenges of its municipal counterpart. **McBride** provides an answer to the questions about the role of campus law enforcement. He also defines the progress of campus agencies in their efforts to blend the philosophy of problem-oriented policing with their environment and goals of professionalization.

Watson and **Young** challenge the conventional wisdom surrounding the roles of criminal investigation functions as they examine why change must take place in the way law enforcement deploys detectives. Their treatise makes it clear that police executives must work toward making criminal cases the responsibility and commitment of their entire organization.

This work, like many others in the field, should be considered a book in transition. Newer perspectives will arise from the ones espoused in these pages that will lead to more innovations and knowledge in this field. Towards that end, the perspectives of these contributors fit nicely.

TABLE OF CONTENTS

xi

ISSUES IN POLICING
New Perspectives

Chapter 1

Police Professionalism: Merging the Rhetoric with Reality

The quest to professionalize policing will always be a never-ending project, but the movement has stalled. What caused the derailment, and what can be done to put it back on track?

by John W. Bizzack

Professionalization of the police establishment would have taken place decades ago had it been an institution invented from scratch. Instead, the idea of professional law enforcement continues to dangle just beyond the immediate reach of the occupation as a whole. Almost an entire century will have passed into history before law enforcement is close to being capable of acting as professional as it likes to sound.

During the Civil War, Lincoln used a story about the tail of a dog to illustrate to his generals the need for accurate labels and perceptions. "If you call a tail a leg, how many legs has a dog?", he asked the generals. Almost collectively, the generals answered, "Five!" "No ... four," Lincoln corrected them, "because calling a tail a leg doesn't make it a leg." The point should be clear.

Police service and its leadership have been in a hurry to professionalize since the late 1960s. This sense of urgency has resulted in many premature declarations insinuating that you can circumvent Lincoln's wisdom and that *instant professionalism* can be achieved by merely adopting the title. In one respect, this has cheapened the notable efforts made toward this end by some genuine leaders and researchers in law enforcement today. Few, inside or outside the genuine group, have ever agreed on what it means for police to be professionalized, and yet they all agree that the police should be professional.

The notion of professionalism in police service is inexorably tied to its leadership, and that leadership has always been haplessly punctuated with the changeable moods of politics.

Since the late 1960s, the word *professional*, when applied to police, has carried with it a certain connotation that unduly complicates and obscures the original ideas conveyed or intended by those who first envisioned a professional police service. The early architects of police science served up the first criteria of professionalism for police based on the influences of their time. August Vollmer's model focused on the careerist orientation complemented by technical efficiency.[1] He sought freedom from political influences for law. There is little difference, if any, from what is called for today, but the quest is overcast with false positives from those who suffer from the effects of the *instant professionalism syndrome*. Unfortunately, the syndrome has been highly contagious throughout police service.

The notion of professionalism in police service is inexorably tied to its leadership, and that leadership has always been haplessly punctuated with the changeable moods of politics. Many police leaders learned early that the image of professionalism was as powerful a sedative against critics as the very reforms they were supposed to be working toward. So, like carnival barkers, they trumpet a self-pronounced professionalism theme, claim their personnel, agency and practices to be above rebuke, and apparently feel this is enough. The ballyhoo does serve as a thin shield that can take on a life of its own. This results in the agency and its personnel to actually believe their own propaganda. Consequently, substance is always sacrificed.

The *instant professionalism syndrome* is an earnest plea for recognition from an occupation suffering from a cultural and sociological neurosis. There are more educated police officers in this country today than have ever been employed at one time. Most are much better suited for the work than many of those they replaced. There are even those who may be described as cosmopolitan in their perspectives on law enforcement. Still, intellectually, policing has yet to come of age, although the fast pace of educated practitioners has increased. Police organizations are still mostly isolated forces which feed on themselves for growth. They have not yet broken out of the intellectual cage that has been created. Perhaps it is the height of the exalted perches that makes it difficult for some of these people to read the pages of the paper cluttering the bottom of the cage. It says the same thing that all crafts and callings have learned: *professional status is earned and appointed -- not yearned then self-anointed.*

The lack of a central and collective professionalism in police service may be placed on a multitude of things. The work has had its devils. But, no matter which way the scales lean, the leadership, or rather the lack of it, is still at the top of the list of reasons for police service being in its current condition.

The urgency created in the late 1960s has been a powerful, thrusting energy for law enforcement. Encouraged by the promise of improved stature, more positive changes have taken place in two decades than have occurred in the previous six combined. This head of steam has been bridled only by the limitations of police leadership. The appeal of professionalism and the desire to attain it have clearly outdistanced the capabilities of many police leaders to establish an environment for creating excellence.

Early Rhetoric

A progressive advance from a lower or simple form to a higher or more complex form cannot be accomplished without a deliberate, comprehensive plan. Laymen are not converted into disciplined, professionally oriented people without a carefully planned process. The plan for law enforcement has never been clear much less uniformly subscribed to by more than 17,000 agencies in this country. A plan, or at least the beginnings of one, was outlined in the late 1960s. The problem was that too few of its ideas were put into place soon enough to make a quick difference; without that quick fix, many agencies seemed to lose interest. The impression was created that as long as some of the ideas were used, then some degree of improvement would be realized. This led to the problem of choosing which of the ideas to use.

The plan emanated from the 1967 Report from the President's Commission on Law Enforcement and Administration of Justice. Armed with this watershed report and thoroughly underwritten by the Federal Government, police agencies embarked on their quest through the 1970s and 1980s. The more years that were put between the Commission's findings and the present, the further away law enforcement seemed to get from the core of the recommendations in the first place.

The appeal of professionalism and the desire to attain it have clearly outdistanced the capabilities of many police leaders to establish an environment for creating excellence.

Although the Commission studied all components of the criminal justice system, it came up with 37 specific recommendations focusing on the police. At first blush, one might think that heaps of praise

A certain drag on momentum has attached itself to law enforcement. Thought is required to break out of this drag ...

should be given to the many agencies that initiated plans to put the recommendations into place, yet a closer look reveals that most recommendations were given the type of lip service most plans tend to get when they accompany grants and funds from the Federal Government. A few far-sighted police leaders and researchers of the period did more. There is no doubt that this era paved the graveled path. With that, however, most of law enforcement could effortlessly coast on the pavement and luxuriate in the stale, predictable attitude still around today, further substantiating the typical police leader's love for action, and hate for thought.[2]

Few executives of the period successfully opposed those recommendations having the allure of the quick fix, i.e. that officers in supervisory positions should be required to have bachelor's degrees, recruiting should focus on the college campus and college graduates, salaries should be separated from other government positions, to name only a few. Other issues, like lateral entry, dividing functions at entry levels, and establishing police standards commissions, were not as attractive to most police executives. Perhaps this was because the ideas were uncharted, untried, and unconventional challenges to the action-loving, thought-hating leadership of the period. Fortunately, the majority did not overwhelm the good sense of the minority, and many recommendations were eventually embraced in some form. Considering the factionalized, jigsaw structure of American policing, this was quite a feat. This was not an experience unique to police service since society has come to expect, without a trace of awkwardness, that the quick fix will work. This had bred impatience and the thirst for instant gratification. The *instant professionalism syndrome* is the bastard offspring of this thinking.

The accomplishment of getting many of the recommendations into the system did not necessarily trumpet a call that all was well. A quarter of a century after the Report, police service is still plodding under the weight of the failure to follow many other recommendations. Obviously major overhauls take time, and changing social conditions also affect long-term planning. A certain drag on momentum has attached itself to law enforcement. Thought is required to break out of this drag, and the thought must come from this and the next era of police leaders. Unfortunately, many already think they have reached professional status and have slowly reverted to being action-loving, thought-hating, reflexive activists, much like the ones they were supposed to have replaced years ago. A dashing example of modern day approach shows in the way most police agencies tackle their community drug problems.

Again, police are viewed as the first-line solution to a social problem (see chapter by Watson and Young). The "get tough" enthusiasm from the public and politicians toward drugs effortlessly spills over into the law enforcement arena because this is one area in which police can demonstrate their love for action. The police are at their best in situations like these, and they have made progress in drug enforcement techniques, but the truth is that drug enforcement is just now at a level at which it should have been 10 to 15 years ago. Some police leaders and most drug enforcement officers realize that sweeps, mandatory sentencing, public housing crackdowns, reverse buys, and interdiction strategies are merely single trends in the tapestry of a more complex solution to a problem that has always been out of control. Still, the police graciously accept the role and image of being the solution. The police are one of the ingredients in a solution, but hardly the solution. Too many police executives who know this fail to speak out and advocate the need for more focus on treatment and education as opposed to enforcement and incarceration. It seems it is just a lot easier to stay on the popular bandwagon, subscribe to the short tern, quick fix approach, and scream for more jail space to hold all the drug offenders being arrested. By doing so, political agendas are massaged and people in the community hear the assuring hard line, but the problem reigns out of control. Some have even claimed victories through enforcement efforts alone in their wars on drugs, but this is like claiming virginity after childbirth: there exists overwhelming evidence to the contrary.

Tough measures are imperative, but there should be no dispute that when other solutions are known to the police, then police leaders should be vocal, in fact instrumental, in working to bring about those other possible solutions. Other avenues should be taken, even at the expense of less action by the police.

The *instant professionalism syndrome* is reflective of values and attitudes that have evolved in our society. Average is too often thought to be enough, and excellence today is rarely cheered or rewarded. Civil Service systems fit quite nicely into this reasoning. While the protection that Civil Service provides law enforcement is, in one way, a necessary safeguard, the system also encourages and even condones the idea that mediocre performance is enough. Police recruits who enter the Civil

The instant professionalism syndrome is reflective of values and attitudes that have evolved in our society.

Service system already conditioned to being satisfied with being average can find very comfortable careers. It would be consoling to think that this was just a phase common to a single generation and that time will take care of it; but as the old guard is slowly replaced, the next generation or two of the new guard does not show a serious departure from the root of this malady. This single issue assures police executives that there will continue to be immediate conflict between what needs to be done and what a young officer may want to do. At a time when executives should be trying to instill service-oriented values, they are confronted with a mood hardly compatible with the duty of delivering a service -- the core of true professionalism.

The Search for Instant Solutions

Instant gratification trends are nothing new to law enforcement. The quick fix has been the staple of most police management, and serves as a host to the value system of many organizations. Issues in policing are often so overwhelming to an ailing agency, or to an ill-prepared police chief, that merely surviving becomes a noble management science. This style is quickly transmitted to every level of supervision and eventually down to the street cop, whose attitude starts to mirror that of the ill-prepared chief. Brush fires burn on and singe the few good ideas that can emerge in this sort of environment. Soon everyone in such an agency focuses exclusively on the fire and never on the measures that can prevent one from starting in the first place.

The quick fix has been the staple of most police management, and serves as a host to the value system of many organizations.

One reason the quick fix style still dominates most police agencies can easily be traced to the fact that all too many police executives today are merely promoted police officers. They cannot really be classified as professional administrators, carefully prepared for demanding roles in the complex enterprise of contemporary policing. Preparation by chance cannot be substituted for preparation by design. Promoting police officers who are not prepared to administer an agency efficiently is a very bad business practice perpetuated by too many mayors, or governmental bodies charged with selecting police chiefs. The repercussions of this practice undercut real progress in law enforcement and contribute to the absence of a meaningless, occupation-wide quest for professional status. While policing is far from saturated with leaders who were developed by design, there are more today than there were before the 1967 President's Commission Report. Still, leaders who may have developed by design are most commonly the property of a limited number of large and mid-sized agencies. A hefty infusion of dispassionate leadership and the exercise of critical reasoning by police administrators is deserved by every agency, its personnel, and the community. Yet all too many are cheated of this need by the befogged and garbled criminal justice agendas customarily designed by uninformed, ignorant politicians. In the unsteady coalition of police departments in this country, it is rare to find many of them working on major law enforcement strategies that are intended to serve law enforcement as a whole. The individualized agendas are what many feel provide the distinct independence and identities that local government and communities strive for. This isolation does permit a community to set the tone for the type of police and law enforcement best suiting their area and interests. At the same time, this very belief also strangles the idea that police departments can ever expect to be professional without being a part of a larger federation that subscribes to a doctrine of quality, standards, codes, and canons.

The professional movement is in dire need of a philosophical autopsy.

That isolationist belief can only buy into a model of professionalism that is at best a graceless vehicle. Irrespective of what's under the hood, the interior is an uncomfortable arrangement of piecemeal parts. The lack of centralization, uniformity, and smooth working parts prevents this belief and the *instant professionalism syndrome* model from evolving beyond a jalopy. Nonetheless, the number of agencies still spending a lot of energy promoting their self-image through this model grows. This further inspires and promotes the false impression that this model is valid, when in fact this model is merely easier to tackle and requires little thought. Chiefs who subscribe to this approach end up with first-rate, second-rate organization: a lot of fluff and very little substance.

Largely deficient and certainly incomplete, the professional movement is in dire need of a philosophical autopsy. There are unique reasons for this situation beyond the impairments that have resulted from the quick fix and the *instant professionalism syndrome*. Self-regulation in policing, for example, is politically infeasible and yet necessary to the sort of professionalism that law enforcement has been seeking. Strangely enough, most of the advances toward professionalism have actually been aimed at restricting the internal control of police while enhancing the external control.[3] The movement, whether or not practitioners realize it, has been stalled for some time. The definitions used so extensively by police to describe their flavor of "professionalism" bear little resemblance to the socially accepted meaning of the term.[4]

Perhaps therein lies the principal reason that a plan, acceptable and applicable to policing in this country, has never been conceptualized, much less adopted. The genesis of such a plan, if it is likely to dawn in this century, would have to be the product of blueprints, designs, and programs that work off the paper as well as on. Such a plan must have the support and understanding of police leaders whose thinking and actions represents a serious departure from most of their reactionary predecessors.

The police leadership shepherding this plan must pilot organizations that reflect and underscore, at the minimum, the following cardinal points of action and thinking:

- change is the only true constant;
- organizations will be effective when errors and mistakes are not repeated;
- police agencies will not isolate themselves from other dynamic organizations in society;
- police executives have an agenda for themselves and their organizations; and
- agencies are unlikely to be better than their leaders.

These concepts, while hardly the last word, do establish the parameters and will result in the model steering away from traditional low-yield strategies. If an agency thinks these cardinal points already serve as their rudder, then the reader should remember that calling a tail a leg doesn't make it a leg. These concepts facilitate the workability of such a plan, but should not be confused with the plan itself. Getting law enforcement to accept a solid plan for professionalism is like giving a child castor oil: the medicine is unpleasant and will draw foul reviews and remarks about its taste; but if used properly, results are conclusive.

Inescapably, should such an overall plan surface, in this decade there are more educated, synoptic and risk-taking police leaders to carry it out than at any other time before in this century. This adds to the likelihood that a solid plan could be sired but is far from the only ingredient necessary. Even if such a plan were to surface, 17,000 agencies would then be expected to take some action toward it. When you multiply 17,000 by the number of politicians and resistant police leaders who could adversely affect such a plan, and divide one plan by the resulting sum, the likelihood of any cohesive professional strategy emerging that would go beyond the 1967 President's Commission Report is dismal.

The Catechism

Police executives and researchers today must assume the posture and role similar to that of a person planting a tree. Nature sees to it that many trees can flourish without the care of a planter, but it is rare that nature allows a tree to live in an environment unsuited for its growth. When man plants a tree, it must be properly planted and sometimes regularly tended. Proper care is what increases its chances of thriving, especially in a hostile environment. The attempt made by law enforcement to plant professionalism has turned out much like an improperly planted tree in a very hostile environment. A more sturdy sapling, one that was more suited to the environment, would have had a better chance of survival. It is unlikely that today's practitioner is going to enjoy the shade from planting any species of professionalism; yet, as the 21st Century nears, the time is here for the right decisions on the question of professionalism. There are three rudimentary questions, and once resolved the castor oil can be mixed.

1. *Can* police service realistically be included in the same professional definitions as the medical and legal fields?
2. If yes, *how*?
3. If no, then *what* direction is necessary?

The past two decades have produced an army of police leaders willing to storm all three of these questions. Most would likely prefer to ignore the first one altogether, perhaps because of the fear of exposing the inappropriateness of instant professionalism thinking. As painful as it may be to some, an honest look produces the responsible answer.

The answer to the first question answers the second. Police service is simply not capable of being a profession in the sense of the medical and legal fields. Those two fields deliver a service to clients who are generally not in a position to evaluate the quality of the service to begin with.[5] Although both services are eventually needed by everyone, choices are available. When a person needs police service, there is no option in selecting the service provider. If the client is not satisfied with the service, there are few if any alternatives. Second opinions are rare in law enforcement service, and one does not change police agencies like one can change attorneys. Policing is a publicly provided, publicly financed service that is expected and demanded. Although policing may earn the right to be respected, it lacks the automatic right to expect elevation to the same professional status as the medical and legal fields.

Credible definitions for police professionalism can only originate outside the police world.

This is not to say that policing cannot or should not be a profession of some definition. Just because law enforcement is not on the professional level of the medical and legal fields does not mean that the work is perfunctory or registers on the same level as "professional car washers," "professional water removal" services, "professional pest control," and the like.

Policing can be professional as long as society agrees with the definition of professional that applies to the work. In order for that to happen, a lot more has to be done in this decade to demonstrate and influence society's thinking. This brings up the third question: What direction is necessary?

The Prescription

Credible definitions for police professionalism can only originate outside the police world. A national focus on this issue is necessary; otherwise progress, if any, will remain piecemeal. The 1967 Report offered such a focus. A similar medium would suffice, but it is very unlikely that such a massive undertaking will come about for this specific purpose unless there are grave, even ugly events in law enforcement to provoke national scrutiny and new calls for reform. Without such a vehicle, leaders must look elsewhere for yardsticks, criteria, scales, and methods of getting society's attention long enough to define police professionalism. Other studies, such as the one in 1973 by the American Bar Association, National Advisory Commission on Criminal Justice Standards and Goals, and the 1984 Panel on the Future of Policing, produced worthy recommendations, but they did not prove to be the mobilizing forces necessary to jump-start a true professionalization movement. In 1983, the Commission on the Accreditation of Law Enforcement Agencies (CALEA) established a core of valid, applicable standards through which to measure or construct policies and procedures for police department management. So far, this Commission, which issues accredited status to those agencies that comply with the standards, is the closest that policing has come to hitting the nail. This voluntary process is a step in the right direction, but many practitioners express reluctance to involve their agencies (see Oettiemier's chapter).

Studies must continue, but they have a way of being shaped by the very atmosphere in which they are created and work. The 1967 Report, for example, was inspired by the 1964 presidential election in which law and order became a political issue. The Commission produced its report in the face of civil unrest and the glaring need for police to get involved in their communities.[6] The recommendations that surfaced in the report had the urgent scent of political and societal appeasement, but still the report fathered a flurry of research projects that enabled policing to move well ahead of most of the leadership and management talent around at the time.

Many television shows, films, books, and some journalism work against progress in this effort every day. Image, a vital ingredient in changing opinion, is questioned as quickly as headway is made. There seems little promise for an embraceable overall plan which is disheartening, which makes it easier to better understand the rationale and sloppy thinking behind the *instant professionalism syndrome*. Professionalism is hard work and requires more thought than action, especially at this stage. The path police service must travel to reach any sort of professional status is just partially graded. There is much more to do before the path can be graveled, much less paved.

Neither the American Bar Association nor the American Medical Association has a counterpart in the law enforcement field. Fraternal associations fall short of representing all law enforcement organizations, such as the International Association of Chiefs of Police, while advancing professional principles are not representative either and cannot assume watchdog roles. The 1967 Report called for states to set standards for police. Most have accomplished this, but the standards that were set usually outlined training criteria for the certification of officers. The various state offices that oversee these standards have few if any teeth, so they can hardly be considered regulatory in the sense of the ABA or the AMA.

The parochial minded who criticize any or all ideas that merely appear to hint at a nationalized police are pleased with the absence of a central regulatory association for police service. They know that without it, local control (which translates into political domination) will never be lessened. Local control is just one of the problems that keep service-wide professionalism from maturing in the first place.

Professionalism is hard work and requires more thought than action.

Through a central commission-association, advances could be made toward another much needed measure -- lateral entry for managers. It makes no sense to maintain a management desert in law enforcement.

Establishing this sort of professional regulatory association for all police service is illusory for many other reasons. So, perhaps the hub of the efforts should be entirely reseated. Instead of concentrating on the professionalization of police service and everyone in it, the convergence of resources should be diverted to professionalizing the one instrument that can ultimately professionalize all police service: its *management and leadership*. Recruiting and drawing on a professionalized management corps will afford more opportunity to actually professionalize agencies regardless of size. This is not a radical idea, but the by-products and offshoots of this notion are immoderate and intense. They also represent a precise and befitting dosage of castor oil to produce the desired outcome. Some may argue that the IACP and other similar associations are already working toward this end. If that is the case, then some of the itinerary in use needs fine tuning. These organizations are not necessarily of the proper design to represent a central regulator or overseer role. Since the organizations are commercialized, they are much less acceptable in overseer or regulator roles. The design of the type of association needed is more like an independent, non-government related commission whose operating budget is underwritten by its membership or grants. Importantly, this commission-association must have the endorsement or at least the consensus of law enforcement leaders and managers in order for its worth to be valued.

Police leadership should find no fault with acquiescing to a well thought out commission-association that would regulate and advance true police management science and leadership development (see Dodenhoff's chapter). After all, a true professional prestige comes with being formally recognized, certified, and declared an expert. That is exactly what this independent commission-association could do if properly created. This commission-association should be empowered to grant and revoke certification of police managers, establish standards of management techniques and practices, and institute continuing education programs. It would also hammer out and initiate plans based on research concerning the future of police management and the service, as well as ratify a code of ethics (see Behan's chapter), found a police command college, and strive for counterpart status with similar commissions, boards and associations whose role is to accredit, license, certify and advance all aspects of their professions.

Through a central commission-association, advances could be made toward another much needed measure -- lateral entry for managers.

This issue creates panic and fear among some police executives and unionized agencies who fear a loss of power or control, or who think that only home-grown management talent is suited for their departments. It makes no sense to maintain a management desert in law enforcement. Few, if any, organizations can truly thrive on only those capabilities that are self-generated. Opening police management up (to more than just the position of chief of police) to lateral entry, portable pensions and all, makes more sense than most other ideas about how to go about professionalizing police service. Those who oppose the concepts are usually more interested in controlling their personnel than leading them. These are the same folks who frequently make up the action-loving, thought-hating group that begs replacement.

The point should be obvious: the leadership and management in policing must be professionalized before police service stands a chance. A professionalized management corps will ultimately professionalize all police service. A resocialized police management perspective will result in managers and leaders identifying with a national professionalism that is much stronger than the potpourri of philosophies that stem from an identifying with only the local idea of professionalism.[7]

Can it be done? Certainly; but as long as the eagerness to professionalize exists, settling for less will probably serve as an acceptable version of progress to many in the field. The most enduring problems in the criminal justice system are neither technical or financial; they are political.[8] Politics in this sense describes not only elected and appointed officials, but also the internal conflicts that exist in the police environment. The lack of professionalism in policing comes from too many diverse agendas and too many interpretations of what little professional stature does exist. The quick fixes and damage from instant professionalism thinking will not dissolve overnight, despite the merit of any one plan. Unraveling this type of ineffectual management style and replacing it with thought is the first move to be made if police are serious about professionalizing. If these ideas seem outrageous, it is precisely this that confirms that changes must be made.

The most enduring problems in the criminal justice system are neither technical or financial; they are political.

It is doubtful if anyone in law enforcement is going to be remembered for being a part of the first professional police department. But there will be a place for those who philosophically, academically, and by deed push for reforms that reflect thought and carry substance through which policing may eventually become a profession.

REFERENCES

Bittner, Egon. *Aspects of Police Work.* Boston: Northeastern University Press, 1990.

NOTES

1. Sykes, Gary W. *Critical Issues in Policing: The Functional Nature of Police Reform.* Prospect, Illinois: Waveland, 1989, p. 285.
2. Strandburg, Kay. "Anthony V. Bouza -- Speaking His Mind," *Law Enforcement Technology*, June 1991, p. 28.
3. Sykes, Gary W., p. 287.
4. Ibid., p. 288.
5. Wilson, James Q. *Varieties in Police Behavior.* Cambridge, MA: Harvard University Press, 1968, p. 79.
6. Walker, Samuel. "Setting the Standards," ABF, *Police Leadership in America*, 1985, p. 359.
7. Sherman, Lawrence W. "The Police Executive as Statesman," ABF, *Police Leadership in America*, 1985, p. 464.
8. Ibid., p. 466.

Chapter 2

Urban General-izations

Now more than ever, police leaders must sound the retreat from military models and metaphors of policing.

by Peter C. Dodenhoff

P residents and other political leaders, beating drums of patriotic fervor, summon the citizenry to back a "war on crime."

-- *In proclamation after hollow proclamation, citizens are reassured that "victory in the war on drugs" is near at hand.*

-- *In police stations from coast to coast, supervisors "muster the troops" at the start of another shift.*

-- *Police organizations annually lift their voices in tribute to "America's domestic soldiers."*

-- *Police executives, commanding sometimes vast cohorts of armed men and women, are touted as our nation's "urban generals."*

Freedom and Responsibility

Language liberates. Anyone who has ever learned a foreign tongue or learned English as a second language, or who has watched a child grow and learn to speak, read and write, or who has seen an adult illiterate free himself from the shackles of a lifelong handicap, know the liberating power that language possesses.

As is often said, however, there is no freedom without concomitant responsibility -- at the very least, the requirement

*We refer idly to patrol offi-
cers as "troops" and "front-
line soldiers" in the "war" on
crime, but would cringe at any
serious suggestion of making
them into real soldiers.*

to exercise one's freedom wisely. Freedom of speech, for example, is a cherished right, but it is well established that this freedom subsumes the burden of not using it to incite -- not shouting "fire" in a crowded theater.

The freedom of language carries with it the daunting responsibility of using such language carefully. In a tongue such as English, with its magnificently rich diversity of words, phrases and idioms, the responsibility is that much greater. Shades of difference in meaning abound. Consider how many different words exist to describe largeness, or quantity, or even the color blue. The freedom of language offers one the choice of describing an object as big, huge, or even gigantic, colored azure, teal, or navy. The responsibility inherent in using language requires one to choose carefully and accurately.

A Pillar of Professionalism

Most professions have, among other attributes, a language, a vernacular unique to that profession. Specificity and clarity of language are touchstones of such vernaculars. Lacking such, the vernacular loses its impact, and one important pillar of that profession is shaken.

What, then, can one make of law enforcement, and its ongoing quest for professional recognition, when its vernacular is so often clogged with empty, ambiguous or misleading words and phrases? We speak unthinkingly of "wars" on crime and drugs. But is it really war we have, or want? We refer idly to patrol officers as "troops" and "front-line soldiers" in the "war" on crime, but would cringe at any serious suggestion of making them into real soldiers.

Bittner (1970) concedes the utility of a rhetorical shift from mere crime control to a war on crime, properly noting that when it comes to mobilizing public sentiment and support, "an aptly chosen phrase may do the work of a thousand good reasons." But he goes on to observe that the war metaphor is laden with both contradiction and conceit. The contradiction lies in the fact that "a community can no more wage war on its internal ills than an organism can 'wage war' against its own constitutional weaknesses." Crime, like organic malfunction, is part of everyday life, and as such is subject to watchful control. But, says Bittner, "the conceit that they can be ultimately vanquished, which is the implicit objective of war, involves a particularly trivial kind of utopian dreaming."

Given the military model from which law enforcement has evolved, the references to war and soldiery may hold a certain romantic charm, but their ring is painfully hollow in the context of the professional status to which law enforcement now aspires and the sociopolitical realities within which law enforcement operates.

"Urban generals"? In the context of the military model, such a term would seem marvelously applicable to police executives, sitting in command of America's domestic anti-crime "armies." (Indeed, more than a few police leaders would seem to have already taken the label to heart, sporting uniforms and comporting themselves after the fashion of some of our more sartorially resplendent military figures.) Yet, as will be explored further in this chapter, the term "urban general," is at best only partly applicable to the new-age police executive, addressing obliquely just one or two of the significant facets of law enforcement leadership. (And, admittedly, the term will be used at various points herein for certain illustrative purposes.) At worst, though, the term, like other military metaphors in the police vernacular, may be dangerously suggestive of directions in which law enforcement leadership, and the profession itself, no longer have any business going, if they ever did.

Fostering and Revealing Attitudes

Language, for all of its power to liberate, also has the capacity to reveal attitudes or intent -- indeed, it is often patterns of language that help to cement attitudes in the first place. Many are the adults, for example, who insist that they are not bigoted, yet who scatter derogatory racial or ethnic epithets throughout their everyday speech. The epithets may speak to an underlying, if unadmitted bias. Yet, even if those individuals are sincere in their assertions of being bias-free, such speech will inevitably galvanize the attitudes of those within earshot, particularly if the listener is young or impressionable to begin with.

Is it really any surprise that some law enforcers act as if policing were the domestic equivalent of war? Such actions have been conditioned by well-fortified attitudes of "us versus them" and "the thin blue line between civilization and chaos.?

In any organizational setting, it's easiest to change behaviors, usually through the promulgation and enforcement of rules, but tougher to change underlying attitudes that may give rise to various behaviors. Discerning such attitudes -- a prerequisite to changing them -- may be helped by taking a look at an individual's vernacular patterns. Is it really any surprise that some law enforcers act as if policing were the domestic equivalent of war? Such actions have been conditioned by well-fortified attitudes of "us versus them" and "the thin blue line between civilization and chaos," to choose but two examples. And what, among other things, fortifies such attitudes and ultimately reveals them? Nothing less than the jargon used too often by too many leaders who think too little about the phrases they choose.

Sending the Wrong Message

In the aftermath of the Rodney King incident in Los Angeles in March 1991, a group of major-city police chiefs -- all "urban generals" of acknowledged professional stature -- met in New York City to discuss the incident and the police issues attendant to it. One of the conclusions drawn was that police managers may be sending their subordinates the wrong message. As one participating chief later observed:

> The whole vocabulary that we use -- war on crime, war on drugs, all of those kinds of terms -- may in fact be causing police officers to react different than they should. They're getting the wrong message that we want to react as if it's a war. We don't. In a war you put the rules aside; in the war we're fighting, in the battle we're fighting, you cannot put the rules aside.

(Rathburn, 1992)

As long as the law enforcement vernacular remains rife with the terminology of war, how much distance can truly be put between law enforcement and the military model? How much progress toward true professionalism can be achieved as long as the professional argot seems to prefer the "sizzle" of rhetoric to the "steak" of accurate, specific, well-chosen words? (See Bouza's chapter, "The Police and the Press.")

Paradigm and Paradox

In the decades since the dawn of the so-called professional era in law enforcement -- under the guiding hand of such "urban generals" as Vollmer, Wilson and Parker -- progress toward true professionalism made some of its greatest strides only in the past 25 years, as such accepted pillars of professionalism as research and advanced education began to gain toe-holds in policing. In a historical coincidence, this thrust toward a new professionalism was concurrent, at least at the outset, with the last major war fought by the United States -- the prolonged and costly Vietnam conflict. Curiously, in many ways it is Vietnam that the current "war on crime," as it has been practiced by our quasi-military police institutions for two decades, most closely resembles. Consider:

>Frequent calls for more money, more personnel, and more equipment.

>A corps of front-line personnel who are given conflicting, unclear directions, by "generals" as well as by civilian superiors, as to the exact nature of the overall mission.

>Armchair "generals" (usually, but not always, political officials) who allow sloganeering to pre-empt substance by issuing lofty, patriotic-sounding calls to arms, while at the same time failing to back up the proclamation with necessary resources and genuine commitment to the long-term goal (if there is one). As importantly, political considerations tend to dictate that everything must lend itself to overnight success. The instant-gratification syndrome (see Bizzack's chapter) erodes all but the most stalwart commitment to get the job done right over the long term.

>The war drags on with no sign of resolution in sight. (This is especially true of the so-called "war on drugs.") The conditions that determine "victory" or "success" in the war go undefined, making any resolution difficult if not impossible to achieve.

With Vietnam as an unwitting paradigm, there is the considerable risk that the military model may turn into the military muddle -- absent a cadre of skillful, insightful police leaders to steer a course away from such shoals. The quasi-military organizational structure, for all of the usefulness it once had (and may still have in a very few respects), is revealed for what it now is in the context of 1990s-style law enforcement: an express lane to a troublesome public-safety quagmire.

Rethinking the Model

The basic problems facing the world today are not susceptible to a military solution.

President John F. Kennedy

A fundamental task for any executive is to define the basic structure of his or her organization (Moore and Stephens, 1991). For most police executives, that task is seen as a done deal. The quasi-military structure, for better or worse, is already in place, and has been for well over a century, leaving the executive with a sense of having nothing to do but tinker, creating a box here and a slot there on the organizational chart. The notion that the quasi-military model might need wholesale rethinking and retooling -- if not outright rejection and replacement -- is anathema to police administrators who operate according to traditional orthodoxy. Even those few administrators who dared challenge this granite block of orthodoxy by applying a flatter, more flexible, less military type of organizational structure inevitably found their efforts unavailing, as their agencies reverted over time to more traditional forms (Guyot, 1979).

Among other well-documented drawbacks, the quasi-military approach tends to stifle, if not stamp out, the discretion inherent in policing, emphasizes internal disciplinary regulations over guidelines for dealing with citizens, and creates large cohorts of middle managers and first-line supervisors whose jobs revolve mainly around insuring subordinates' compliance with departmental rules.

The quasi-military model -- with its standard design features of strict chain of command, hierarchical control of communication and authority, elaborate rules, regulations, policies and procedures, specialization, and well-defined jobs -- served a useful, even noble purpose at one time, and became the conventional wisdom of policing until roughly the mid-20th century (Roberg and Kuykendall, 1990). Using this approach, police administrators were able to launch law enforcement on a path to reform, purging the sloth, corruption and political manipulation that characterized many departments (Bittner, 1990). The late Chief William Parker of Los Angeles achieved particularly noteworthy results in applying military-style structure and management to his department, and thereby creating a nationally recognized example of the slick, incorruptible, "professional" police agency (as well as forging an undisputed reputation for himself as an "urban general").

Whatever the military model's success in cleaning up police departments and promoting discipline, esprit de corps and, in embryonic form at least, professionalism, it has not been without its shortcomings.

Among other well-documented drawbacks, the quasi-military approach tends to stifle, if not stamp out, the discretion inherent in policing (Moore, 1988), emphasizes internal disciplinary regulations over guidelines for dealing with citizens (Bittner, 1990), and creates large cohorts of middle managers and first-line supervisors whose jobs revolve mainly around insuring subordinates' compliance with departmental rules (Moore, 1988). In addition, effective communications tend to be strangled or distorted by the military-style hierarchical structure. Such a system attaches the least emphasis, authority, pay and prestige to the critically important police officer rank -- the part of the work force that has the most, and most important, ongoing contact with the clientele -- and fosters an insularity that not only keeps the police apart from the community, but from fellow professionals as well (Guyot, 1979). Police leaders cling to this bureaucratic rock despite the fact that behavioral science research has long since documented that a more organic, more humanistic approach might improve individual and organizational performance (Roberg and Kuykendall, 1990).

Policing takes a shot at being more military than the military itself. Where the armed forces encourage recruits to "be all you can be," too often the quasi-military style of law enforcement seems to be saying to practitioners, "be what we say you'll be."

To top matters off, the quasi-military organizational structure of policing has also been identified as a source of employee stress (Lacey, 1983). Given, then, its several and significant shortcomings, it may be no great wonder that Moore (1988) expresses "doubts about whether [the quasi-military model] was a suitable form in the past and even more, therefore, about whether it's a suitable form for the future."

Out-Militarying the Military

It follows that such a structure would have a stultifying impact on efforts to generate true police leaders from within. Indeed, in at least this respect, policing takes a shot at being more military than the military itself. Where the armed forces encourage recruits to "be all you can be," too often the quasi-military style of law enforcement seems to be saying to practitioners, "be what we say you'll be." This is not to deny or take away from the many leaders who have emerged at various times to lend a new vitality, if only temporarily, to the profession, despite the hamstringing effect of the quasi-military system surrounding them. That such leaders have emerged at all is likely due more to their own personal attributes and motivations than to any cultivation effort done by the law enforcement system.

It seems scarcely short of miraculous, given Goldstein's observation (1977):

> [I]f one set out to design a system to prevent and discourage the police from developing their own leadership capability, it would be difficult to come up with a more surefire scheme than that which currently exists.

In Search of the New Order

Along with military metaphors that bog down and misdirect law enforcement, the quasi-military model appears to have outlived its usefulness. That aspects of the military model -- carefully chosen, adapted and applied -- may have some utility and relevance is not to be denied. However, if policing is to effect any meaningful and lasting change in the way it does business, the first step, according to Braiden (1991), is a Bureaucratic Garage Sale, gutting the conventional organizational chart to accommodate the new way of doing business. "If you try to superimpose the new on top of the old," he rightly observes (having history as his best evidence), "convention will win out...."

Even the Bureaucratic Garage Sale, however, needs an antecedent step. Before any organizational structure can be rethought, revised or replaced, one must first consider what the mission, priorities and values of the organization are, and let those values and priorities drive how the department is structured and what strategies will be used, rather than the other way around, as is now the norm (Sherman, 1990).

Braiden notes, somewhat more emphatically:

> Conventional policing does not have a core value. If it does, I have missed it.... For sure, there are goals and objectives, but these need a "faith" to guide them. This being the case, when there is no core value, there is bound to be drift. To correct that drift, we must start with a core value, entrench it and then evaluate everything and everyone against it. If this is done, I forecast the collapse of many organizational chart boxes [and] a shift in career paths....

Obviously, though, it's not enough merely to collapse the old structure and leave nothing in its place. If the military model no longer does the job, some other organizational construct will be needed to fill the void. A number of potentially useful models are available, and careful research can evaluate which elements of these various models can be adopted to create the new-age, post-military model police department (Sherman, et al., 1978).

Help From the Private Sector

The approach that has received perhaps the greatest attention in recent years is the corporate perspective. More a strategy than an organizational format, strictly speaking, the corporate paradigm is one that recognizes that "the police represent a certain bundle of assets, and the task of the management ... is to find the highest value of those assets for a particular city or at a particular point in time" (Moore, 1988). The strategy also supports the idea of a fluid approach to the nature of services provided to "customers," and to the ways in which the organization will come together to provide those services. Customer contact -- or, for policing, citizen contact -- also helps to foster innovation, Moore observes, noting that "the closer the corporations are in touch with their markets, the more innovative and the more useful the innovations turn out to be" (1988).

The corporate approach, combined with other strategic revisions, can also help law enforcement stanch its current loss of "market share" in the security and safety industry. The balance of investment in this area is tipping in favor of private security, personal protection and other non-police measures. The public perception that the police cannot protect them, and that police agencies are not sufficiently responsive to public needs and desires, fuels the imbalance and contributes to a diminished quality of urban life and an inequality in access to security (Moore, 1988).

In seminars and training programs from coast to coast, police executives are already learning how to adapt corporate methods to law enforcement, such as "quality circles" and participative management. The state of Washington pioneered one excellent approach in its Operation Bootstrap program, which exposes police officials of all ranks to some of the best in corporate leadership and management training (Bruns, 1989). Many such strategies are to be found in the practices of successful private-sector companies, with Moore and Trojanowicz (1988) suggesting three criteria for evaluating and choosing among them:

The value of the strategy if successfully implemented;

Feasibility (whether the strategy is "internally consistent in terms of the products, programs, and administrative arrangements emphasized, and whether it is based upon solid information and proven technologies"); and

The degree of risk associated with a given strategy.

A future corporate strategy of policing begins to develop that Moore and Trojanowicz suggest might be called a "professional, strategic, community, problem-solving policing." Wisely, they acknowledge that realizing such a vision poses serious challenges for police executives, who must overcome, among other hurdles, the potent claims of tradition in articulating the mission and organizing their departments. What such executives -- police *leaders* -- will be doing is nothing less than building the new-age, post-military model police department.

Looking to Other Professions

The corporate sector is not the only realm from which policing can draw organizational models in the march toward a new professionalism. Sherman (1990) suggests that the model most appropriate to policing may be found in two kindred professions: higher education and medicine.

> The pay structure should be such that the people who do the work the best make a lot more money than the people who are in charge of the organization. That's the way universities are organized; that's the way hospitals are organized. The senior surgeons make a lot more money than the hospital administrators, senior professors are paid -- both in salary and outside consultation -- compensation that is far in excess of the university president. We need to set a similar system for police departments whereby line police officers can grow in income, status, and perhaps even authority while they are actually doing police work, rather than taking them out of doing police work as the only way they can get ahead in life.

Earlier, Sherman et al. found another respect in which the hospital or university model fit in with law enforcement, speculating that advanced education on the part of police officers would lend itself to a more collegial, less hierarchical structure (1978):

> If all police officers were well educated, and considered themselves professionals committed to a code of ethics, the traditional bureaucratic structures of central control could be replaced with neighborhood-based teams of officers who would be of equal status within the team. A central coordinating staff, under this model, would provide only training and support services, as well as investigating possible violations of ethics. The theory of this proposal is that a collegial organization would produce better police-community relations and better police morale. Whether educated officers would adapt better to this kind of organizational design is an open question, but it is true that other collegial organizations (law firms, hospitals, universities) usually have well-educated personnel.

Law enforcement's quest for professionalism is hindered, perhaps fatally, by the almost universal lack of lateral entry at any rank other than police chief or, occasionally, police officer.

Finally, higher education offers law enforcement one other bit of food for thought. It is frequently observed that law enforcement's quest for professionalism is hindered, perhaps fatally, by the almost universal lack of lateral entry at any rank other than police chief or, occasionally, police officer. Certainly the insularity of thousands of individual police departments is one obstacle -- largely an attitudinal one -- to a broad lateral-entry effort. On a more practical level, the potential loss of pension accruals tends to deter officers from moving to another agency. College professors, by contrast, are able to participate in the national retirement system known as TIAA/CREF, which is private and portable, allowing the professor who changes jobs to remain in the same pension system. The idea of developing a similar national police retirement system, which would permit inter-agency transfers without loss of benefits, has been around at least since the President's Crime Commission recommended it in 1967 (Walker, 1983). If law enforcement is serious about the idea of developing leadership from within (more on this issue later), a greatly enhanced lateral-entry system would seem an idea whose time has come.

Leadership For a New Age

*The question "Who ought to be boss?" is like asking
"Who ought to be the tenor in the quartet?" Obviously,
the man who can sing tenor.*

Henry Ford

Law enforcement has plenty of managers, administrators, and even executives. What it needs, now or ever, is more leaders. (It may be argued whether a true profession can ever have too many leading professionals.) If law enforcement is to shake itself free from the restrictive aspects of the quasi-military model and move on to a new organic footing, leaders are desperately needed to pave and guide the way. What kind of individual should answer the call? Start with the observation of Professor Harold Hill in *The Music Man*: "It takes judgment, brains and maturity to score in this game." Then throw in ample helpings of courage, insight, diplomacy and perseverance, and what begins to emerge is a rough picture of the new-age police leader.

Leadership talents must be allowed to flower at the top, the middle and the bottom, and this is all the more true if the new-age, post-military model of law enforcement embodies generous doses of the community-service and problem-solving philosophies now growing in popularity.

As importantly, the organic, post-military model of law enforcement will not reserve the term "leaders" only for those who head agencies. In the fashion of true professionalism, leaders will be found -- and must be encouraged -- at all levels of the organization, regardless of how hierarchical that organization may turn out to be (Davis, 1978). Leadership talents must be allowed to flower at the top, the middle and the bottom, and this is all the more true if the new-age, post-military model of law enforcement embodies generous doses of the community-service and problem-solving philosophies now growing in popularity.

Role Revision

Leaders lead; administrators administer; managers manage. And what do supervisors do? They supervise, of course. Taking a "strict constructionist" view of that term, it means they check up on other people. This is exactly the wrong posture for a post-military model police agency. As the new-age police department chugs along toward true professionalism, the sense of entrepreneurship, proprietorship and nascent leadership at the police officer level -- the client contact level -- will simmer with potential energy just one level below the first-line supervisors, rocking their vocational boat with growing vigor. That energy has the power to alter the role of the first-line supervisor in dramatic ways. And what of the second-line supervisors (or are they first-line managers)? In the hierarchy of the military model, their job, again by a "strict constructionist" definition, is to supervise ... the supervisors!

As professionals, these first- and second-line supervisors will necessarily find themselves facing role redefinition in the new-age, post-military model police department. Only so many can be kept in slots where they merely manage and supervise, inasmuch as the new-age department should see a reduced need for supervision in the traditional sense. Corruption and misconduct will be kept in check, as they must be, through such means as vigilant internal affairs, the informal citizen oversight that is a normal outgrowth of increased contact with the community, and the constant emphasis on values, values, values! Since the new-age police department is supposed to be cultivating and encouraging leadership *throughout* the organization, the rest of the one-time supervisors can now be redirected toward new projects that develop, challenge, and apply their creative and intellectual energies (Moore and Stephens, 1991).

Why, after all, should chiefs and front-line officers have all the fun?

Who Are the Generals?

As previously noted, "urban generals" may well be a metaphor that, like "war on crime," is more perilous and misdirecting than it is useful. For purposes of discussion and analysis, however, there is one respect in which the term may have a considerable usefulness.

Consider that in a military context, not all generals are equal or alike. There are generals who are consummate strategists; there are those who are master tacticians; there are planners, logisticians and more. History offers such examples as George C. Marshall, who coordinated much of the American effort in World War II and later applied the same leadership abilities to the European recovery plan that was to bear his name. General George S. Patton, on the other hand, was one example of the many generals who show consummate skill in taking command of a battlefield but appear disturbingly deficient when it comes to such strategic arts as planning, politicking and diplomacy. The pioneering General Billy Mitchell, one of the founding fathers of modern air power, provides another model -- that of the visionary leader who stuck courageously to his principles and his perceptions, even at the cost of his own career.

So, too, in law enforcement should the term "urban generals" be viewed as an umbrella covering strategists and tacticians alike. To derive maximum benefit, any working definition of "urban generals" -- police leaders -- must be flexible enough to include a Goldstein, a Moore, a Sherman, and a Skolnick along with the Vollmers, the Wilsons, the Parkers, and the Murphys.

Too often, non-practitioner analysts are unwisely and unfairly written off as "armchair generals," whose views on topical issues are to be tolerated as part of the cost of doing business as usual. How parochial and far from the truth. Since the late 1960s, law enforcement has benefited in no small way from the activities and acumen of these research-minded strategists and thinkers, some of them former practitioners, many of them not. Their willingness to ask tough questions of "why" and "how" has helped to create a body of knowledge that is helping to elevate law enforcement to the professional status it craves.

Too often, non-practitioner analysts are unwisely and unfairly written off as "armchair generals," whose views on topical issues are to be tolerated as part of the cost of doing business as usual. How parochial and far from the truth.

To snub the researchers, scholars and analysts, to fail to include them in a broader definition of "urban general," is unwise on several levels. Quite obviously, such a rejection would be unsupported by the weight of evidence. Moreover, it would fly in the face of examples set by other professions, such as the medical community, wherein the researcher is not less important and accorded no less recognition than the practitioner.

There's also a bottom-line consideration. Looking at law enforcement from the corporate perspective favored by Moore (1988) and others, it is inconceivable that a large corporation (a police agency) or a major industry (law enforcement in general) would go about its business with no investment in or concern for research and development. The researchers and number crunchers, provided that they are astute enough to be researching the right issues and crunching numbers the right way, play at least as critical a role as the executives running the corporation or industry. With the billions of dollars invested in law enforcement as an industry, it can ill afford to undervalue the contributions, role and standing of these non-practitioner "urban generals."

The Leading Edge

Be not afraid of greatness: some are born great, some achieve greatness, and some have greatness thrust upon them.

William Shakespeare

Some people may have greatness thrust upon them. Very few have excellence thrust upon them.

John Gardner

Where does the search for the new-age police leaders begin? Historically, the search for "urban generals" has begun -- and ended -- with the individual police agency itself. Police agencies are right to take pride in trying "to do everything in-house" (Minetti, 1987), from conducting original research to promoting from within. The risk, however, lies in the fact that many departments do not actively seek out *leaders* among their home-grown personnel. Under the constraints of the traditional quasi-military structure, officers see promotion as one of the very few ways of advancing themselves professionally, and the department all too often ends up being run by "promoted police officers" who have not received the kind of careful and thorough preparation needed for demanding, complex leadership roles in a modern police agency (Bizzack, 1991).

When a vacancy occurs at the police chief level, the issue of appointing from within or without becomes a considerable source of discussion for those in the ranks. The mere mention of the words "national search" is often enough to make members of a given police agency bristle with indignation. Even the jargon used, "insider vs. outsider," is suggestive of a raw-nerve issue that is out of step with true professionalism. Notwithstanding the pride a departing chief can feel at knowing his subordinates have been well-groomed to succeed him, and despite the fact that Civil Service realities often make looking outside the agency a practical impossibility, the failure to look far and wide for the best possible leader, wherever he or she may be, speaks to a shortsightedness that works against the achievement of true professionalism.

Regrettably, for all of the recent growth in managerial and executive training, law enforcement still lacks for outright *leadership* development programs. (Perhaps tellingly, there are few if any programs that incorporate the word "leadership" into their name. There are numerous command colleges, executive institutes, management seminars and schools of police administration, but rare is the program that directly proclaims itself to be a leadership school.) America's "urban generals," such as they are, have no West Point, no R.O.T.C. program to train them for the leadership roles they will one day fill. One cannot take away from the contributions made by established programs from Cambridge, Massachusetts, to Quantico, Virginia, to Louisville, Kentucky, and countless places in between, but law enforcement does not have a true analog to West Point -- turning out *leaders* for the profession -- in the same sense that, say, England's Bramshill Police College is analogous to the military academy at Sandhurst (even allowing for the vastly greater fragmentation of the police system in the United States as compared to the United Kingdom).

Off the Beaten Track

It should hardly surprise one that police departments almost never go completely outside the profession for new sources of leadership. They can barely find the will to go outside the agency.

Considering the "insider/outsider" dilemma that so often arises when selecting a police chief (a dilemma that may well be unique to police among established professions), it should hardly surprise one that police departments almost never go completely outside the profession for new sources of leadership. They can barely find the will to go outside the agency, so why bother looking beyond law enforcement at large, no matter how capable the leaders that may be found?

Granted, isolated exceptions do exist. Robert McGuire, a former Federal prosecutor and son of a police lieutenant, creditably ran the New York City Police Department for six years in the late 1970s and early 1980s. George Napper, a one-time probation officer, community organizer and college professor, held the top posts in the Atlanta Police Bureau and the Department of Public Safety. Still others have come from the officer corps of the U.S. military to serve capably as heads of police agencies. And, to be sure, the elective nature of most sheriff's positions opens wide the possibility that literally anyone can aspire to and attain the top leadership post in the agency. (Notwithstanding the potential perils of having elections for law enforcement executives, there are potential lessons to be derived from the example of sheriff's departments.)

But is it enough, necessarily, to end the search in the fields of law, politics and academia? Not if the ultimate goal is to uncover pure leadership talent. As programs like Operation Bootstrap are demonstrating, managing a large organization requires skills that translate neatly from one type of business to another. And, certainly, many are the police executives who go on to successful careers leading private corporations in diverse, even unlikely fields. The door does not swing both ways, however, and by ignoring personnel resources to be found outside of policing, law enforcement does itself a disservice and retards its own development as a profession (Dees, 1991).

As the new-age, post-military model police department evolves, the opportunities for talented leaders in other fields to make executive-level contributions should expand. (Again, though, the desirability of cultivating leaders from within should never be minimized.) Even under the military model, most policing does not revolve around the kinds of hard, tactical scenarios that only a through-the-ranks police manager can handle. With the emergence of a new-age model, it will become more evident that good leadership techniques are good leadership techniques, whether in law enforcement, higher education, law or heavy industry. Good leaders can be effective in almost any business environment (and remember the corporate perspective of law enforcement as big business). Police experience may be invaluable, even absolutely necessary at the line level, but it need not be and can even prove counterproductive at the executive level (Dees, 1991).

This is not to say that corporate executives or other leaders can only be used to good effect at the police chief level. With the growth of civilization often providing a way to work around over-restrictive Civil Service considerations, outside talent can be brought in on an as-needed basis at other levels, say by creating a slot for a deputy commissioner here or a project director there. If a suitable research manager, training director or public relations executive cannot be found within the ranks, bring one in until home-grown talent can be cultivated. The spirit of true professionalism will not suffer in the short term, and in the long term it will be enhanced if department personnel are given the opportunity to hone their skills by learning from top-quality executives brought in from other fields.

As Braiden (1991) put it in his call for a Bureaucratic Garage Sale, "Start out with a few mavericks (it helps if the chief is one) and give them freedom to attack convention."

Now More Than Ever

The quasi-military model, with its focus on hierarchy, strict chain of command, and authoritarian controls, is fundamentally at odds with community-based policing, especially the kind based on problem-solving models. The quasi-military model cannot give you quality policing. "Rules and regulations ... cannot give it to you because you cannot order people to be energetic, imaginative or creative."

As the decade of the 1990s unfolds, it would seem the time could never be more right for a sweeping assault on the traditional orthodoxy of policing, including the quasi-military model and the pervasive, misguided use of military metaphors.

For starters, consider these factors: It is now 25 years -- roughly a police career -- since the President's Commission on Law Enforcement and Administration of Justice issued its clarion call for progressive reforms of policing. In that time, during which an entire generation of policing has come and gone, higher education for police has moved steadily if slowly toward becoming the norm, and applied research on critical law enforcement has grown to maturity. Few practitioners any longer question the relevance or importance of these two developments, which, as recognized benchmarks of professional status, have helped in no small way to move law enforcement ahead. As importantly, the organizational design of the educated police department can be very different from existing quasi-military designs, which pre-date even the most primitive educational standards for police (Sherman, et al., 1978).

Then, too, nearly an entire generation has passed during which there has been no military draft. Military service, once a standard part of most young men's passage into adulthood, no longer supplies the significant numbers of American police officers that it once did. By extension, it is no longer supplying the mortar that cemented the quasi-military model as a police institution.

With higher education and applied research in place, and with military service fading out as a factor, these provide some of the reasons why the new-age police department *can* become a reality. The reason why it *must* is seen in another development that has been taking place in recent years.

That development is the growing trend toward community-based policing, by whatever name that philosophy and style may be known. The quasi-military model, with its focus on hierarchy, strict chain of command, and authoritarian controls, is fundamentally at odds with community-based policing, especially the kind based on problem-solving models. The quasi-military model, Braiden observes, cannot give you quality policing. "Rules and regulations ... cannot give it to you because you cannot order people to be energetic, imaginative or creative" (1991).

Community policing has been picking up steam of late, despite its prevailing lack of a definition or set of parameters. Generally speaking, it has fallen into the category of being the "politically correct" thing to do (Rosen, 1992; Koby and Lucy, 1992). At this point, though, it has ceased to be debated whether the police alone can control crime, and the community policing philosophy seems to offer some of the greatest promise for law enforcement in some time. Despite all the claims of police organizations that they are "into" community policing, Braiden remains skeptical. Most efforts have entailed the writing of copious policy or the creation of a new box or two on an existing organizational chart, "but little structural or intellectual change at the management level has occurred" (1991).

If community policing is to succeed in fullest flower, it requires the abandonment of the outdated quasi-military model. Otherwise, it risks becoming a grander attempt at team policing, which was a noble concept brought to ruin by the futile effort to weld it onto an existing and incompatible organizational structure.

Conversely, if the quasi-military model is to pass into the history books, as it should, it requires that the community-based, problem-solving approach succeed. The abandonment of the former and the success of the latter, then, are locked together in symbiotic fashion, and the best-case outcome is nothing less than an accelerated march toward true professionalism, exponential growth in innovation and creativity, new and challenging roles for mid-level personnel, and increased opportunities for the development of individual leadership at all levels.

References

Bittner, Egon. *The Functions of the Police in Modern Society.* Rockville, Md.: National Institute of Mental Health, 1970.

Bittner, Egon. *Aspects of Police Work.* Boston, Mass.: Northeastern University Press, 1990.

Bizzack, John. *No Nonsense Leadership.* Lexington, Ky.: Autumn House Publishing, 1991.

Braiden, Chris. "Who Paints a Rented House?" *Law Enforcement News,* April 30, 1991.

Bruns, Bill. "Operation Bootstrap, Opening Corporate Classrooms to Police Managers," *Research in Action.* Washington, D.C.: National Institute of Justice, August 1989.

Davis, Edward M. *Staff One: A Perspective on Effective Police Management.* Englewood Cliffs, N.J.: Prentice-Hall, 1978.

Dees, Timothy M. "Modernizing Police Management," *Law & Order,* Sept. 9, 1991.

Goldstein, Herman. *Policing a Free Society.* Cambridge, Mass.: Ballinger, 1977.

Guyot, Dorothy. "Bending Granite: Attempts to Change the Rank Structure of American Police Departments," *Journal of Police Science and Administration,* 5 (September 1979).

Koby, Thomas G. and Lucy, Virginia M. "Two Promising Concepts in Trouble," *Law Enforcement News,* Feb. 14, 1992.

Lacey, Robert T. Interview, *Law Enforcement News,* Nov. 7, 1983.

Minetti, Pat G. Interview, *Law Enforcement News,* May 26, 1987.

Moore, Mark H. Interview, *Law Enforcement News,* April 15, 1988.

Moore, Mark H. and Stephens, Darrel W. *Beyond Command and Control: The Strategic Movement of Police Departments.* Washington, D.C.: Police Executive Research Forum, 1991.

Moore, Mark H. and Trojanowicz, Robert C. "Corporate Strategies," *Perspectives on Policing,* No. 6 (Washington, D.C.: National Institute of Justice and Harvard University, Nov. 1988).

Rathburn, William. Unpublished Interview, *Law Enforcement News,* January 1992.

Roberg, Roy R. and Kuykendall, Jack. *Police Organization and Management: Behavior, Theory and Processes.* Pacific Grove, Calif.: Brooks Cole, 1990.

Rosen, Marie Simonetti. "1991 in Review: Graphic Images Paint a None-Too-Pretty Picture," *Law Enforcement News,* Jan. 31, 1992.

Sherman, Lawrence W. Interview, *Law Enforcement News,* March 31, 1990.

Sherman, Lawrence W., et al. *The Quality of Police Education.* San Francisco: Jossey-Bass, 1978.

Walker, Samuel. *The Police in America: An Introduction.* New York: McGraw-Hill, 1983.

Chapter 3

Values

In spite of shortcomings, police have fewer moral breakdowns than most other professions.

Leaders should not run their organization by rules or procedures manuals, but by policies and philosophies.

by Cornelius J. Behan

"**A** police officer is authorized to make decisions about the lives of others, an enormous power the rest do not have. Such power should be exercised only by those whose public and private behavior befits authority."

Character and Cops
by Ed Delattre

The *Baltimore Sun* of April 29, 1991, carried the banner headline: "Survey of Americans' beliefs finds nation lacking a moral consensus." The conclusion came from a book published a month later entitled *The Day America Told the Truth: What People Really Believe About Everything That Really Matters*, by J. Walter Thompson and Peter Kim. "Americans are making up their own rules and laws," say the authors. The survey they conducted showed that only 13 percent of the people believe in all 10 Commandments, and 9 out of 10 lie regularly.

While the findings are shocking, they should not surprise even the casual observer of the American scene. We are surrounded by the evidence. On the December 13, 1990 CBS Morning Show, a discussion, inspired by a survey, concerned cheating. When questioned, approximately 35 percent of grade school students said they would cheat on exams, while 65 percent of high school students said they would cheat. Other surveys revealed that in some colleges, it was 100 percent. What a statement about America's youth.

U.S. News and World Report called the Savings and Loan scandal "not just a financial crisis but a moral crisis." Five U.S. senators are now known as the "Keating Five" for using their influence with bank regulators in behalf of financier Charles Keating, Jr. Perhaps the least guilty in receiving $1.3 million from Keating is Sen. John McCain. He and his family took vacations at Keating's expense and began reimbursement after the business became public. According to one newspaper account, when he appeared before the Senate Ethics Committee on January 4, 1991, McCain said, "You not only have to be careful about how and what you do, but you have to be careful about what you appear to do." Can you imagine a member of Congress not knowing the basic concept that perception is as important as reality? He had to be found coming up short before it dawned on him. What does this suggest about other law makers?

Continuing in his testimony, Sen. McCain excused his actions by saying that, "obviously, I did not have a proper procedure." The Code of Ethics for federal government service forbids accepting "favors and benefits under circumstances which might be construed by reasonable persons as influencing the performance of government duties." In other words, the senator doesn't find himself guilty of unethical conduct, but of using faulty procedures. Values are in the mind and heart, not in a rule book.

It took two years to come to grips with the last of the Keating Five. On November 20, 1991, the Senate Ethics Committee rebuked Sen. Alan Cranston for "violating unwritten but commonly understood standards of Senate behavior." By rebuking him rather than any other action, the committee avoided a Senate floor vote. The senator said that "nothing I did violated any law or specific Senate rule" in his reply to the findings of "substantial credible evidence" that his solicitation of more than $800,000 in charitable contributions was linked to his official duties. Later at a news conference, he and his lawyer, Harvard Law Professor Alan Dershowitz, said they could prove that many senators engaged in comparable linkage.

On February 11, 1991, The *New York Times* reported the indictment of seven Arizona state legislators for taking money in exchange for their support to legalize gambling. One was to get the shrimp concession, another the gift shop. Much of the questionable activities were recorded on video camera. The quotes are unbelievable. One state representative said, "I don't give a [expletive] about issues. There is not an issue in this world that I give a [expletive] about. My favorite line is what's in it for me." Another said, "I sold too cheap." Another said she wanted to "die rich."

Governor Evan Mecham, of Arizona, was impeached for concealing a $350,000 campaign loan and lying about it. In California, a state senator and a former state senator were convicted last year of accepting bribes. In South Carolina, 11 state legislators were indicted for accepting bribes; some have pled guilty. Sen. Dave Durenberger of Minnesota was *reprimanded*, not *censured*, for false expense accounts and illegal honorariums. Representative Gus Savage of Illinois was not even reprimanded for making improper unwanted advances to a female Peace Corps volunteer in Zaire, because he wrote a letter of apology. Representative Barney Frank of Massachusetts fixed 33 parking tickets for a companion who was on probation. The same Barney Frank, who called for an investigation of the Savage case, says he did not know that a former male employee of his was operating a prostitution ring out of Frank's apartment. Not only is there a leadership vacuum in America, but Congressional Ethics Committees do not care to hold their colleagues accountable.

What about the pollution in our culture by such groups as 2 Live Crew? Almost 2 million records have been sold with the group singing about forcing anal sex on a girl and then forcing her to lick the excrement. Ten-to twelve-year-olds chant the lyrics. The *New York Times* noted that "the history of music is the story of innovation, even outrageous styles that interacted, adapted, and became mainstream." The absence of condemnation is appalling. According to the *U.S. News and World Report*, "the president of the New York School for Social Research says we are witnessing a collision between those comfortable with change and those yearning for a simpler era." Other notables chimed in, supporting the music which debases women and is directed at children.

Gratefully, some people opposed this outrage. Stanley Crouch, critic and essayist, called 2 Live Crew "spiritual cretins and slime." Jewelle Taylor Gibbs, author, said "censorship is a red herring in this case. The real issue is values, the quality of life." This kind of reference to values is springing up all over America -- from the heartland, not from high places.

The word *hypocrisy* comes from the ancient Greek *Hypo* (less than) and *Krinein* (to choose); that is, not making true choices. Not only is hypocrisy observed at the top, but we lie about it. We wouldn't ever trade arms for hostages. Pragmatism abounds. Do whatever is necessary to succeed and beat the competition. "People come to feel like suckers if they're honest," said Gary Edwards, Executive Director of the Ethics Resource Center in Washington, D.C., "if the companies they're competing against are not." Imagine feeling bad because one is honest.

In 1985, baseball commissioner Peter Uberroth, on urging drug testing for baseball players, said that "the integrity of the game is everything ... baseball is a public trust." Yet, in September 1991, much was said about Otis Nixon's suspension from the Atlanta Braves after testing positive for cocaine -- for the third time. There was no mention of what this does to the country, to the sport, to the millions of young people who hold baseball stars as role models. Plenty was said about his loss to the Braves in the final days of the pennant race.

Sports moguls are making "some" statements about the use of illegal substances by players. Steve Howe was disciplined six times for drug and alcohol abuse, but was invited last spring to the Yankee training camp. The *Edmonton Journal* alleged that Grant Fuhr had a substance abuse problem since the early 1980s. The National Hockey League is tough on abusers; so when the story broke, Fuhr was suspended. He went back to work as a goalie for the Oilers. Defensive lineman Dexter Manley, after flunking a drug test for the third time, was suspended for life -- which lasted one year, then the Phoenix Cardinals picked him up. If you can throw or catch a ball, make or prevent goals, or tackle or block your opponent, the owners and players don't seem to care about drug abuse. So much for a drug-free work place. What are we telling our youth and society about the evils of drugs and the values of life?

For years, the medial profession failed to acknowledge the existence of AIDS or its killing capability. When the mortality figures climbed, the truth could no longer be avoided. Now, even though there is general agreement that all human immunodeficiency virus (HIV) carriers will get AIDS and all AIDS victims will die, the medical folks still argue in favor of privacy over public safety. The Center for Disease Control is subjected to heavy criticism for "trying to develop a list of procedures that doctors and dentists infected with the AIDS virus should not perform" on patients. According to the *New York Times* of

November 5, 1991, numerous medical organizations claim the effect has no scientific validity, is too costly, lacks sufficient data, and should not be imposed. They ignore the facts that surgeons are injured during operations, that five patients were infected by a Florida dentist, and that hepatitis B has been transmitted from health care workers to patients in a number of cases. What value system is operating when doctors and other health care practitioners put themselves ahead of their patients when treating a murderous disease? Has their age-old ethical code changed?

Earvin "Magic" Johnson, star of the Los Angeles Lakers basketball team, announced on November 7, 1991, that he had contracted HIV, indicating that he got it from imprudent heterosexual activity. Although it shouldn't have, it seems to have shocked the heterosexual world. To his credit, Magic intends to carry the message of caution to all who will listen. There are three main ways for heterosexuals to avoid the disease: sexual abstinence, faithfulness, and use of condoms with spermicide. Yet, the next day in a discussion about the case, a prominent Baltimore radio talk show host talked down to a caller who suggested restraint in sexual matters, and quickly went to another call. Ball players, he said, were young, under stress, rich, possessed active glands, and therefore had active sexual lives. Constraint was a ludicrous notion. The host must have forgotten that professional athletes also have brains and common sense. We must remember that the essence of being a talk show host is the art of hanging up on people.

In a *U.S. News - CNN* survey by Roper, of those polled, 54 percent thought people were less honest than they were ten years ago. In the same poll:

> 69% thought employees steal at work
> 60% thought expense accounts are padded
> 53% thought government officials take payoffs
> 49% thought people fake illness to stay home from work
> 47% thought labor leaders use union funds for personal reasons
> 45% thought citizens cheat on their income tax,
> but only 25% thought police took payoffs from law breakers

"Don't Let Your Babies Grow Up To Be Lawyers" is an article that appeared in *The Washingtonian* in November 1990. John Sansing conducted a survey of the trust people have for those working in certain occupations. From the data, he created a "trust index." Lawyers ranked fourth from last above cab drivers, politicians and car salesmen, and below plumbers and journalists. Police ranked third below teachers and dentists, and tied with doctors.

Police rate high even though the papers focus almost daily on police corruption and brutality. Police have their problems and are held to higher accountability because they carry the public trust. The March 3, 1991 Rodney King beating incident will remain in the public consciousness for years. Four officers are indicted and now await trail. Last May 30, current and former Cleveland police officers were arrested for shielding gambling operations. Two Baltimore City officers were arrested for drugs in June, and on November 8, 1991, another pled guilty to theft. Milwaukee fired two officers for inefficiently handling an encounter with the serial killer, Jeffrey Dahmer. The items could go on and on because no industry experiences greater scrutiny than law enforcement.

Police are held in high regard by many segments of the population for a number of reasons. Americans deplore dishonesty, hate being lied to, and consider dignity as the way to treat their friends and loved ones. They believe politicians should not make promises they can't keep, and lawyers should not deceive to save clients. Bernard Kalb, a respected State Department spokesman, said that "one of the most regrettable by-products of any sense of deception would be if the American public were suddenly to dilute its own perception of what America stands for, if there were a ... resignation that this is the way it goes. That would be a terrible loss and tragedy." We may be approaching that point, but we haven't reached it yet.

Police rate high in many surveys because they make a strong contribution to the quality of life in this country. In 1990, officers across the United States investigated 14,475,613 serious crimes and arrested 2,328,221 for those same offenses. Almost 2 million Maryland citizens called for some kind of police assistance -- that's 40 percent of the state's population. Projecting that nationally, it means police responded to 100 million 911 calls in 1990 and millions more that remained unrecorded. Police help at births, deaths, sickness, injuries, gas leaks, dangerous conditions, missing persons, lost children, and whatever the public feels requires assistance. So regardless of the weak individuals in their ranks, millions of people, without hesitation, call and receive wanted help from police officers every year. When people need help, they call a cop. It's hard to know how police do so much when there are only 600,000 of them in the country, but the large amount of favorable citizen contacts explains why the corruption in their ranks fades into the background.

In spite of their shortcomings, I maintain that police have fewer moral breakdowns than most other professions. What's more, they try to correct the deficiencies. Most police departments have their own "internal affairs" units to investigate misconduct and hold many training sessions to minimize it (see chapter by Bouza and Sherman). In addition, there are state prosecutors, special prosecutors, grand juries, special commissions (such as the New York City's Knapp Commission), civilian review boards and investigative reporters, who investigate allegations of police wrongdoing. There are procedures encouraging the public to file complaints with the police or any agency they choose.

Such is not the case in other professions. Officers are fired for lying, particularly under oath. How many persons lose their jobs for lying, or stealing, or assaulting someone, or using illegal drugs while working in the private sector? Repeated incidents of drug abuse in police circles are dealt with as soon as they are discovered. In most departments, officers are fired after the first discovery is proven. In the Baltimore County Police Department, 99 percent of the sworn members voted for unannounced random drug testing of themselves to prove and set an example that they are drug free. Only about 50 percent of the civilian employees made the same commitment. Cheating on exams in the police academy is grounds for dismissal. There is 0 percent tolerance. We, in the police service, can take pride in our systems and the actions we take when our codes are violated.

Officers are fired for lying, particularly under oath. How many persons lose their jobs for lying, or stealing, or assaulting someone, or using illegal drugs while working in the private sector?

Up to now, I've painted a dismal picture of American values. I believe they have slipped. Many don't even know or care about our once proud values -- the values that made this country great. However, I see signs of a reversal. The signals are not coming from on high as a national policy, but from right-thinking citizens who realize we must get back to basics. People of influence, like police officials, are speaking out. Every day, if you're tuned in, you will read or hear from the media some expression of values.

For example, business ethics are being reborn. Since 1988, Harvard Business School requires its students to take a 3-week course in ethics.

Admittedly, you can't teach ethics and values in that period of time, but you do make a statement. Professors by example and teaching methods can put them in all their courses.

In the same year, Arthur Andersen and Co., the large accounting firm, started a $5 million project to teach values. College professors are trained to use the case study method and lead discussions of ethics and values in their marketing, economics, finance and management courses. The company wants to instill ethical decision-making in its 40,000 employees, according to Duane Kullerg, a managing partner.

Last year, Governor William Donald Schaeffer of Maryland congratulated Catholic and Jewish religious leaders for teaming up to promote a national campaign to enhance the teachings of moral values in the nation's public schools. For the first time ever, the Ecumenical and Interreligious Affairs Committee of the National Conference of Catholic Bishops and the Interreligious Affairs Committee of the Synagogue Council of America joined together to address a prime problem in American society. The joint document stated: "Children lack fundamental values -- like honesty, integrity, tolerance, loyalty, and belief in human worth and dignity. All of these values are grounded in our respective religious traditions, the Constitution, the Bill of Rights, much of the world's great literature, and ethical business practices."

Normally, these values are taught by the family, churches and synagogues, schools, and government. "But in recent years, there has been a growing reluctance to teach values in our public educational system out of fear that children might be indoctrinated with a specific religious belief." The two organizations recommended establishing committees, convening conferences, and placing values education in the curricula, and asked the media to join the effort. They said, "To raise a generation without an understanding of values is to assure disaster. Children are the future. The specter of a nation with an amoral citizenry is terrible to contemplate. The damage would be irreversible."

Nine months before the Rodney King incident, in *Public Management*, a monthly publication by the International City Management Association (ICMA), appeared an article by Stephen J. Bonczek entitled "Ethics: Challenge of the 1990s." He noted the negative impact of unethical behavior in government, the waste of energy it causes, the spread of suspicion from the guilty to the innocent public servants, the time taken from our duties in order to respond to reporters, and the discouraging effect on morale. After the King beating, the four indicted officers became all officers in the country. The Attorney General of the United States asked for a 5-year review of past brutality cases. Community groups and individuals are accusing police officers of brutality, whether it exists or not. Reporters besieged the Los Angeles Police Department and departments all over the country for interviews. The action video will be shown on national TV for years to come. Stephen Bonczek was right.

The Woodstock Theological Center engages in research and publishes books on a variety of topics. After a 2-year study, in December 1990 it issued a report called *Creating and Maintaining an Ethical Corporate Climate*. Top executives from Chase Manhattan Bank, BankAmerica Corporation, Salomon Brothers, Inc., Manufacturers Hanover Trust, The Kaempfer Company, Chemical Bank, The World Bank and ITT Corp. joined university professors, lawyers, and academics to analyze key ethical values needed for success and responsibility in business. They found that massive business and cultural changes have taken place in American society. Among them were the break-up and re-configuring of corporations, changing from a manufacturing to a service economy, and an emphasis on individual rights.

Leadership from the top is the single most important factor in creating and maintaining an ethical climate in any business.

The report's executive summary begins with the statement that "leadership from the top is the single most important factor in creating and maintaining an ethical climate in any business." Therefore, corporate leaders play an important part in developing, articulating, and maintaining values at all levels of corporate life. They listed eight values as a starting point for any CEO who wants to stress ethics in his or her business:

> Responsibility of purpose
> Responsibility to constituencies
> Honesty
> Reliability
> Fairness
> Integrity (including loyalty)
> Respect for the individual
> Respect for property

Leaders should not run their organizations by rules and procedure manuals, but by policies and philosophies.

There was no mention of making money. The report did say that "incompetence, carelessness, or the production of flawed goods injures the firm's constituencies and increases the pressure to violate other ethical principles." This document supports the contention that a movement to spread values is on the way.

In the *Maryland Business Weekly* of February 4, 1991, Blair Walker stated that many companies are implementing codes of ethics. Ronald Berenbeim, a business ethics expert, said, "I don't suppose an ethics code is going to make you a lot of money, but it could save you a lot of money." Using police parlance, we paraphrase Berenbeim by saying it may not get you more arrests, but it will reduce brutality, corruption, discrimination, and bring us closer to the people.

Stephen E. Loeb, Chairman of the Accounting Department, University of Maryland, says that "ethics is more than moralizing and saying this is right and this is wrong." People should be able to identify an ethical conflict and "have the reasoning skill and the ability to think it through and deal with the particular situation." Loeb says there is a large movement to integrate ethics into business curricula. This last thought was clearly emphasized when I heard Father Ed Molloy, President of Notre Dame University, say they were examining all the schools in the university to see where ethics could be emphasized greater than ever before.

Yes, a grass roots movement is underway. But, where do the police fit? Well, we can stand on the sidelines and cheer on those involved, or we can get into the action and make a fine contribution. We enjoy a unique place in society. We have more credibility than most. We have a noble mission -- the protection of life and property. Our organizations are goal oriented and respond to direction. We have harsh discipline and get rid of our bad apples. All of these can be brought to bear on values, and we can make our departments value-driven.

Chiefs of police and ranking officers are required to lead to get the job done. We make policy and speeches, influence committees, argue for budgets, and motivate our people toward police objectives. Why not extend that leadership to living and articulating ethical standards.

Police departments are famous for their rule books. There are rules for everything -- from how to wear the uniform to the preparation of every form used in the agency. Leaders should not run their organizations by rules and procedure manuals, but by policies and philosophies.

I surprised the members of the Baltimore County police department when, a few years ago, I informed them that I never read the rule books. True, they have their place, but not at the top. Values are not a set of rules, but rather beliefs held so strongly that they effect the way we think and act.

For the most part, police officers work unsupervised. In most jurisdictions, they work alone and make quick decisions without prior consultation. The actions they take are the result of the values they possess. What value system are they following? Take brutality as an example. When an officer in a heated situation uses the correct amount of force, is it because: it's the law, or it's the rules and regs, or people are watching, or you get in trouble if you act otherwise -- or is it because he or she believes in the dignity of man and that everyone is entitled to fair and just treatment. If it's the latter, our missteps will be minimal; with the others, slippage will be more frequent.

All police officers are leaders and role models. Look at the success of the Drug Abuse Resistance Education program (DARE). More than 8,000 cops are teaching values in our grade schools, most of them full-time. They teach children the right values and show them how to use peer pressure to stay away from drug abuse. A DARE graduation is a moving sight when all the youngsters in the 6th grade rise to their feet and scream at the top of their lungs, "NO" to drugs.

The ancillary benefits of the program have surprised us all. Children have forced their friends to go to the school principal or the DARE officer and talk as an alternative to using drugs. Absenteeism has been reduced, and problem kids have improved their behavior. The rapport and trust of the DARE officer by the children and the faculty result in the discovery of many child abuse cases.

In most jurisdictions, they work alone and make quick decisions without prior consultation. The actions they take are the result of the values they possess. What value system are they following?

Our Baltimore County P.D. values led us to our Racial, Religious, and Ethnic (RRE) policy against hate crimes. When a cross is burned, a swastika painted, or tombstones overturned, the traditional response is to investigate, gather the evidence, and try to solve the crime. Now, we go much farther. We assess the psychological and emotional damage to the victim and neighborhood. A painted swastika conjures up memories of Dachau or Buchenwald; the cross-burning -- a lynching. At the very least, fear is instilled that more is coming. We remove all signs of the offense, gather neighbor support, and visit and counsel the victims until the fear is at an irreducible level. It has meant drilling out sidewalk slabs, washing or repainting walls -- even on bridges, getting neighbors and realtors to drop by and show their concern.

I've often said that as chief I may not be able to change an attitude, but I can surely effect behavior.

When you think about it, it's amazing that all police departments don't have a written set of values just as our legal mandates are recorded. In state and municipal government charters appear directions to preserve the peace, prevent crime, arrest offenders, and protect people and property. These are values. The courts, media, crime commissions, and the public have more to say about what we should believe in than we do. Now, the Congress is busy trying to pass laws to curtail police brutality, and no doubt sexual harassment will follow. With the way it handled the Keating Five, the Barney Frank affair, and other legislators who broke the code, Congress is a fine bunch to tell us what our values ought to be. However, it's our fault if we don't have our own.

We often refer to ourselves as professionals -- a term that began in the Middle Ages. It was given to those who devoted their life to the service of God or mankind. In theory, professionals put values ahead of personal gain. I realize we all know some in the professional class who are sleazy and avaricious, or are so called because they get paid for what they do. We know many who are not.

Police have to be professional leaders in the true meaning of the word. The American people have given up certain rights and freedoms, handed them to us in order to obtain order in their lives. What kind of society would we have if no one enforced the traffic laws or dealt with outrageous behavior? The oath we take comes closer to a value system than anything else. For the power given, we swear to uphold the Constitution of the United States, the Constitution of our respective states, to obey their laws and to enforce the law fairly and impartially. But, so much is left out. Robinette, in his article "Police Ethics," January 1991 issue of the *Chief*, says we cannot teach character, but leadership "plays an important role in the conduct of organizational members." I've often said that as chief I may not be able to change an attitude, but I can surely effect behavior. Now, I state it differently. If we can improve the value systems of our agencies, if more of our people adopt the values we espouse, then we can and will change attitudes.

The Baltimore County P.D. is a value-driven agency with a long way to go. We've come a long way. We began talking about values and their importance in 1987. It is not easy to focus on values when one has a full plate and working hard to serve the community. Police executives are busy. We were greatly influenced by Edwin J. Delattre, author of *Character and Cops*, who on December 2, 1986, gave a talk on values to our executive corps. In September 1987, we issued a special order announcing that the department would undertake a values study.

In January 1988, we formed a Values Committee comprised of every rank in the department. Their mission was to establish the set of values their department was to follow and be known by. For two years it worked with others in and out of the department. At times, it was sidetracked by the press of business and their notion that this was not the most important thing to worry about. True, the chief could have drafted a set of values in a few hours. But they would have been the chief's values, not the department's. So with gentle and sometimes not so gentle nudging, the committee kept to its task.

Besides examining the literature, we received information from the police departments of Fort Collins, Colorado; Chicago, Illinois; Lynchburg and Newport News, Virginia; Madison, Wisconsin; and the Federal Bureau of Investigation. We knew that no matter what we learned from others, the values would have to fit our own organization.

The committee was also charged with determining how to disseminate and inculcate the values throughout the agency. When finalized and approved, we gave each member a copy of the value statement and a small condensed version to be carried in a wallet. No orders were issued demanding compliance nor checking to see if the small cards were being carried.

The values fell into three broad categories:

AS PUBLIC SERVANTS ...

> We shall preserve and advance the principles of democracy and freedom in our pluralistic society.

> We are accountable to higher authority and the community se serve.

AS MEMBERS OF THE POLICE DEPARTMENT ...

> We aspire to professionalism in all aspects of our operation.

> We shall maintain the highest standards of integrity.

> We shall treat each other with mutual trust, fairness, and dignity, as we strive to accomplish the Police Department's mission.

IN SERVICE TO THE COMMUNITIES OF
BALTIMORE COUNTY ...

> We are committed to fair and impartial enforcement of the laws, reduction of fear, prevention of crime, vigorous pursuit of offenders, and compassionate assistance to victims of crime.

> We are committed to community policing.

"In-service training" is an annual requirement under Maryland law. All 2,000 members of the department must attend for one week. Lesson plans are prepared and discussions held. Each week, the chief of police and his command staff spend three to four hours with the class in a segment known as "Communicating with the Administration." We chose to lead a discussion on values.

In our presentation to the class, we took a simple premise. Pointing out that police, by pursuing the violent and helping those in need, provide an important element to a free society. What we do as peace-makers enables us to lead and join the growing army dedicated to revitalizing our inherited values. No one else is in a better position to do so. The Preamble to the Constitution makes it clear: "We the people of the United States, in Order to form a more perfect Union, establish Justice ..." Police are at the front end of the justice system. The arrests we make, the relief we offer citizens to their physical injuries and victimizations starts the ball rolling. To do this with respect and dignity for the individual is essential. "[To] insure domestic tranquility ...," police respond to all disputes -- from domestic quarrels to riots. The military are brought in as a last resort, and then without bullets in their guns. The citizens need us to settle matters with impartiality and fairness.

Too often, citizens see the police as mere regulators, a necessary evil to endure. The vital role they play in society is obscure.

"[To] promote the general Welfare, and secure the Blessings of Liberty ...," by maintaining order, the police give assurances that everyone's rights are important. By helping the sick and indigent, by keeping voluminous records used in court or to settle claims, by risking our lives to safeguard others, by being accountable for what we do -- we, the police, perhaps more than any others, are positioned to keep the tenants dreamed of by our forefathers. With such an important role, isn't it absolutely necessary that we carry out our responsibilities using all the good values that exist?

Too often, citizens see the police as mere regulators, a necessary evil to endure. The vital role they play in society is obscure. Think for a moment what it would be like without them. What would substitute for the citizen volunteers who make policing their life's work. Who would maintain order? Every society demands order and rules, and someone to enforce them. Even the hippie generation of a few years ago, who went off to the countryside and set up communes to escape the regulations of the civilized world, as the first order of business established rules about sanitation, eating, and sharing work -- and a way to enforce them. Any other system of order than the one we have now will result in less freedom. That is my fear. If our current police design fails, the result will be a new America with less freedom and the shattering of our democratic ideals. Therefore, police must renew the concepts that made America the country with the most individual freedom in the history of man.

Margaret Chase Smith summed it up very well: "My creed is that public service must be more than doing a job efficiently and honestly. It must be a complete dedication to the people and to the nation, with full recognition that every human being is entitled to courtesy and consideration, that constructive criticism is not to be expected but sought, that smears are not only to be expected but fought, that honor is to be earned but not bought."

Chapter 4

The Blue Milieu: Police as a Vocational Subculture

Law enforcement is not just a job, nor is it a vocation. It is a way of life.

Scholars have often called the police bureaucracy semi-military. However, the military bureaucracy has become flexible. The police bureaucracy has not. It is a part of the blue milieu, part of the police way of life.

by Edward A. Thibault, Ph.D.

"**A**bout three months after I left the department, I was double-parked on Third Avenue. I had the parking permit in the windshield. Some sergeant from Internal Affairs comes over and he sees the permit and he asks for my badge. I said, 'What for?' He says I better just cooperate or else he's gonna pull me in ..."

"'Hey, I'm not on the ... job, asshole,' I tell him.... Meanwhile, a sergeant from the One Seven comes along and sees what's going on. 'Hey, Bo,' he says. 'How ya doin'?' 'Tell this asshole to go screw.' The asshole calls for backup, and a lieutenant comes down from the borough. He sees me. 'Hey, Bo!' I felt some satisfaction."[1]

This police officer had, as he himself admits, been a thorn in the side of the New York City police brass and had resigned because he felt he was not appreciated. Sure, he had made 1,400 felony arrests in 15 years and was awarded 75 medals, but he and the "clout" did not get along.

Yet, he couldn't give up one of the trappings of power, a police parking permit, so he could park anywhere he pleased in Manhattan. He cried on the way to putting in his shield for retirement. He felt more than some satisfaction when his fellow officers recognized him. His language is vulgar, "street language" as some scholars call it. He is rough and tough. His identification with reality, his very personality, is permeated with the blue milieu.

Is policing somehow different than other jobs?

He describes how he feels when a clerk uses a perforation stamp, stamping "retired" into his police identification card. He writes about the "little holes spelling out the end of my police career. She might as well have been punching holes in my heart."[2]

How does this feeling come about? Is policing somehow different than other jobs? The answer is a strong Yes! Being a police officer is very different than almost any job. It is not the potential for violence or upholding the law or anything that you might read in a newspaper or news magazine. It is more than that. It is the blue milieu.

Law enforcement is not just a job, nor is it just a vocation. It is a way of life. Your wife is a police officer's wife. Your children are daughters and sons of a police officer (see Howard's chapter). You have two families -- your own family and the greater police family. It is a police community that surrounds and operates in one of the most rigid bureaucracies in the nation. Scholars have often called the police bureaucracy semi-military. However, the military bureaucracy has become flexible -- even having quality circles during Operation Desert Storm. The police bureaucracy is not semi-anything. It is part of the blue milieu, part of the police way of life.

Westley's Police Culture

Police culture was discovered in a 1950 dissertation (published in 1970) about the Gary, Indiana Police Department, by William Westley. The subheadings in Westley's dissertation give all scholars of law enforcement the topics which have since been covered over and over again in various textbooks, topics, and articles on police culture:

> Police [as] dirty work
> The public as enemy
> The morality of secrecy and violence
> The roots of [police] morality: silence, secrecy, and solidarity
> The identification of norms in the legitimization of action
> Legitimization for violence[3]

Dirty Work

The dirty work is dealing with drunks, insane, and vice-ridden.[4] Like professionals in corrections and mental health, police can take on the stigma of that population they deal with. This can socially isolate a police officer and make that officer feel that the public does not respect him or her.

Public Hostility: Real and Imagined

Westley documents these feelings of public hostility by the police, time and again. "The public does not like a policeman. They think he is just a hard head, that's all. You take your average person who says he is a good citizen. But when I pinch him, I am just an asshole."[5]

In 1985, Van Maanen wrote an article, "The Asshole," where the police use stigma attached to a public they interact with to provide justification for police actions so that police are always right. He quotes one officer: "I guess what our job really boils down to is not letting the assholes take over the city.... They're the ones that make it tough on decent people out there. You take the majority of what we do and it's nothing more than asshole control."[6]

In a 1988 article, Shernock asked police in eleven police departments in small and medium size cities in New Hampshire and New York about public respect. "78.7% of the sample responded that the general public lacks appropriate respect for the police."[7] In 1950, Westley found that 73 percent of the police felt that the public was "against the police, hates the police."[8]

The Not-So Hostile Public

However, the police are generally wrong about general public hostility to police. As Walker[9] documents in his textbook on police, showing through both national and local surveys over time, "The vast majority of Americans have a generally positive attitude toward the police in their community." In a 1986 national survey, only 8 percent of Americans rated police performance poor; for Blacks it was only 11 percent and for Hispanics 6 percent.[10]

In rating police in terms of honesty and ethical standards, in a 1988 national survey, police ranked below college teachers, clergy and medical doctors, but they rated above bankers, journalists, lawyers, national, state and local office political holders, and labor union leaders. Walker points out that "the percentage of people rating the ethical standards of the police 'very high' and 'high' rose from 37% in 1977 to 47% in 1988."[11]

Law enforcement is not just a job, nor is it just a vocation. It is a way of life.

This may be changing. The Gallup Poll asked a national sample how much they respect the police in their area, and found:[12]

	1965	1967	1991
A great deal	70%	77%	60%
Some	22%	17%	32%
Hardly any	4%	4%	7%
Don't know	4%	2%	1%

This is not a large erosion of public confidence. However, a series of questions on police brutality shows some erosion.

"In some places in the nation, there have been charges of police brutality. Do you think there is any police brutality in your area or not?" In 1965, 9 percent said yes; and in 1991, 35 percent said yes.

Scholars have often called the police bureaucracy semi-military. However, the military bureaucracy has become flexible. The police bureaucracy is not semi-anything. It is part of the blue milieu, part of the police way of life.

What is more disturbing is a 1991 question: "Do you happen to know anyone who has been physically mistreated or abused by the police?" One in five, that is 20 percent, answered yes! This is a national sample and something we all need to worry about.

Before we can go on to explore the police norms of silence, secrecy, solidarity and social isolation and their relation to police behavior, we need to look for explanations for these police attitudes, especially the police officer's social construction of a reality that the public is hostile.

Study after study documents these attitudes and subcultural norms. However, few authors give an explanation besides Westley's that the public doesn't like us, or Van Maanen's that the attitudes defend even unreasonable police action. Both authors show, as others have, that such a construction of reality can lead to a justification for police violence. But why? Why do police feel this way -- especially if it is not true?

The Police as a Subculture

First, the police do show the characteristics of a subculture. A standard textbook in sociology defines subculture as "a group that shares in the overall culture of the society but also has its own distinctive values, norms and life style."[13] What we have been describing are the norms of the police subculture; as Robertson states,[14] "norms -- shared rules or guidelines that proscribe the behavior appropriate in a given situation."

When you enter the blue milieu, you become part of a life-style with distinctive norms which guide your behavior as a police officer, both on and off the job.

Protecting the Status of the Police

Goffman[15] shows us how groups manage the impressions they make on each other and why they manage these impressions:

> The structural and dramaturgical perspective seems to intersect most clearly in regard to social distance. The image that one status grouping is able to maintain in the eyes of an audience of other status groupings will depend upon the performers' capacity to restrictive communicative contact with the audience.... The cultural values of an establishment will determine how the participants are to feel about many matters and at the same time establish a framework of appearances that must be maintained....

The police need to create a reality for themselves that give them status in the country compared to other groups. Thus, the public is perceived to be hostile, filled with assholes. The police create a behavior and a morality that protects themselves and the public from these awful people. The police then create a framework of appearances that gives them a good status in relation to other groups in society and protects them from being stigmatized by the creeps and crooks that police interact with on a daily basis. By creating a social distance between the police and the crooks and creeps, the police also isolate themselves form the rest of society.

In 1970, Westley wrote, "As change escalates, they [the police] must band together and in doing so they withdraw from the community, build a wall of secrecy, and live by their own rules."[16]

After all the professionalism, education, affirmative action, the bringing in of minorities and women, police culture is almost a time capsule. Silence, secrecy, solidarity, hostility to outsiders, a perception of violence are part of ongoing norms that still shape the police agencies in every community in the nation.[17]

To most people, we seem to be inhuman, somehow separate and apart. Almost like another species. Maybe they're right but I'll tell you, I'd trust even my worst enemy in this department before I'd trust the people out there.

Blumberg's 1985 List of Police Cultural Norms

In 1985, Blumberg in the *Ambivalent Force*[18] gives us another list, not too different than Westley's but adding to it. Westley has written about many of these but did not identify by current labels. We have the standard, secrecy, solidarity, social isolation and loyalty. His social isolation goes a step further where police view themselves as a minority group.

Blumberg also adds a construction of reality that entails suspicion, perception of danger and cynicism. Police are trained in the field to view the public with suspicion and a perception of danger and violence. After all, police deal with a lower class public that lies to them and on occasion may take a shot at them. This is not an unreasonable view.

A Police Myth:
Dangerousness of Domestic Disturbances

Police may have pushed this perception too far. For example, most police consider domestic disturbances to be extremely dangerous for police officers. However, it has been documented that this one of the calls generally is not a dangerous call compared to other calls such as burglary.

Most police consider domestic disturbances to be extremely dangerous for police officers.

In 1982, the FBI reclassified disturbance class separating domestic violence. Stanford and Mowry,[19] in their study of domestic disturbance danger rate for police officers, cite a study which showed that domestic disturbances were only responsible for 5.7 percent of police deaths during the years 1973-1982. They cite other studies which showed domestic calls accounting for 8.6 percent of all assaults on police and 4 percent of officer injury. In their study of the Tampa Police Department, they conclude:[20] "Domestic disturbance situations constituted fewer calls handled by the dispatch system and occupied less time per call. Therefore, the amount of activity neither fosters the perception of increased danger nor increases the probability of injury." Needless to say, "this study does not provide support for the argument that domestic disturbance calls constitute the greatest danger to law enforcement."

Gail A Goolkasian,[21] in her monograph on domestic violence, states, "Police officers, police managers, police researchers and family violence researchers have commonly believed that domestic disturbances pose an exceedingly high physical threat to responding to officers. Training materials from the International Association of Chiefs of Police and other organizations regularly emphasize the dangerousness of domestic disturbances."

This is part of the mythology of police culture: the perception of violence and the need to deal with violence on a continuing basis. It serves to protect the police and justify police actions.

This is part of the mythology of police culture: the perception of violence and the need to deal with violence on a continuing basis. As with the perception of a hostile public, the myth persists over and beyond any objective reality. It serves to protect the police and justify police actions.

Perception of Violence: The Reality

Police work can be dangerous. It is not the same as civilian jobs, and this helps shape police culture. If you look at the period from 1980 to 1989, 801 officers were killed, with 328 in arrest situations, 132 in disturbances, broken down to 76 in bar fights and a man with gun, and 56 in domestic quarrels. The next most dangerous category is investigating suspicious persons/circumstances with 115 deaths, traffic pursuits/stops with 108 deaths, and 70 officers killed by being ambushed.[22]

However, the most dangerous thing a police officer could do from 1980 to 1989 was be anywhere near an automobile while on duty. In this period, there were 713 accidental deaths. Automobile accidents, motorcycle accidents, and being struck by vehicles (directing traffic, traffic stops, etc.) accounted for 73 percent of the deaths. Accidental shootings accounted for 60 deaths. In 1989, there were 62,172 assaults on police officers.

Police officers also kill people in the line of duty, and it can be a major trauma. John Stratton,[23] Director of Psychological Services for the Los Angeles County Sheriff's Department for twelve years, remarking on officers who are involved in traumatic incidents, wrote, "Approximately one-third have minimal, if any, problems; one-third have moderate problems; and another third have severe difficulties that affect their families...." He also added:

Trauma and upheaval are part and parcel of a police officer's job. They might witness a partner being killed or a critically injured officer narrowly escaping death; they might accidentally shoot a fellow officer or shoot and kill a suspect; they might see a child killed or abused; they will often be on the scene of fatal traffic accidents, plane crashes, and bizarre criminal cases.

The strength of Stratton's text is in his quotes from his case studies. They give you a feel for the flesh-and-blood police officer:[24]

Jim S. shot and killed an armed-robbery suspect who was leaving a store. The shooting was necessary and the officer did his job.... He told me: "I saw you three years ago after a shooting.... I lost 20 pounds. I'm divorced. I've screamed in the middle of the night and have been startled out of nightmares. I don't have the same drive, and my interest in work is lost."

In another case, he shows the importance of what he calls a support group and police culture scholars call police solidarity. Eight police officers were serving a warrant on a suspect on Monday at 8:30 at night, when another suspect killed one of the officers. One officer could not fire his gun, and the police killer ran out of the house where another officer killed him. They met two weeks later with the police psychologist:[25]

Each officer cried when expressing his feelings. One frustrated officer, sitting on the floor, was slamming his fist into the carpet. There were concerns about the dead officer's widow and her children. The officer who had been unable to shoot wondered if he would be able to shoot next time. Another officer wondered how he would act when he returned to the streets. Many of the officers were concerned about the welfare of the officer who shot and killed the suspect.

Precisely two weeks after the incident, each officer knew exactly where he was at 8:30 on a Monday night. As Stratton remarks, "It was as if each of them checked his watch at 8:30 and said to himself: 'This is the time that our fellow officer Bill was killed.'"

This is the reality of police work, even though it doesn't happen often. However, because of the intense emotions and feelings of solidarity that the perception of violence creates, it helps shape police culture. One officer told me how he opened a door for a family disturbance and a man stuck a shotgun in his stomach. The man finally submitted to be arrested. This incident stuck with the officer for his lifetime, over thirty years in police work. Incidents such as these do not have to happen often to shape a police officer and structure a subculture.

Police Cynicism

Police cynicism has been documented time and again since Niederhoffer's classic work *Behind the Shield.*[26] This was often considered part of Skolnick's[27] working police personality. There really is no police personality type. However, there is a police job and a police culture that creates certain police attitudes related to subcultural norms, such as cynicism, suspicion, perception of violence, etc.

One of the main reasons behind police cynicism is internal politics in a police department.

Blumberg, inadvertently, documents one of the main reasons behind this cynicism: internal politics in a police department. Blumberg calls it respect for power and authority. But his explanation does not show a great deal of respect. He shows how a police officer's career in the New York City police department may be helped by a rabbi (or a hook in other departments). A rabbi is an older police officer of superior rank who helps another police officer up the ranks in terms of assignments and promotion. It could be a friend of the family, a kin, etc. Since promotion is supposed to be objective in civil service, this could create a certain amount of cynicism.

Thibault, Lynch and McBride[28] have shown how a police duty manual made up of trivial rules and used to "get" officers also creates a certain disrespect for authority. Since the police officer's own rule book for running the department has often been trivialized and used unfairly and in large departments, officers may feel that they can only get "good" assignments, etc. with the help of a rabbi. The internal workings of the police department creates a certain cynicism.

Police as a Minority Group

This attitude results in the police feeling that they are a minority group. As Shernock[29] states, "As a result of police perception of public hostility toward them, police officers have assumed many of the characteristics of a minority group." Blumberg[30] agrees with this and adds, "The police, prosecution and criminal courts represent a closed community manifesting a defensive attitude toward 'outsiders' and 'critics'."

Blumberg also shows how the feeling of social isolation has gradually turned into a feeling of the police as a minority group. Since they feel the public does not support them, the police often develop a "we and they" attitude, treating the public almost as an enemy.

He then worries about the role of professionalism and the police, and concludes, "For too long, the police as an occupational group has been out of the mainstream of society."[31] It could be 1950, but instead it is 1985 and nothing has changed.

Stan Shernock's 1988 fine research article on police and community stated:[32] "They tend to socialize almost exclusively with other police officers and their families in order to avoid unpleasant interactions with civilians who view them only in terms of their police identity." His next subheading is, what else, "Solidarity and Secrecy."

Productivity: The Pressure to Produce

Finally, Blumberg shows a fairly new phenomenon in local police departments -- the pressure to produce.[33] "There is in police departments an emphasis on 'activity,' 'batting averages,' 'quotas,' and 'collars' as yardsticks to measure the worth of performance for purposes of promotion or assignment to less onerous duties." J. Edgar Hoover was, of course, the master at this as he created meaningless statistics about stolen cars and communist infiltrators while ignoring organized crime for years.[34]

Hoover's FBI developed, for example, the crime clock which states that a crime would be committed every so many seconds. There is a finite number of seconds in a year while the population and crime grows every year. Thus, happily for the FBI, Hoover could document to the Congress that more crimes were committed for each second of the year, and it went up every year. Every year, partially through blackmail and such erroneous devices as the crime clock, Hoover received more resources to fight the war on crime.

According to Walker,[35] "In 1960 only 20% of all sworn officers had had any college education; by 1988 the figure had reached 65% with 22.6% of officers holding four year degrees or more." With the prestige of the FBI as a model of using figures to justify funding, our professional, college-educated administrators also discovered figures. As the saying goes, "figures don't lie, but liars figure." This attitude has created a performance measure for personnel that is close to such items as traffic ticket quotas, and has placed increased pressure on personnel to perform in order to have good figures for budget time.

This is part of some large police departments. All departments do not operate this way, especially not in small towns and rural areas. However, where this system has been implemented, it will help shape the professional lives of each police officer.

One of the criticisms of the police culture concept is that police departments have changed considerably in terms of personnel and that police culture is no longer relevant.[36] As has been noted, the subcultural norms of police culture have been documented time and again from 1950 to the 1990s, and they have not changed.

We may have a more professionally oriented police department, but it is still one that is governed by police culture norms.

Higher Education and Police Culture

As has been pointed out, we have a more educated force; however, as Thibault and Weiner[37] noted in their article "The Anomic Cop" back in 1973, police culture overwhelms the effects of higher education. Today, this still seems to be the case. For example, Wycoff and Susmilch,[38] in examining the relevance of college education for policing, reviewed a number of studies and concluded that "a college education does not appear to be significantly related to the attitudes which have interested researchers." We may have a more professionally oriented police department, but it is still one that is governed by police culture norms.

Women Police Officers and Police Culture

Women have been police officers since Allice Stebbins Wells joined the Los Angeles Police Department in 1910. It was only in 1968 when women first went on a regular patrol in Car 47 in Indianapolis.[39] Now it is the 1990s, and after a number of successful affirmative action cases, women do have a larger role in police departments.

In a study[40] of all police departments serving populations of 50,000 or more and all state police departments, in 1978 women were roughly 5 percent of police personnel in the metropolitan departments. In 1986, this had grown to roughly 10 percent. In state police departments, the total female police went from .9 percent in 1978 to 3.7 percent in 1986.[41] In 1987, the U.S. Department of Justice reported that the percentage of women in the 59 largest city police departments was 9.3 percent.[42] Of the 25 largest municipal police departments in 1987, the following five had the largest percentage of female police officers:

Detroit	18.9%
Pittsburgh	15.4%
Washington, D.C.	14.0%
Atlanta	13.4%
San Diego	12.2%

There were also departments like Newark with 1 percent and San Antonio with 5.6 percent.

The reality is that in major metropolitan police departments, only one in ten officers is a female; and in rural areas where there generally have been no affirmative action cases, the percentage should be much lower.

One female police officer states what has been happening to many of these women throughout the country:[43]

> My first year as a police officer was spent in constant battle with men who refused to accept women in patrol. This was complete with practical jokes, calling in sick, sexist remarks, and men who just outwardly refused to work with women. There were days when some of the female officers left the precinct cursing, crying, but stubbornly returning the next day to face the same harassment they had vowed and sworn they didn't have to take.

The female police officer does want to be accepted and still be female. As one officer stated:[44]

> Does the fact that you carry a gun, have killed a man, make you any less feminine? Or does the fact that you

have proven you can protect yourself as well as your
male partner make you less of a woman or him less of
a man? No!!

Joseph Balkin[45] titled his article "Why Policemen Don't Like Policewomen." He went on to document from numerous studies that women
police officers were competent and did fine police work. Other studies
have documented that women with their less aggressive attitude than
the men handle violent confrontations better than the men, the men are
more likely to discharge their gun, and there is no difference in the
amount of injuries sustained by men and women police officers.[46]
However, in case after case, policemen were hostile to policewomen.[47]
"A policewoman reported that the men were very interested in whether
policewomen were lesbians. If not, the men flirted or teased them. 'If
you are sleeping with someone you are a slut; if not you are a dyke.'" The
reason why policemen do not like policewomen is police solidarity.
"This solidarity is in the service of ameliorating the men's sense of
isolation from the public and the dangerousness of their work. Women
in policing undermine this solidarity. They are not like them and are
[therefore] opposed."[48]

African American and Latino
Police Officers and Police Culture

When you look at the research on African American and Latino police
officers, their attitudes are obvious -- they want to be part of police
culture, and their only complaints relate to promotions and being
excluded socially from the white police officer's social world.[49] Unlike
the female officer, they have fairly large numbers. For the 59 large
police departments in the United States, African Americans and Latinos
in 1987 make up 22 percent of the full-time sworn officers; e.g., Detroit
49.1 percent, Washington D.C. 57.1 percent, San Antonio 43.8 percent,
and Atlanta 52.6 percent.[50] These are significant numbers.

What is happening is that they are being assimilated by the police
culture. As Walker[51] points out, "Black officers tend to arrest black
suspects more often than white officers." They use their guns on an
equal basis and have a bit more positive attitude toward the neighborhood in which they are assigned.

Gay Police Officers

A new group -- gay police officers -- has become organized and public. Even here, the complaint is much like the women officers' complaint of lack of acceptance. The president of the New York Police Department's Gay Officers Action League, Sgt. Charlie Cochrane,[52] states: "There is no conflict in being a cop and being gay.... My goal, although it may never be fully realized in my lifetime, is to erase this stigma." He wants the gay cop to be simply accepted by the police culture.

The Undercover Police Officer

Given the sense of loyalty and unity in most police departments, being undercover, as pointed out in Gary Marx's brilliant book, can lead to some real identity problems. Marx[53] has a number of quotes from undercover officers, all on one page, that gives us a feeling for the problem:

> You're working with dope fiends and perverts all day, and a guy on the vice squad usually goes down, he deteriorates; he becomes like the people you work with.

> I knew it was a role playing thing, but I became total, 100 percent, involved. I became what I was trying to tell people I was, and it confused me. Believe me, it confused me a lot.

> I began to wake up in the morning and look at myself in the mirror and see my reflection -- and I didn't like what I was.... I didn't like the way I was dressing. We all started wearing pinkie rings. I hated them, but I found myself wearing one.... I started looking like Mafia guys.

> ... one day ... something snapped. I just felt it like a jolt going through ... and I was no longer afraid or nervous. It was like I had a handle on things.... A short time after that ... I didn't believe I was a cop.

Some of the police officers started identifying more with the bad guys than the good guys. Some were turned. Many had identity crises.

One police officer, after he had worked undercover with drug dealers for a number of years, told me he went into a Chinese restaurant for dinner with his wife. The manager told him he could only eat there if he sat in the back. The police officer's wife was mortified. He soon switched back to the uniform division, under pressure from his wife. After all, she was a police officer's wife, not the wife of some "asshole."

The police have constructed their own social reality: police culture.

Most of the time, the social solidarity of the police agency is an excellent support system. However, the undercover police officer becomes isolated from his fellow officer, dresses and acts like the deviants he is supposed to be arresting, and becomes isolated from the other officers.

Conclusion

The police have constructed their own social reality: police culture. The vocational social norms of social isolation, secrecy, perception of danger, perception of a hostile public, for example, have survived professionalism, upgrading in the education of police officers and the successful implementation of affirmative action. Minority, female, and even gay police officers want to be part of the police culture and accepted as police officers.

Why does police culture persist? The police deal with roughly 5 percent of the population, and most of them are not pleasant people. The police officer deals with them in high stress, tension-filled situations. The job can also be dangerous, and the true stories of danger become part of the mythology of the police profession.

Police need to protect themselves and develop strong social support among themselves in order to survive as human beings. The police administration was never seen as supportive by the line officer. The new "production" systems of accountability will further alienate the line officer from "the brass." Given their perception of a hostile public, who is there left to draw on for social support for the line officers but themselves?

A knowledge of police culture is especially useful for programs that attempt to involve the line officers deeply with the local community. If social isolation and perceptions of hostility of the local citizens are high, then the line officer simply won't cooperate with these programs.

Three current approaches to policing are *community policing,*[54] which seems to be the old team policing concept without the teams, but still working closely with community groups (see Murphy's chapter). *Problem-centered policing*[55] is a type of task force approach where police departments concentrate a large number of resources on specific problems in specific neighborhoods and eliminate these problems. If organized well, over a long period of time, this sometimes works, or at its worst it simply displaces crime to other neighborhoods. Finally, there are projects aimed at *fear reduction,*[56] so the citizens have less fear in terms of living in their neighborhoods. All of these have admirable aims and some good concepts that might even work with a good police management team.

Police managers have to educate their own departments about the support for police activities that already exist for the police, even in minority neighborhoods. Police managers have to mitigate the social isolation of the police, or these programs simply won't work. Most police managers are not willing to do this, so most of these programs are doomed to failure. Where you have a progressive, proactive police management that is willing to come to grips as to how their own police agencies actually work within the context of the social reality of police culture, then these and similar programs stand a chance.

Proactive police managers need to distance themselves from the blue milieu if they are to understand how their own departments and officers operate.

Police culture is good when it functions as a solid support system for the individual officers. However, police culture has its negative aspects. It doesn't work well for the female and gay police officers who are seen as threats to that social solidarity. It protects police corruption and brutality. It does not support undercover officers who are crucial in corruption and drug investigations. It can also be hostile to the very communities that the police are sworn to protect.

Whatever the judgment, positive or negative, the cultural norms of police culture are alive and well, and operating on a daily basis in every police department in the nation. Proactive police managers need to distance themselves from the blue milieu if they are to understand how their own departments and officers operate. Police managers, if they are to operate their departments on a proactive basis, have to understand how police culture both supports and undermines their departments.

REFERENCES

Balkin, Joseph. "Why Policemen Don't Like Policewomen," *Journal of Police Science and Administration*, March 1988, pp. 29-38.

Blumberg, Abraham. "The Police and the Social System: Reflections and Prospects," in Blumberg, Abraham and Niederhoffer, Elaine (Eds.), *The Ambivalent Force*. Hinsdale, Illinois: Dryden Press, 1985, pp. 3-26.

Blumberg, Abraham and Niederhoffer, Elaine. *The Ambivalent Force*. Hinsdale, Illinois: Dryden Press, 1985.

Broderick, J. *Police in a Time of Change*, 2nd ed. Prospect Heights, Illinois: Waveland, 1987.

Dietl, Bo and Cross, Ken. *One Tough Cop*. New York: Pocket Books, 1988.

Garner, J. and Clemmer, E. *Danger to Police in Domestic Disturbances -- A New Look*. Washington, D.C.: U.S. Department of Justice, 1986.

Gentry, Curt. *J. Edgar Hoover*. New York: W.W. Norton, 1991.

Goffman, Erving. *Presentation of Self in Everyday Life*. Garden City, New York: Doubleday, 1959.

Goldstein, Herman. *Problem Oriented Policing*. New York: McGraw-Hill, 1990.

Goolkasian, Gail A. *Confronting Domestic Violence: A Guide for Criminal Justice Agencies*. Washington, D.C.: U.S. Department of Justice, 1986.

Grennan, Sean A. "Findings on the Role of Officer Gender in Violent Encounters with Citizens," *Journal of Police Science and Administration*, Vol. 15, No. 1, March 1987, pp. 78-85.

Kelling, George L. "Police and Communities: The Quiet Revolution," in Siegel, Larry J. (Ed.), *American Justice: Research of the National Institute of Justice*. St. Paul, Minnesota: West, 1991, pp. 121-128.

Leinen, S. *Black Police, White Society*. New York: Basic Books, 1984.

Macquire, Kathleen and Flanagan, Timothy J. (Eds.), *Sourcebook of Criminal Justice Statistics 1990*. U.S. Department of Justice, Bureau of Justice Statistics, 1991.

Marx, Gary T. *Undercover: Police Surveillance in America*. Berkeley: University of California Press, 1988.

Mitteager, Jim. "NYPD's Gay Cops," *The National Centurion*, Vol. 2, No. 1, February 1984, pp. 33-36, 71.

Moore, Mark H. and Trojanowicz, Robert C. "Policing and Fear of Crime," in Siegel, Larry J. (Ed.), *American Justice: Research of the National Institute of Justice*. St. Paul, Minnesota: West, 1991, pp. 129-136.

Nicholas, Alex. *Black in Blue*. New York: Appleton-Century-Crofts, 1969.

Niederhoffer, Arthur. *Behind the Shield*. Garden City, N.Y.: Doubleday, 1967.

Niederhoffer, Arthur and Blumberg, Abraham. *The Ambivalent Force*. Hinsdale, Illinois: Dryden Press, 1976.

Police Foundation. *On the Move: The Status of Women in Policing*. Washington, D.C.: Police Foundation, 1990.

Reicher, Lisa M. and Roberg, Roy R. "Community Policing: A Critical Review of Underlying Assumptions," *Journal of Police Science and Administration*, June 1990, Vol. 17, No. 2, pp. 105-114.

Robertson, Ian. *Sociology*, 3rd edition. New York: Worth Publishers, Inc., 1987.

Shernock, Stan K. "An Empirical Examination of the Relationship Between Police Solidarity and Community Orientation," *Journal of Police Science and Administration*, Vol. 16, No. 3, September 1988, pp. 183-194.

Skolnick, Jerome H. "A Sketch of the Policeman's Working Personality," in Blumberg, Abraham and Niederhoffer, Elaine (Eds.), *The Ambivalent Force*. Hinsdale, Illinois: Dryden Press, 1985.

Skolnick, Jerome H. and Gray, Thomas C. *Police in America*. Boston: Little, Brown, 1975.

Stanford, Rose Mary and Mowry, Bonney Lee. "Domestic Disturbance Danger Rate," *Journal of Police Science and Administration*, Vol. 17, No. 4, December 1990, pp. 240-244.

Stratton, John G. *Police Passages*. Sandusky, Ohio: Glennon Publishing Company, 1984.

Tauber, Ronald K. "Danger and the Police: A Theoretical Analysis," *Issues in Criminology*, Vol. 3, Summer 1967, pp. 69-81.

Thibault, Edward and Weiner, Norman L. "The Anomic Cop," *Humboldt Journal of Social Relations*, Fall 1973, reported in *Human Behavior*, 1974.

Thibault, Edward A., Lynch, Lawrence M. and McBride, R. Bruce. *Proactive Police Management*, 2nd edition. Englewood Cliffs, New Jersey: Prentice Hall, 1990.

Van Maanen, John. "The Asshole," in Manning, Peter K. and Van Maanen, John (Eds.), *Policing: A View From the Street.* Santa Monica, California: Goodyear Publishing, 1978.

Walker, Samuel. "Racial Minority and Female Employment in Policing: The Implications of 'Glacial' Change," *Crime and Delinquency,* Vol. 31, October 1985, pp. 355-572.

Walker, Samuel. *The Police in America.* New York: McGraw-Hill, Inc., 1992.

Westley, William A. *Violence and the Police.* Cambridge, Mass.: Massachusetts Institute of Technology, 1970.

Weiner, Norman. *The Role of the Police in Urban Society: Conflicts and Consequences.* Indianapolis, Indiana: Bobbs-Merrill, 1976.

Wilson, James Q. *Varieties of Police Behavior.* Cambridge, Massachusetts: Harvard University Press, 1968.

Wycoff, Mary Ann and Susmilch, Charles E. "The Relevance of College Education for Policing: Continuing the Dialogue," in Petersen, David M. (Ed.), *Police Work.* Beverly Hills, California: Sage, 1979, pp. 17-36.

NOTES

1. Dietl, Bo and Cross, Ken. *One Tough Cop*. New York: Pocket Books, 1988, p. 276.
2. Ibid., p. 274.
3. Westley, William A. *Violence and the Police*. Cambridge, Mass.: Massachusetts Institute of Technology, 1970, pp. xx, xxi.
4. Ibid., p. 15.
5. Ibid., p. 94.
6. Van Maanen, John. "The Asshole," in Manning, Peter K. and Van Maanen, John (Eds.), *Policing: A View From the Street*. Santa Monica, California: Goodyear Publishing, 1978, p. 221.
7. Shernock, Stan K. "An Empirical Examination of the Relationship Between Police Solidarity and Community Orientation," *Journal of Police Science and Administration*, Vol. 16, No. 3, September 1988, p. 188.
8. Westley, P. 93.
9. Walker, Samuel. *The Police in America*. New York: McGraw-Hill, Inc., 1992, p. 231.
10. Ibid., p. 226.
11. Ibid., p. 229.
12. Macquire, Kathleen and Flanagan, Timothy J. (Eds.) *Sourcebook of Criminal Justice Statistics, 1990*. U.S. Department of Justice, Bureau of Justice Statistics, 1991, p. 67.
13. Robertson, Ian. *Sociology*, 3rd edition. New York: Worth Publishers, Inc., p. 76.
14. Ibid., p. 62.
15. Goffman, Erving. *The Presentation of Self in Everyday Life*. Garden City, New York: Doubleday, 1959, pp. 240-241.
16. Westley, p. 192.
17. Van Maanen, p. 121.
18. Blumberg, Abraham. "The Police and the Social System: Reflections and Prospects," in Blumberg, Abraham and Niederhoffer, Elaine (Eds.), *The Ambivalent Force*. Hinsdale, Illinois: Dryden Press, 1985, pp. 1-19.
19. Stanford, Rose Mary and Mowry, Bonney Lee. "Domestic Disturbance Danger Rate," *Journal of Police Science and Administration*, Vol. 17, No. 4, December 1990, p. 244.
20. Ibid., p. 248.

21. Goolkasian, Gail A. *Confronting Domestic Violence: A Guide for Criminal Justice Agencies*. Washington, D.C.: U.S. Department of Justice, 1986, p. 6.
22. Macquire and Flanagan, p. 394.
23. Stratton, John G. *Police Passages*. Sandusky, Ohio: Glennon Publishing Company, 1984, pp. 225-226.
24. Ibid., p. 228.
25. Ibid., p. 232.
26. Niederhoffer, Arthur and Blumberg, Abraham. *The Ambivalent Force*. Hinsdale, Illinois: Dryden Press, 1976.
27. Skolnick, Jerome H. "A Sketch of the Policeman's Working Personality," in Blumberg, Abraham and Niederhoffer, Elaine (Eds.), *The Ambivalent Force*. Hinsdale, Illinois: Dryden Press, 1985, pp. 80-90.
28. Thibault, Edward A., Lynch, Lawrence M., and McBride, R. Bruce. *Proactive Police Management*, 2nd edition. Englewood Cliffs, New Jersey: Prentice Hall, 1990, pp. 28-54, 128-132.
29. Shernock, p. 184.
30. Blumberg, "The Police and the Social System: Reflections and Prospects," pp. 12-14.
31. Ibid., pp. 12-24.
32. Shernock, p. 185.
33. Blumberg, "The Police and the Social System: Reflections and Prospects," p. 19.
34. Gentry, Curt. *J. Edgar Hoover*. New York: W.W. Norton, 1991.
35. Walker, *The Police in America*, p. 23.
36. Ibid., pp. 333-335.
37. Thibault, Edward and Weiner, Norman L. "The Anomic Cop," *Humboldt Journal of Social Relations*, Fall 1973, reported in *Human Behavior*, 1974.
38. Wycoff, Mary Ann and Susmilch, Charles E. "The Relevance of College Education for Policing: Continuing the Dialogue," in Petersen, David M. (Ed.), *Police Work*. Beverly Hills, California: Sage, 1979, p. 26.
39. Balkin, Joseph. "Why Policemen Don't Like Policewomen," *Journal of Police Science and Administration*, March 1988, p. 30.
40. Police Foundation. *On the Move: The Status of Women in Policing*. Washington, D.C.: Police Foundation, 1990, p. 31.
41. Ibid., p. 186.

42. Macquire and Flanagan, p. 37.

43. Stratton, pp. 195-196.

44. Ibid., p. 197.

45. Balkin, p. 29.

46. Grennan, Sean A. "Findings on the Role of Officer Gender in Violent Encounters with Citizens," *Journal of Police Science and Administration*, March 1987, p. 84.

47. Balkin, p. 33.

48. Ibid., p. 35.

49. Nicholas, Alex. *Black in Blue.* New York: Appleton-Century-Crofts, 1969. Leinen S. *Black Police, White Society.* New York: Basic Books, 1984. Walker, Samuel. "Racial Minority and Female Employment in Policing: The Implications of 'Glacial' Change," *Crime and Delinquency*, Vol. 31, October 1985, pp. 355-572.

50. Macquire and Flanagan, p. 37.

51. Walker, *The Police in America*, pp. 337-338.

52. Mitteage, Jim. "NYPD's Gay Cops," *The National Centurion*, Vol. 2, No. 1, February 1984, pp. 33-36, 71.

53. Marx, Gary T. *Undercover: Police Surveillance in America.* Berkeley: University of California Press, 1988, p. 164.

54. Kelling, George L. "Police and Communities: The Quiet Revolution," in Siegel, Larry J. (Ed.), *American Justice: Research of the National Institute of Justice.* St. Paul, Minnesota: West, 1991, pp. 121-128. Reicher, Lisa M. and Roberg, Roy R. "Community Policing: A Critical Review of Underlying Assumptions," *Journal of Police Science and Administration*, Vol. 17, No. 2, June 1990, pp. 105-114.

55. Goldstein, Herman. *Problem Oriented Policing.* New York: McGraw-Hill, 1990.

56. Ibid.

Chapter 5

The Ethics of Deceptive Interrogation

Should police ever employ trickery and deceit during interrogation in a democratic society?

Although lying is considered immoral, virtually no one is prepared to forbid it categorically.

How are we to balance our respect for truth and fairness with our powerful concern for public safety?

by: **Jerome H. Skolnick[1]**
Richard A. Leo[2]

As David Rothman and Aryeh Neier have recently reported, "third degree" police practices -- torture and severe beatings -- remain commonplace in India, the world's largest democracy.[3] Police brutality during interrogation flourishes because it is widely accepted by the middle classes.[4] Although this may seem un-civilized to most Americans, it was not so long ago that American police routinely used physical violence to extract admissions from criminal suspects.[5] Since the 1960s and especially since *Miranda*, police brutality during interrogation has virtually disappeared in America. Although one occasionally reads about or hears reports of physical violence during custodial questioning,[6] police observers and critics agree that the use of physical coercion during interrogation is now infrequent.[7]

This transformation occurred partly in response to the influential Wickersham report,8 which disclosed widespread police brutality in the United States during the 1920s; partly in response to a thoughtful and well-intentioned police professionalism, as exemplified by Fred Inbau and his associates; and partly in response to changes in the law which forbade police to "coerce" confessions but allowed them to elicit admissions by deceiving suspects who have waived their right to remain silent. Thus, over the last 50 to 60 years, the methods, strategies, and consciousness of American police interrogators have been transformed.

Psychological persuasion and manipulation have replaced physical coercion as the most salient and defining features of contemporary police interrogation. Contemporary police interrogation is routinely deceptive.[9] As it is taught and practiced today, interrogation is shot through with deception. Police are instructed to, are authorized to -- and do -- trick, lie, and cajole to elicit so-called "voluntary" concessions.

Police deception, however, is more subtle, complex, and morally puzzling than physical coercion. Although we share a common moral sense in the West that police torture of criminal suspects is so offensive as to be impermissible -- a sentiment recently reaffirmed by the violent images of the Rodney King beating -- the propriety of deception by police is not nearly so clear. The law reflects this ambiguity by being inconsistent, even confusing. Police are permitted to pose as drug dealers, but not to use deceptive tactics to gain entry without a search warrant; nor are they permitted to falsify an affidavit to obtain a search warrant.

The acceptability of deception seems to vary inversely with the level of the criminal process. Cops are permitted to, and do, lie routinely during investigation of crime -- especially when, working as "undercovers," they pretend to have a different identity.[10] Sometimes they may, and sometimes may not, lie when conducting custodial interrogations. Investigative and interrogatory lying are each justified on utilitarian crime control grounds. But police are never supposed to lie as witnesses in the courtroom, although they may lie for utilitarian reasons similar to those permitting deception at earlier stages.[11]

In this chapter, we focus on the interrogatory stage of police investigation, considering (1) how and why the rather muddled legal theory authorizing deceptive interrogation developed; (2) what deceptive interrogation practices police, in fact, engage in; and -- a far more difficult question -- (3) whether police should ever employ trickery and deceit during interrogation in a democratic society that values fairness in its judicial processes.

Police deception is more subtle, complex, and morally puzzling than physical coercion.

The Jurisprudence of Police Interrogation

The law of confessions is regulated by the Fifth, Sixth and Fourteenth Amendments. Historically, the courts have been concerned almost exclusively with the use of *coercion* during interrogation. Although a coerced confession has been inadmissible in federal cases since the late Nineteenth Century, the Supreme Court did not proscribe physically coercive practices in state cases until 1936.[12] In *Brown v. Mississippi*, three black defendants were repeatedly whipped and pummeled until they confessed. This was the first in a series of state cases in which the Court held that confessions could not be "coerced" but had to be "voluntary" to be admitted into evidence.[13]

Whether a confession meets that elusive standard is to be judged by "the totality of the circumstances." Under that loose and subjective guideline, an admission is held up against "all the facts" to decide whether it was the product of a "free and rational will" or whether the suspect's will was "overborne" by police pressure. Over the years, however, certain police practices have been designated as presumptively coercive. These include physical force, threats of harm or punishment, lengthy or incommunicado interrogation, denial of food and/or sleep, and promises of leniency.[14] In 1940, the Supreme Court ruled -- in a case in which a suspect was first threatened with mob violence, then continuously questioned by at least four officers for five consecutive days -- that psychological pressure could also be coercive.[15]

One reason for excluding admissions obtained through coercion is their possible falsity. But, beginning with *Liesnba v. Califonia*[16] in 1941, and followed by *Ashcraft v. Tennessee*[17] three years later, the Supreme Court introduced the criterion of *fairness* into the law. Whether in the context of searches or interrogations, evidence gathered by police methods that "shock the conscience" of the community or violate a fundamental standard of fairness are to be excluded, regardless of reliability.[18] This rationale is sometimes twinned with a third purpose: deterring offensive or unlawful police conduct.

In its watershed *Miranda* decision, the Supreme Court in 1966 prescribed specific limitations on custodial interrogation by police.[19] The five-to-four majority deplored a catalog of manipulative and potentially coercive psychological tactics employed by police to elicit confessions from unrepresented defendants. In essence, the court could not reconcile ideas such as "fairness" and "voluntariness" with the increasingly sophisticated and psychologically overbearing methods of interrogation. In response, it fashioned the now familiar prophylactic rules to safeguard a criminal defendant's Fifth Amendment right against testimonial compulsion. As part of its holding, *Miranda* requires that (1) police

The case law of criminal procedure has rarely addressed the troubling issue of trickery and deceit during interrogation.

advise a suspect of his right to remain silent and his right to an attorney, and (2) the suspect "voluntarily, knowingly and intelligently" have waived these rights before custodial interrogation can legally commence. An interrogation is presumed to be coercive unless a waiver is obtained. Once obtained, however, the "due process-voluntariness" standard governs the admissibility of any confession evidence. In practice, once a waiver is obtained, most of the deceptive tactics deplored by the majority become available to the police.

In retrospect, *Miranda* seems to be an awkward compromise between those who argue that a waiver cannot be made "intelligently" without the advice of an attorney, who would usually advise the client to remain silent, and those who would have preferred to retain an unmodified voluntariness standard because police questioning is "a particularly trustworthy instrument for screening out the innocent and fastening on the guilty," and because the government's obligation is "not to counsel the accused but to question him."[20]

In sum, then, three, sometimes competing, principles underlie the law of confessions: first, the truth-finding rationale, which serves the goal of *reliability* (convicting an innocent person is worse than letting a guilty one go free); second, the substantive due process or *fairness* rationale, which promotes the goal of the system's integrity; and third, the related *deterrence* principle, which proscribes offensive or lawless police conduct.

The case law of criminal procedure has rarely, however, and often only indirectly, addressed the troubling issue of trickery and deceit during interrogation. We believe this is the key issue in discussing interrogation since, we have found, interrogation usually implies deceiving and cajoling the suspect.

Police deception that intrudes upon substantive constitutional rights is disallowed. For example, the Supreme Court has ruled that an officer cannot trick a suspect into waiving his *Miranda* rights. But apart from these constraints, the use of trickery and deceit during interrogation is regulated solely by the due process clause of the Fourteenth Amendment, and is proscribed, on a case-by-case basis, only when it violates a fundamental conception of fairness or is the product of egregious police misconduct. The courts have offered police few substantive guidelines regarding the techniques of deception during interrogation. Nor have the courts successfully addressed the relation between fairness and the lying of police, or the impact of police lying on the broader purposes of the criminal justice system, such as convicting and punishing the guilty. As we shall see, the relations among lying, conceptions of fairness, and the goals of the criminal justice system raise intriguing problems.

Typology of Interrogatory Deception

Because police questioning remains shrouded in secrecy, we know little about what actually happens during interrogation. Police rarely record or transcribe interrogation sessions.[21] Moreover, only two observational studies of police interrogation have been reported, and both are more than two decades old.[22] Most articles infer from police training manuals what must transpire during custodial questioning. Our analysis is based on Richard Leo's dissertation research. It consists of a reading of the leading police training manuals from 1942 to the present, from attending local and national interrogation training seminars and courses, from listening to tape recorded interrogations, from studying interrogation transcripts, and from ongoing interviews with police officials.

"Interview" versus "Interrogate"

The Court in *Miranda* ruled that warnings must be given to a suspect who is in custody, or whose freedom has otherwise been significantly deprived. However, police will question suspects in a "non-custodial" setting -- which is defined more by the suspect's state of mind than by the location of the questioning -- so as to circumvent the necessity of rendering warnings. This is the most fundamental, and perhaps the most overlooked, deceptive stratagem police employ. By telling the suspect that he is free to leave at any time, and by having him acknowledge that he is voluntarily answering their questions, police will transform what would otherwise be considered an interrogation into a non-custodial interview. Thus, somewhat paradoxically, courts have ruled that police questioning outside of the station may be custodial,[23] just as police questioning inside the station may be non-custodial.[24] The line between the two is the "objective" restriction on the suspect's freedom. Re-casting the interrogation as an interview is the cleanest deceptive police tactic since it virtually removes police questioning from the realm of judicial control.

Re-casting the interrogation as an interview is the cleanest deceptive police tactic.

Miranda Warnings

When questioning qualifies as "custodial," however, police must recite the familiar warnings. The Court declared in *Miranda* that police cannot trick or deceive a suspect into waiving *Miranda* rights.[25] The California Supreme Court has additionally ruled that police cannot "soften up" a suspect prior to administering the warnings.[26] However, police routinely deliver the *Miranda* warnings in a flat, perfunctory tone of voice to communicate that the warnings are merely a bureaucratic ritual. Although it might be inevitable that police would deliver *Miranda* warnings unenthusiastically, investigators whom we have interviewed say that they *consciously* recite the warnings in a manner intended to heighten the likelihood of eliciting a waiver. It is thus not surprising that police are so generally successful in obtaining waivers.[27]

Misrepresenting the Nature or Seriousness of the Offense

Once the suspect waives, police may misrepresent the nature or seriousness of the offense. They may, for example, tell a suspect that the murder victim is still alive, hoping that this will compel the suspect to talk. Or police may exaggerate the seriousness of the offense -- overstating, for example, the amount of money embezzled -- so that the suspect feels compelled to confess to a smaller role in the offense. Or the police may suggest that they are only interested in obtaining admissions to one crime, when in fact they are really investigating another crime. For example, in a recent case, *Colorado v. Spring*, federal agents interrogated a suspect on firearms charges and parlayed his confession into an additional, seemingly unrelated and unimportant admission of first degree murder.[28] Despite their pretense to the contrary, the federal agents were actually investigating the murder, not the firearms charge. This tactic was upheld by the Supreme Court.

Role Playing: Manipulative Appeals to Conscience

The most well-known role that interrogators act out is the good cop/bad cop routine.

Effective interrogation often requires that the questioner feign different personality traits or act out a variety of roles.[29] The interrogator routinely projects sympathy, understanding, and compassion in order to play the role of the suspect's friend. The interrogator may also try to play the role of a brother or father figure, or even to act as a therapeutic or religious counselor to encourage the confession. The most well-known role that interrogators act out is, of course, the good cop/bad cop routine, which may be played out by a single officer. While acting out these roles, the investigator importunes -- sometimes relentlessly -- the suspect to confess for the good of his case, his family, society, or conscience. These tactics generate an illusion of intimacy between the suspect and the officer while down-playing the adversarial aspects of interrogation.

Misrepresentation is advertised by police training manuals and firms as one of their most effective.

The courts have routinely upheld the legitimacy of such techniques -- which are among the police's most effective in inducing admissions -- except when such role-playing or manipulative appeals to conscience can be construed as "coercive," as when, for example, an officer implies that God will punish the suspect for not confessing.[30]

Misrepresenting the Moral Seriousness of the Offense

Misrepresentation of the moral seriousness of an offense is at the heart of interrogation methods propounded by Inbau, Reid, and Buckley's influential police training manual.[31] Interrogating officials offer suspects excuses or moral justifications for their misconduct by providing the suspect with an external attribution of blame that will allow him to save face while confessing. Police may, for example, attempt to convince an alleged rapist that he was only trying to show the victim love or that she was really "asking for it"; or they may persuade an alleged embezzler that blame for his actions is attributable to low pay or poor working conditions. In *People v. Adams*, for example, the officer elicited the initial admission by convincing the suspect that it was the gun, not the suspect, that had done the actual shooting.[32] Widely upheld by the courts, this tactic is advertised by police training manuals and firms as one of their most effective.

The Use of Promises

The systematic persuasion -- the wheedling, cajoling, coaxing, and importuning -- employed to induce conversation and elicit admissions often involves, if only implicitly or indirectly, the use of promises. Although promises of leniency have been presumed to be coercive since 1897, courts continue to permit vague and indefinite promises.[33] The admissibility of a promise thus seems to turn on its specificity. For example, in *Miller v. Fenton*, the suspect was repeatedly told that he had mental problems and thus needed psychological treatment rather than punishment. Although this approach implicitly suggested a promise of leniency, the court upheld the validity of the resulting confession.[34]

Courts have also permitted officers to tell a suspect that his conscience will be relieved only if he confesses, or that they will inform the court of the suspect's cooperation, or that "a showing of remorse" will be a mitigating factor, or that they will help the suspect out in every way they can if he confesses.[35] Such promises are deceptive insofar as they create expectations that will not be met. Since interrogating officials are single-mindedly interested in obtaining admissions and confessions, they do not always feel obliged to uphold their promises.

Misrepresentations of Identity

A police agent may try to conceal his identity, pretending to be someone else, while interrogating a suspect. In *Leyra v. Denno*, the suspect was provided with a physician for painful sinus attacks he began to experience after several days of unsuccessful interrogation.[36] But the physician was really a police psychiatrist, who repeatedly assured the defendant that he had done no wrong and would be let off easily. The suspect subsequently confessed, but the Supreme Court ruled here that the confession was inadmissible. It would be equally impermissible for a police official or agent to pretend to be a suspect's lawyer or priest. However, in a very recent case, *Illinois v. Perkins*, a prison inmate, Perkins, admitted a murder to an undercover police officer who, posing as a returned escapee, had been placed in his cell-block.[37] The Rehnquist Court upheld the admissibility of the confession. Since Perkins was in jail for an offense unrelated to the murder to which he confessed, the Rehnquist Court said, Perkins was not "in custody" for *Miranda* purposes. Nor, for the same reason, were his Sixth Amendment *Massiah* rights violated.[38] Thus, the profession or social group with which an undercover officer or agent identifies during the actual questioning may -- as a result of professional disclosure rules or cultural norms -- be more significant to the resulting legal judgment than the deceptive act itself.[39]

Perhaps the most dramatic physical evidence ploy is to stage a line-up, in which a coached witness falsely identifies the suspect.

Fabricated Evidence

Police may confront the suspect with false evidence of his guilt. This may involve one or more of five gambits. One is to falsely inform the suspect that an accomplice has identified him. Another is to falsely state that existing physical evidence -- such as fingerprints, bloodstains, or hair samples -- confirm his guilt. Yet another is to assert that an eyewitness or the actual victim has identified and implicated him. Perhaps the most dramatic physical evidence ploy is to stage a line-up, in which a coached witness falsely identifies the suspect. Finally, one of the most common physical evidence ploys is to have the suspect take a lie-detector test and, regardless of the results -- which are scientifically unreliable and invalid in any event -- inform the suspect that the polygraph confirms his guilt.[40] In the leading case on the use of police trickery, *Frazier v. Cupp*, the Supreme Court upheld the validity of falsely telling a suspect that his crime partner had confessed.[41]

The Consequences of Deception

Although lying is, as a general matter, considered immoral, virtually no one is prepared to forbid it categorically. The traditional case put to the absolutist is that of the murderer chasing a fleeing innocent victim, whose whereabouts are known by a third party. Should the third party sacrifice the innocent victim to the murderer for the cause of truth? Few of us would say that he should. We thus assume a utilitarian standard regarding deception. So too with respect to police interrogation.

Interrogatory deception is an exceedingly difficult issue, about which we share little collective feeling. How are we to balance our respect for truth and fairness with our powerful concern for public safety and the imposition of just deserts? We are always guided by underlying intuitions about the kind of community we want to foster and in which we want to live. Which is worse in the long run -- the excess of criminals or the excess of authorities?

Few of us would countenance torture by police in the interests of those same values. One reason is that violence may produce false confessions. As Justice Jackson observed in his dissent in *Ashcraft*: "... [N]o officer of the law will resort to cruelty if truth is what he is seeking."[42] But that is only partly correct. Cruelty can also yield incontrovertible physical evidence. We reject torture for another reason -- we find it uncivilized, conscience-shocking, and unfair, so most of us are repelled by it. That leads to a third reason for opposing torture. If effective law enforcement requires public trust and cooperation, as the recent movement toward community-oriented policing suggests, police who torture can scarcely be expected to engender such confidence.

What about police deception? Does it lead to false confessions? Is it unfair? Does it undermine public confidence in the police? A recent and fascinating capital case in Florida Court of Appeals, *Florida v. Cayward*, the facts of which are undisputed, is relevant to the above questions.[43] The defendant, a 19-year-old male, was suspected of sexually assaulting and smothering his 5-year-old niece. Although he was suspected of the crime, the police felt they had too little evidence to charge him. So they interviewed him, eventually advised him of his rights, and obtained a written waiver.

Cayward maintained his innocence for about two hours. Then the police showed him two false reports which they had fabricated with the knowledge of the state's attorney. Purportedly scientific, one report used Florida Department of Criminal Law Enforcement stationery; another used the stationery of Life Codes, Inc., a testing organization. The false reports established that his semen was found on the victim's underwear. Soon after, Cayward confessed.

"Of course the police should lie to catch the murdering rapist of a child," said one. "I don't want to live in a society where police are allowed to lie and to falsify evidence," said another.

Should this deception be considered as akin to lying to a murderer about the whereabouts of the victim? Or should police trickery, and especially the falsification of documents, be considered differently? We un-systematically put this hypothetical to friends in Berkeley and asked about it in a discussion with scholars-in-residence at the Rockefeller Study Center in Bellagio, Italy. For some, the answer was clear -- in either direction. "Of course the police should lie to catch the murdering rapist of a child," said one. "I don't want to live in a society where police are allowed to lie and to falsify evidence," said another. Most were ambivalent, and all were eager to know how the Florida court resolved the dilemma.

To be more systematic, we administered a questionnaire to our students in an undergraduate criminal justice class, and to police in the patrol division of the Hayward, California police department. We told them that the questionnaire was intended to gauge public sentiment about the propriety of police interrogation tactics and that answers would remain anonymous and used only for academic purposes. The basic facts of the questionnaire were grounded in the Florida case, with three variations. The basic facts were stated as follows.

> A 19-year-old male is suspected of sexually assaulting and smothering his 5-year-old niece. After two hours of police questioning, the suspect still denies having committed the crime.

In the first variation:

> The interrogating officer momentarily steps out of the
> room and returns with a rubber hose. After the suspect
> is beaten with the rubber hose for 15 minutes, he
> screams out in pain and confesses.

The police and the students were asked whether this interrogation was
"fair"? As we anticipated, all of the police and all of the students
reported that it was not, and approximately the same percentages, 81
percent (n = 71) of the students and 83 percent (n = 52) of the police felt
it should be excluded. We had anticipated a strong exclusionary
response with this set of facts, and had intended to use the first variation
to have respondents commit themselves to the principle of exclusion
based on unfairness, even when the crime was shocking. Respondents
were then presented with the second variation, based on the true facts of
Florida v. Cayward:

> The interrogating officer momentarily steps out of the
> room and returns with two fabricated scientific reports:
> One is prepared on the stationery of the State Department
> of Criminal Law Enforcement; the other is prepared on
> the stationery of Life Codes, Inc., a private testing
> organization. These false reports indicate that a scientific
> test establishes that the semen stains on the victim's
> underwear came from the suspect. Proclaiming the
> suspect's guilt, the police officers show the reports to
> the suspect. The suspect confesses.

Here we find, however, quite striking and statistically significant
differences between the students and the police. Of the police, 83
percent felt the interrogation was fair, while only 17 percent of the
students thought so. Similarly, 11 percent of the officers and 46 percent
of the students thought the confession should be excluded. (Note that
when the suspect was beaten instead of deceived, 83 percent of the
officers thought the confession should be excluded.) In variation 3,
there is again deception; but instead of showing false reports to the
suspect, the police pretend that they have just received phone calls from
scientific laboratories indicating that the semen stains on the victim's
underwear were the suspect's. That is, here the police lie, but without
showing forged documents. Almost all the police (94 percent) thought

the interrogation was "fair" and only 8 percent said its results should be excluded. But almost two-thirds of the students (64 percent) disagreed that it was fair, and 53 percent thought its results should be excluded.

What did the Florida Court decide? Citing *Frazier v. Cupp* and other cases, the court recognized "that police deception does not render a confession involuntary *per se.*" Yet the court, deeply troubled by the police deception, distinguished between "verbal assertions and manufactured evidence." A "bright line" was drawn between the two on the following assumption: "It may well be that a suspect is more impressed and thereby more easily induced to confess when presented with tangible, official-looking reports as opposed to merely being told that some tests have implicated him."[44]

Although we do not know the accuracy of the conjecture, it assumes that false police assertions such as "Your fingerprints were found on the cash register" are rarely believed by suspects unless backed up by a false fingerprint report. But in these deception cases, we do not usually encounter prudent suspects who are skeptical of the police. Such suspects rarely, if ever, waive their constitutional rights to silence or to an attorney. As in *Cayward*, and many deception cases, the suspect, young or old, white or black, has naively waived his right to remain silent and to an attorney.

Would such a suspect disbelieve, for example, our third scenario?: After two hours of questioning, the telephone rings. The detective answers, nods, looks serious, turns to the suspect and says, "We have just been informed by an independent laboratory that traces of your semen were found, by DNA tests, on the panties of the victim. What do you say to that?"

A verbal lie can be more or less convincing, depending upon the authority of the speaker, and manner of speaking, its contextual verisimilitude, and the gullibility of the listener. False documentation adds to verisimilitude, but a well-staged, carefully presented verbal lie can also convince. The decision in *Cayward*, however well-written and considered, is nevertheless bedeviled by the classic problem of determining whether Cayward's confession was "voluntary."

No *contested* confession, however, is ever voluntary in the sense of purging one's soul of guilt, as one would to a religious figure.

"The principal value of confession may lie elsewhere, in its implicit reaffirmation of the moral order," writes Gerald M. Caplan. "The offender by his confession acknowledges that he is to blame, not the community."[45] That observation focuses on the offender. Sometimes that is true, often times it is not. Those who contest their confessions claim that they were unfairly pressured, and point to the tactics of the police. The claim is that the police violated the moral order by the use of unfair, shady, and thus wrongful tactics to elicit the confession. Had the police, for example, beaten a true confession out of Cayward, it would indeed seem perverse to regard his confession as a reaffirmation of the moral order.

If Cayward had been beaten, and had confessed, we would also be concerned that his confession was false. Assuming that all we know are the facts stated in the opinion, which say nothing of corroborating evidence or why Cayward was suspected, should we assume that his confession was necessarily true? However infrequent they may be, false confessions do occur. Moreover, they do not result *only* from physical abuse, threats of harm, or promises of leniency, as Fred Inbau and his associates have long maintained;[46] nor are they simply the result of police pressure that a fictionalized reasonable person would find "overbearing," as Joseph Grano's "mental freedom" test implies.[47] They may arise out of the manipulative tactics of the influence and persuasion commonly taught in police seminars and practices by police and used on Cayward.

A coerced-internalized" false confession causes an innocent person to temporarily internalize the message(s) of his interrogators and falsely believe himself to be guilty.

Psychologists and others have recently begun to classify and analyze the logic and process of these false confessions,[48] which are among the leading causes of wrongful conviction.[49] Perhaps most interesting is the "coerced-internalized" false confession, which is elicited when the psychological pressures of interrogation cause an innocent person to temporarily internalize the message(s) of his interrogators and falsely believe himself to be guilty.[50] Although Cayward was probably factually guilty, he might have been innocent. Someone who is not altogether mature and mentally stable, as would almost certainly be true of a 19-year-old accused of smothering and raping his 5-year-old niece, might also have a precarious and vague memory. When faced with fabricated, but supposedly incontrovertible, physical evidence of his guilt, he might falsely confess to a crime of which he has no recollection, as happened in the famous case of Peter Reilly,[51] and, more recently, in the Florida case of Tom Sawyer,[52] both of which were "coerced-internalized" false confessions.[53]

If Cayward was, in fact, guilty, as his confession suggests, the court was nevertheless willing to exclude it. Presumably, he will remain unpunished unless additional evidence can be produced. Characterizing the falsified evidence as an offense to "our traditional notions of due process of law," the Florida court was evidently alarmed by the *unfairness* of a system which allows police to "knowingly fabricate tangible documentation or physical evidence against an individual."[54] In addition to its "spontaneous distaste" for the conduct of the police, the court added a longer-range utilitarian consideration. Documents manufactured for such purposes, the court fears, may, because of their "potential of indefinite life and the facial appearance of authenticity,"[55] contaminate the entire criminal justice system. "A report falsified for interrogation purposes might well be retained and filed in police paperwork. Such reports have the potential of finding their way into the courtroom."[56] The court also worried that if false reports were allowed in evidence, police might be tempted to falsify all sorts of official documents "including warrants, orders and judgments," thereby undermining public respect for the authority and integrity of the judicial system.

Yet the slippery slope argument applies to lying as well as to falsification of documents. When police are permitted to lie in the interrogation context, why should they refrain from lying to judges when applying for warrants, from violating internal police organization rules against lying, or from lying in the courtroom? For example, an *Oakland Tribune* columnist, Alix Christie, recently received a letter from a science professor at the University of California at Berkeley who had served on an Alameda County (Oakland) murder jury. He was dismayed that a defendant, whom he believed to be guilty, had been acquitted because most of the jurors did not believe the police, even about how long it takes to drive from west to east Oakland. "The problem," writes Christie, "predates Rodney King. It's one familiar to prosecutors fishing for jurors who don't fit the profile of people who distrust cops." She locates the problem in "the ugly fact that there are two Americas." In the first America, the one she was raised in, the police are the "good guys." In the other, police are viewed skeptically.

Police misconduct -- and lying is ordinarily considered a form of misconduct -- undermines public confidence and social cooperation, especially in the second America. People living in these areas often have had negative experiences with police, ranging from an aloof and legalistic policing "style" to corruption, and even to the sort of overt brutality that was captured on the videotape of the Rodney King beating in Los Angeles. Community-oriented policing is being implemented in a number of American police departments to improve trust and citizen cooperation by changing the attitudes of both police and public.

Police deception may thus engender a paradoxical outcome. Although affirmed in the interest of crime control values by its advocates like Fred Inbau -- who, along with his co-author John Reid, has exerted a major influence on generations of police interrogators -- it may generate quite unanticipated consequences. Rarely do advocates of greater latitude for police to interrogate consider the effects of systematic lying on law enforcement's reputation for veracity. Police lying might not have mattered so much to police work in other times and places in American history. But today, when urban juries are increasingly composed of individuals disposed to be distrustful of police, deception by police during interrogation offers yet another reason for disbelieving law enforcement witnesses when they take the stand, thus reducing police effectiveness as controllers of crime.

Police and prosecutors affirm deceitful interrogative practices not because they think these are admirable, but because they believe such tactics are necessary.

Conservatives who lean toward crime control values do not countenance lying as a general matter. They approve of police deception as a necessity, measuring the cost of police deceit against the benefits of trickery for victims of crime and the safety of the general public. Police and prosecutors affirm deceitful interrogative practices not because they think these are admirable, but because they believe such tactics are necessary.[57]

The Florida police officers who fabricated evidence did so for the best of reasons. The victim was a 5-year-old girl, and the crime was abhorrent and hard to prove. Nevertheless, the Florida court excluded the confession on due process grounds, arguing that police must be discouraged from fabricating false official documents. Many persons, but especially those who, like Fred Inbau, affirm the propriety of lying in the interrogatory context, tend to undervalue the significance of the long-term harms caused by such authorized deception: namely, that it tends to encourage further deceit, undermining the general norm against lying. And if it is true that the fabrication of documents "greatly lessens," as the Florida court says, "the respect the public has for the criminal justice system and for those sworn to uphold and enforce the law,"[58] doesn't that concern also apply to interrogatory lying?

There is an additional reason for opposing deceitful interrogation practices. It does happen that innocent people are convicted of crimes -- not as often, probably, as guilty people are set free, but it does happen. Should false evidence be presented, a suspect may confess in the belief that he will receive a lesser sentence. In a study in 1986 of wrongful conviction in felony cases, Ronald Huff and his colleagues conservatively estimated that nearly 6,000 false convictions occur every year in the United States.[59] Hugo Bedau and Michael Radelet, who subsequently studied 350 known miscarriages of justice in recent American history, identified false confessions as one of the leading sources of erroneous conviction of innocent individuals.[60]

There are no easy answers to these dilemmas, no easy lines to suggest when the need to keep police moral and honest brushes up against the imperatives of controlling crime. Phillip E. Johnson, who has proposed a thoughtful statutory replacement for the *Miranda* doctrine,[61] would not allow police to "intentionally misrepresent the amount of evidence against the suspect, or the nature and seriousness of the charges,"[62] as well as other, clearly more coercive tactics. But he would allow feigned sympathy or compassion, an appeal to conscience or values, and a statement to the suspect such as "A voluntary admission of guilt and sincere repentance may be given favorable consideration at the time of sentence."[63] Johnson states no formal *principle* for these distinctions, but does draw an intuitively sensible contrast between, on the one hand, outright *misrepresentations*, which might generalize to other venues and situations; and, on the other, *appeals* to self-interest or conscience, which seem to draw upon commonly held and morally acceptable values. If however, as we have argued, rules for police conduct, and the values imparted through these rules, produce indirect, as well as direct, consequences for police practices and the culture of policing, Johnson's distinctions are persuasive. This resolution, we suggest, is quite different from the direction recently taken by the Rehnquist Court.

We have earlier argued that when courts allow police to deceive suspects for the good end of capturing criminals -- even as, for example, in "sting" operations -- they may be tempted to be untruthful when offering testimony. However we think we ought to resolve the problem of the ethics of deceptive interrogation, we need always to consider the unanticipated consequences of permitting police to engage in what would commonly be considered immoral conduct -- such as falsifying evidence. The Supreme Court has moved in recent years to soften the

A thoughtful statutory replacement for the __Miranda__ doctrine would not allow police to "intentionally misrepresent the amount of evidence against the suspect, or the nature and seriousness of the charges.

control of police conduct in interrogation. In *Moran v. Burbine*, for example, the Court let stand a murder conviction even though the police had denied a lawyer -- who had been requested by a third party, but without the suspect's knowledge, prior to his questioning -- to the suspect during interrogation. The dissenters decried the "incommunicado questioning" and denounced the majority for having embraced "deception of the shabbiest kind."[64]

More recently, the notoriety of the beating of Rodney King overshadowed the significance of the Rehnquist Court's most significant self-incrimination decision, *Arizona v. Fulminante*.[65] Here, a confession was obtained when a prison inmate, an ex-cop who was also an FBI informer, offered to protect Fulminate from prison violence, but only if he confessed to the murder of his daughter. In a sharply contested 5-to-6 opinion, the Court reversed the well-established doctrine that a coerced confession could never constitute "harmless error." Whether the ruling will be as important in *encouraging* police coercion of confessions as the King videotape will be in discouraging future street brutality remains to be seen. But in concert with other recent U.S. Supreme Court decisions that have cut back on the rights of defendants, the *Fulminante* decision may also send a message that police coercion is sometimes acceptable, and that a confession elicited by police deception will almost always be considered "voluntary."

NOTES

1   Jerome H. Skolnick, author of *Justice Without Trial: Law Enforcement in a Democratic Society*, is Claire Clements Dean's Professor of Law and the University of California at Berkeley; Richard A. Leo, a graduate student at the University of California at Berkeley, is currently researching police interrogation for his doctoral dissertation.

2.   For helpful advice, criticism, and counsel, we would like to thank the following individuals: Albert Altschuler, Jack Greenberg, James Hahn, Sanford Kadish, Norman LaPera, Gary Marx, Paul Mishkin, Robert Post, Peter Sarna, Jonathan Sither, Jeremy Waldron, and, especially, Phillip Johnson.

3.   Rothman & Neier, "India's Awful Prisons." New York review of books (1991), pp. 53-56.

4.   Ibid., p. 54.

5.   Hopkins, *Our Lawless Police: A Study of Unlawful Law Enforcement* (1931), and Lavine, *The Third Degree: A Detailed and Appalling Expose of Police Brutality* (1930).

6.   "Confessions at Gunpoint?" 20/20, ABC News. March 29, 1991.

7.   Caplan, "Miranda Revisited," 93 *Yale Law Review*: 1375-1385 (1984).

8.   National Commission on Law Observance and Enforcement, *Lawlessness in Law Enforcement* Washington, 1931).

9.   Richard Leo, "From Coercion to Deception: The Changing Nature of Police Interrogation in America," *Law, Social Change, and Crime* (July 1992).

10.   Marx, *Undercover: Police Surveillance in America* (1988).

11.   Skolnick, *Deception by Police, Criminal Justice Ethics* (Summer, Fall 1982), pp. 40-54.

12.   *Brown v. Mississippi*, 297 U.S. 278 (1936).

13.   Caplan, "Questioning Miranda," 38 *Vanderbilt Law Review*: 1417 (1985).

14.   The Supreme Court's very recent ruling that coerced confessions may be "harmless error" will undermine this general rule. *Arizona v. Fulminante*, U.S. Lexis 1854 (1991).

15.   *Chambers v. Florida*, 309 U.S. 227 (1940).

16.   314 U.S. 219 (1941).

17.   322 U.S. 143 (1944).

18.   See *Rochin v. California*, 342 U.S. 165 (1952); *Spano v. New York*, 360 U.S. 315 (1959); and *Rogers v. Richmond*, 365 U.S. 534 (1961).

19. *Miranda v. Arizona*, 384 U.S. 436 (1961).

20. Op. Cit., Caplan (1985), pp. 1422-23.

21. The state of Alaska requires, as a matter of state constitutional due process, that all custodial interrogations be electronically recorded. See *Stephen v. State*, 711 P.2d 1156 (1989).

22. Wald, et al., "Interrogations in New Haven: The Impact of Miranda," 76 *Yale Law Journal*: 1519-1648 (1967), and Milner, *Court and Local Law Enforcement: The Impact of Miranda* (1971).

23. *Orozco v. Texas*, 394 U.S. 324 (1969).

24. See *Beckwith v. United States*, 425 U.S. 341 (1976); *Oregon v. Mathiason*, 429 U.S. 492 (1977); and *California v. Beheler*, 463 U.S. 1121 (1983).

25. However, police may deceive an attorney who attempts to invoke a suspect's constitutional rights, as to whether the suspect will be interrogated, and the police do not have to inform the suspect that a third party has hired an attorney on his behalf. *People v. Moran*, 475 U.S. 412 (1986).

26. *People v. Honneycutt*, 570 P.2d 1050 (1977).

27. See Stephens, Jr., *The Supreme Court and Confessions of Guilt* (1973), pp. 165-200, for a useful summary of studies assessing the impact of *Miranda* in New Haven, Los Angeles, Washington, D.C., Pittsburgh, Denver, and rural Wisconsin. These studies indicate that police obtain waivers from criminal suspects in most cases. Additionally, the Captain of the Criminal Investigation Division of the Oakland Police Department told one of the authors that detectives obtain waivers from criminal suspects in 85-90% of all cases involving interrogations.

28. *Colorado v. Spring*, 107 S.Ct. 851 (1987).

29. Consider the following passage from Royal and Schutt, Op. Cit. (p. 65): "To be truly proficient at interviewing or interrogation, one must possess the ability to portray a great variety of personality traits. The need to adjust character to harmonize with, or dominate, the many moods and traits of the subject is necessary. The interviewer/interrogator requires greater histrionic skill than the average actor.... The interviewer must be able to pretend anger, fear, joy, and numerous other emotions without affecting his judgment or revealing any personal emotional about the subject."

30. *People v. Adams*, 143 Cal.App.3d 970 (1983).

31. Inbau, Reid and Buckley, *Criminal Interrogation and Confessions* (1986).

32. Op. Cit., *People v. Adams*.

33. *Bram v. United States*, 168 U.S. 532 (1897).

34. *Miller v. Fenton*, 796 F.2d 598 (1986).

35. Kaci and Rush, "At What Price Will We Obtain Confessions?", *Judicature*, Vol. 71 (1988), pp. 256-257.

36. *Leyra v. Denno*, 347 U.S. 556 I (1954).

37. *Illinois v. Perkins*, 110 S.Ct. 2394 (1990).

38. In *Massiah v. United States*, 377 U.S. 201 (1964), the U.S. Supreme Court held that post-indictment questioning of a defendant outside the presence of his lawyer violates the Sixth Amendment.

39. Cohen, "Miranda and Police Deception in Interrogation: A Comment on *Illinois v. Perkins*," *Criminal Law Bulletin*: 534-546 (1990).

40. Skolnick, "Scientific Theory and Scientific Evidence: Analysis of Lie Detection," 70 *Yale Law Journal*: 694-728 (1961); and Lykken, *A Tremor in the Blood: Uses and Abuses of the Lie-Detector* (1981).

41. *Frazier v. Cupp*, 394 U.S. 731 (1969).

42. Op. Cit., *Ashcraft v. Tennessee*, p. 160.

43. *Florida v. Cayward*, 552 So.2d 971 (1989).

44. Op. Cit., *Florida v. Cayward*, 977.

45. Op. Cit., Caplan (1984).

46. Inbau, *Lie-Detection and Criminal Interrogation* (1942).

47. Grano, "Voluntariness, Free Will, and the Law of Confessions," 65 *Virginia Law Review*: 859-945 (1979).

48. Kassin and Wrightsman, Confession Evidence in Kassin and Wrightsman (Eds.), *The Psychology of Evidence and Trial Procedure* (1985); Gudjonsson and Clark, *Suggestibility in Police Interrogation: A Social Psychological Model* (1985); Ofshe, "Coerced Confessions: The Logic of Seemingly Irrational Action, 6 *Cultic Studies Journal*: 6-15 (1989); Gudjonsson, "The Psychology of False Confessions," 57 *Medico-Legal Journal*: 93-110 (1989); and Ofshe and Leo (1991), *The Social Psychology of Coerced-Internalized False Confessions,"* paper presented at the Annual Meetings of the American Sociological Association, August 23-27, 1991.

49. Bedau and Radelet, "Miscarriages of Justice in Potentially Capital Cases, 40 *Stanford Law Review*: 21-179 (1987).

50. Ibid., Kassin and Wrightsman.

51. Bartel, *A Death in Canaan* (1976); and Connery, *Guilty Until Proven Innocent* (1977).

52. *State of Florida v. Tom Franklin Sawyer*, 561 So.2d 278 (1990). See also Philip Weiss, "Untrue Confessions," *Mother Jones* (September 1989), pp. 22-24, 55-57.

53. Op. Cit., Ofshe and Leo (1991).

54. Op. Cit., *Florida v. Cayward*, p. 978.

55. Ibid.

56. Ibid.

57. Inbau, "Police Interrogation -- A Practical Necessity," 52 *Journal of Criminal Law, Criminology, and Police Science*: 412 (1961).

58. Op. Cit., *Florida v. Cayward*, p. 983.

59. Huff et al., "Guilty Until Proven Innocent: Wrongful Conviction and Public Policy," 32 *Crime and Delinquency*: 518-544 (1986); Rattner, "Convicted But Innocent: Wrongful Conviction and the Criminal Justice System," 12 *Law and Human Behavior*: 283-293 (1988).

60. Op. Cit., Bedau and Radelet (1987).

61. P. Johnson, *Criminal Procedure* (1988), pp. 540-550.

62. Ibid., p. 542.

63. Ibid.

64. *Moran v. Burbine*, 475 U.S. 412 (1986).

65. Op. Cit., *Arizona v. Fulminante* (1991).

Chapter 6

Can Accreditation Survive the '90s?

Accreditation promises more for police organizations than other management tools, but why has it failed to acquire the overwhelming support that other types of law enforcement programs have received?

Does accreditation make an agency responsive to community needs and demands?

by Timothy N. Oettmeier, Ph.D.

Accreditation has been a part of the law enforcement scene for over a decade. Spearheaded by the formation of the Commission on Accreditation for Law Enforcement Agencies (CALEA) in 1979, police departments are now afforded an opportunity to become accredited if they can demonstrate compliance with a specified number of "professionally" developed standards. Agency size will dictate various levels of compliance when determining a department's qualification status. Irrespective of agency size, accreditation is touted by CALEA (1984) as being able to: 1) increase an agency's capabilities of preventing and controlling crime; 2) enhance the effectiveness and efficiency of service delivery; 3) improve cooperation and coordination with other law enforcement agencies and other components of the criminal justice system; and 4) increase citizen and staff confidence in the goals, objectives, policies, and practices of the agency. Whether or not these "goals" are actually attained on a consistent basis is open to serious debate.

CALEA (1984) also purports to claim that an accredited agency will reap many benefits -- among them, nationwide recognition of professional excellence, continued growth and improvement, employee confidence-esprit, proactive management systems, access to the latest law enforcement practices, etc. These benefits are derived by virtue of having a police agency comply with standards spread throughout six major law enforcement areas, inclusive of: 1) role, responsibilities, and relationships with other agencies; 2) organization, management, and administration; 3) personnel administration; 4) law enforcement operations, operations support, and traffic law enforcement; 5) prisoner and court-related services; and 6) auxiliary and technical services. Accreditation, according to CALEA (1984), is designed to reflect the best professional practices in each of these six areas. Collectively, the standards deal with "what" to do, leaving the decisions of "how" to do it up to the agency.

Neil Behan (1984), Chief of Baltimore County which was one of the first large-scale agencies to become accredited, has stated that his agency has supported and espoused, since its inception, the concept of establishing standards of accreditation by which our (agency's) professionalism, programs, training, and general performance can be measured.

As enticing as it may sound, accreditation is not without its critics. Probably one of the most visibly recognized opponents is Daryl Gates, the embattled Chief of the Los Angeles Police Department. Gates (1985) is on record claiming that "the accreditation program is costly, unnecessary, serves no long-standing useful purpose to law enforcement, and threatens the very foundation of local government."

Research regarding the status of accreditation within this country is minuscule at best.

Research regarding the status of accreditation within this country is minuscule at best. The most intriguing descriptive research conducted on accreditation has been performed by David Carter (et al., 1991). Contained within his survey of contemporary police issues were a number of questions pertaining to accreditation.

Of the 340 responding agencies, Carter (et al., 1991) found that 68 percent were not accredited nor in the process of being accredited. When asked about the likelihood of nonaccredited departments willing to seek accreditation, only 22 percent indicated that they "definitely" will or that there is a "good" likelihood that they will seek accreditation. Another 30 percent stated that they "will" consider seeking accreditation, while the remaining 47 percent said they "probably will not seek" or "definitely will not" seek accreditation.

When the respondents were asked what they thought the benefits would be as a direct result of becoming accredited, the predominant responses included: 1) establishing a standard for evaluation, 2) modernizing policies and procedures, and 3) projecting higher status and recognition from the public and one's peers. What is obviously missing from these responses is a belief that accreditation will improve service delivery capabilities, reduce crime, enhance the agency's capacity to prevent crime, or facilitate the formation of a partnership with the public in order to address community problems of crime and disorder. Curiously enough, some of these excluded beliefs are the very things CALEA claims will occur by virtue of becoming accredited.

According to Carter's (et al., 1991) findings, the major problems encountered by the respondents who have attempted to become accredited include: 1) the amount of time it takes to become accredited, 2) the amount of resources expended to become accredited, 3) the costs of making operational changes and rewriting policies and procedures, and 4) garnering acceptance by the officers and labor organizations.

If Carter's responses are indicative of a national trend, one could cautiously conclude that the accreditation process is far from being accepted by the majority of police chiefs in this country. Unfortunately, as of this writing only CALEA knows how many of their 17,000 plus targeted agencies are presently: 1) seeking to become accredited, 2) have become accredited and are pursuing reaccreditation, 3) have been accredited and are not opting to become reaccredited, or 4) have failed to become accredited and why. What is blatantly obvious, absent this information, is recognizing that police chiefs are not "beating down the door" to have their departments become accredited.

Contrast this lack of a large-scale, bona fide movement for accreditation with the late 1970s when the Field Training and Evaluation Program (FTEP) burst onto the law enforcement scene. Here was a program that was unquestionably perceived by police departments as a valid management tool. As a consequence, FTEPs were implemented within agencies throughout the country at breakneck speed. The strength of FTEPs can also be measured in terms of their durability. With the promulgation of the nationally distributed *Field Training Quarterly* magazine[1] and emergence of the National Association of Field Training Officers,[2] FTEPs are assured of continued growth and development.

On the surface, accreditation promises so much more for police organizations than FTEPs. Why, then, has accreditation failed to acquire the overwhelming support other types of law enforcement programs have received? The answer may be as simple as acknowledging that many police chiefs are not convinced that the accreditation process, as presently conceived, is a viable management tool to help strengthen organizational development. The purpose of this chapter is to provoke serious thought about the accreditation process within a management context.

A major premise of this article is the notion that if a police department has developed an effective management system and is addressing the problems and concerns of the community in a competent manner, it may not need to be accredited. Even if a department is perceived to be "weak" on policies and procedures but is considered to be well managed and well led, accreditation probably won't fly because the chief will perceive the process as not being able to add substantive value to the agency's mode of operation. The implication of this premise is that adjustments should be made to the accreditation process so it will be perceived as being useful to all agencies.

CALEA operates on the assumption that administrative compliance will enhance organizational control which, in turn, will promote the attainment of results

What is the Purpose of Accreditation?

From a practitioner's perspective, accreditation is an illusive concept. CALEA (1984) insists that the purpose for creating the commission was to provide law enforcement agencies with an opportunity to voluntarily participate in a process to demonstrate that they meet professional standards. CALEA operates on the assumption that administrative compliance will enhance organizational control which, in turn, will promote the attainment of results. Point of fact, the accreditation process does not measure the effect of administrative compliance. Accreditation seeks only to standardize procedures and then determine if those procedures are being adhered to by agency personnel. The accreditation process does not attempt to determine if there is a direct relationship between a standard and the attainment of a specific result -- the reason for developing the standard in the first place.

Should we be surprised, then, when practitioners claim that the accreditation process will have little practical impact? Probably not. As noted by Morrison (1987), for the working policeman, it really doesn't seem to have much of an effect other than to hopefully make regulations a little clearer.

If this perception is predominant within police agencies, then one must wonder if the stated purpose of accreditation really has any meaningful value to a community. Are police chiefs so incredibly caught up with

The decision to pursue accreditation is probably based on the chief's assessment of whether the "gain is going to be worth the pain."

the "me-too syndrome" that they will pursue the process of accreditation solely on the "belief" that it will make their agency more responsive to community needs and demands absent any tangible proof that this will happen? As plausible as this may sound, surely it can't be true -- can it?

In actuality, the decision to pursue accreditation is probably based on the chief's assessment of whether the "gain is going to be worth the pain." This quandary is similar to the following analogy.

Let's assume you haven't been feeling well for a number of days. You have tried the obvious home remedies but to no avail. You begin to think about the prospects of having to go see a doctor. Chances are the doctor will ask you why you don't feel good -- to wit, you don't know, otherwise you wouldn't need to see the doctor. Eventually, you know the doctor will want to begin poking and jabbing, sticking things down your throat, scraping for samples, and conducting other assorted tests. Since this is not very appealing and is certainly going to be more time-consuming than you desire, doubt begins to set in. You begin to think about this whole process a little bit more, before asking yourself the inevitable question: Do I really want to be subjected to all of this? Your answer hinges on what you perceive to be the impending outcome.

If your answer is yes, then you don't mind the uncomfortableness, because in the long run you feel better knowing that your condition has been properly diagnosed and treated. If your answer is no, you are gambling that with the passage of time, everything will revert back to a state of normalcy. Basically, you feel that the trip to the doctor's office will do nothing more than affirm your own suspicions that you're perfectly healthy, "other than the reaction you got from eating a bad piece of food the other night (or whatever)."

The decision to pursue accreditation isn't much different from this analogy. In both instances, the decision is based on what is perceived to be the value of subjecting oneself or the organization to an unpleasant process.

In the case of deciding whether or not to pursue becoming accredited, the chief must realize that an affirmative answer will subject his department to a very lengthy, intensive, and rigorous self-assessment process. Herein lies a very dangerous pitfall for unsuspecting chiefs. The process of accreditation becomes an end in itself, rather than a means to an end.

Police chiefs must come to grips with the prospect that when they commit their agency to becoming accredited, the entire organization will become subservient to the process of standardization. Just about every action taken within the agency will be reviewed in terms of how it will help or hinder the prospects of complying with the accreditation standards. It makes little difference if these actions were prompted by the need to address community problems of crime and disorder. If it is inconsistent with an accreditation standard, it will probably be perceived as not being vital to the operation of the organization.

The accreditation process also requires literally hundreds of directives, policies, or procedures to be reviewed, revised, created, or deleted. Larger agencies are required to produce up to as many as 50 reports, all under the rhetoric that it will make the department more efficient and effective.[3]

Some departments have been known to refer to the production of this massive amount of paperwork as a "paper tiger phenomenon." A by-product of this phenomenon is having police managers split their valuable time between the performance of their normal responsibilities and ensuring compliance with accreditation standards. In other words, police managers spend more of their time working on policies and procedures, for the sake of accreditation, than on managing their available resources in association with addressing local community crime and disorder problems.

In this context, accreditation is a static process, as opposed to being a dynamic and facilitative one. Compliance is measured only in terms of matching directives, policies, and procedures to specific standards, which in some instances totally impede operational efficiency. "Measurable compliance" is a hollow concept because it simply means that a department either has and adheres to the standards or it doesn't. There is no firm link between compliance with the standards and the *quality* of services delivered. This problem appears to be inherent no matter where accreditation is used.

Police managers spend more of their time working on policies and procedures, for the sake of accreditation, than on managing their available resources in association with addressing local community crime and disorder problems.

Look at the educational systems, the health care systems, or correctional systems in operation today throughout this country. Many of these organizations, if not all, purport to abide by accreditation standards. Despite this fact, each of these professions is struggling to provide quality services.

Obviously, accreditation can't shoulder the entire blame for all of the problems occurring within the attending organizations. But it certainly doesn't minimize the importance of the following question to law enforcement: "Are we heading down the same path?" Are politically motivated police chiefs misleading the public into thinking that just because an agency is accredited, crime will diminish and violence will disappear only to be replaced by a state of peace, harmony and eternal bliss? A police chief may stand before the mayor, the city manager, or city council and boast of being accredited; but, if crime is rampant in the streets and the perception of fear drastically affects the quality of community life, accreditation isn't going to mean much to the average citizen.

What, then, should police chiefs expect from accreditation? The answer will ultimately depend upon the "health" of the organization. If a department is considered to be disorganized, is viewed as being non-responsive or non-caring by the community, is facing extensive litigation from improper or unethical actions taken by officers or managers, constantly experiences difficulty, or is failing to properly manage dispatch, patrol, investigative or tactical operations -- then the accreditation process, as it is now structured, will be of value to the chief, the department, and the community.

The reason accreditation is valuable is because it helps establish organizational structure where none exists. It assists in defining fundamental functions which are useful in helping employees attain consensus on roles and responsibilities. Accreditation uses administrative compliance as a means of establishing and then maintaining organizational control, which these departments are in desperate need of.

Are politically motivated police chiefs misleading the public into thinking that just because an agency is accredited, crime will diminish and violence will disappear only to be replaced by a state of peace, harmony and eternal bliss?

In the context of another medical analogy, accreditation helps organize the anatomy of a department. It helps managers determine which bones are out of wack and suggests steps which, if taken, will help the bones so the skeleton is anatomically correct. Accreditation serves as a blueprint, a reference guide, a checkpoint station, or a monitoring process for managers working within these departments. Accreditation tells the chief what his or her organization has or does not have. For many departments, accreditation represents the first step of organizational development. Unfortunately for CALEA, not all departments in this country possess these types of problems, and therefore are not in need of this type of assistance.

Does that mean that accreditation is incapable of helping "healthy" organizations? Of course not, but CALEA must allow the accreditation process to evolve. CALEA must understand that not all police chiefs are in need of establishing an operational foundation within their organization. Many departments are "anatomically sound;" their structure is properly aligned. What these chiefs need is a tool that will help them examine the organization's managerial capacity. The challenge confronting CALEA is to develop a management platform that includes an evaluative device that will assess behavior and actions taken in relationship to outcomes and results.

The reason accreditation is valuable is because it helps establish organizational structure where none exists.

Reformulating the Intent of Accreditation

If a police agency is going to be "results-oriented," it must seek to integrate the desires and expectations of citizens with actions taken by the department to identify and address conditions that negatively impact a community's neighborhoods. This union or partnership between the police officers and citizens requires a commitment to work together to prevent and control crime in a city's neighborhoods.

According to Oettmeier and Bieck (1988), the formation of this union is dependent upon the internal development of more appropriate management systems to build and better utilize available resources in working with the public to promote neighborhood tranquility and ensure justice through equitable enforcement of municipal codes and state laws, while acknowledging allegiance for democratic axioms that espouse the dignity of individual rights of citizens that comprise the community.

The strength of an effective police department, therefore, lies in its ability to develop efficient management systems as opposed to developing highly structured bureaucracies. What CALEA needs to recognize is that the administration of police work is dependent upon the efficient utilization of two components: organization and management. The organizational component, states Souryal (1977), is the structural framework within which administration is conducted. It provides the framework, tasks, and rules for the administrative process. Organization establishes a blueprint designed to assign functions, positions, and tasks. As such, claims Souryal (1977), it sets up the groundwork for the realization of common goals.

The strength of an effective police department lies in its ability to develop efficient management systems as opposed to developing highly structured bureaucracies.

Theodore Levitt (1976) claims that management consists of goals and purposes (what is to be done?); the systematic development of strategies to achieve these goals; the marshalling of the required resources; the rational design, organization, direction, and control of the activities required to attain the selected purposes; and, finally, the motivating and rewarding of people to do the work. Mintzberg (1983) suggests that a manager's effectiveness is significantly influenced by insight into his own work. Thus, managers who can be introspective about their work are likely to be effective at their jobs.

What is so disheartening today is that police managers are not trained to be introspective. In fact, Peters (1985) claims that the #1 managerial productivity problem in America is, quite simply, managers who are out of touch with their people and out of touch with their customers. One of the reasons this axiom holds true for policing is because police managers have perceived their roles and responsibilities from a very narrow perspective.

According to Goldstein (1990), lessons drawn from the studies that questioned the value of standard procedures demonstrated that the police erred in doggedly investing so much of police resources in a limited number of practices, based, in retrospect, on some rather naive and simplistic concepts of the police role. Furthermore, Goldstein (1990) contends that the majority of changes that have been advocated in policing over the past several decades reflect a continuing preoccupation with means over ends; with operating methods, process, and efficiency over effectiveness in dealing with substantive problems; and with the running of the organization rather than with the impact of the organization on community problems that the police are expected to handle.

Nowhere is Goldstein's observation more poignantly revealed than in CALEA's (1984) insistence on telling police departments "what to do." The accreditation process is so inundated with standards designed to "run the organization," that the need to have departments redirect their managerial commitment toward addressing substantive community problems is completely ignored. Conversely, many community-oriented departments are working with community representatives to draft an acceptable framework for service delivery that aligns department resources in response to community expectations. The challenge confronting these departments is not in knowing *what* to do, but in determining *how* to get it done in an effective and efficient manner.

Given the diversity found in large cities, flexibility vis-a-vis uniformity may be required, i.e. different strokes for different folks.

Today's innovative police agencies are discarding traditional and bureaucratic control-oriented management systems. They are looking to develop a more progressive alternative that extends beyond participatory management and involves input from the citizenry in addressing community concerns for public safety. By way of comparison, police administrators and managers working in accredited police agencies have come to rely on accreditation as a management system. Evidence of this occurs whenever an existing or new policy, procedure, or directive is sent to the accreditation manager or team prior to any action being taken by the department's command staff. If it is found to be inconsistent with accreditation standards, it is sent back for review and rewrites or is discarded.

The problem with this approach is multifaceted. First, departments are being forced to meet a standard because it is perceived to be good in and of itself and not because it improves the capacity of the organization to achieve results. Second, you don't manage the affairs of a police department in accordance with accreditation standards. Police operations are managed in accordance with the availability of resources, motivated employees, and a genuine willingness to direct organizational strengths toward effectively addressing diverse community problems of crime and disorder. Third, accreditation should not be used as a device to maintain organization control. If you want to instill control throughout the department, then allow people the opportunity to participate in the building of organizational products and in developing and implementing a variety of different service delivery strategies. Ownership is the key to organizational control, not blind compliance to administrative edicts.

CALEA needs to step back and rethink what the intent of accreditation should encompass. Telling police departments "what" to do represents nothing more than a smoke screen for most of them. Granted, there are probably a large number of agencies who are searching for someone or something to tell them what to do; and, in these instances, accreditation performs a very valuable role (see Bizzack's chapter). However, if CALEA expects to provide a service to progressive agencies, it must begin reformulating its intentions.

If CALEA expects to provide a service to progressive agencies, it must begin reformulating its intentions.

A new breed of managers is beginning to permeate public and private sector enterprises. Their management practices, states Peters (1988), are aimed at ensuring that the organization is externally focused, always sensing change or impending change before it sneaks up. Their primary task is to convert stagnant organizations into adaptive ones. An adaptive organization is one that is in touch with the community; it senses change and is capable of adapting to change via constant contact with and reaction to citizen needs and demands by every person within the organization.

If accreditation is to become an effective management tool, it must be perceived by police managers as being capable of helping them convert stagnant organizations into adaptive ones. The accreditation process must evolve beyond determining what to do and begin thinking how it can assist managers in their quest to be more responsive to community needs and demands.

Accreditation is a static process. It does not spark management vision or initiative. What accreditation can do is insure that the organization is anatomically sound.

Building a New Platform

The accreditation process is like a rocket sitting on a launch pad but incapable of going anywhere because it lacks propellant; or, put even more simply, it's like a car without a driver. Accreditation is a static process. It does not spark management vision or initiative. Mandating benign administrative compliance, accreditation is not a substitute for good management. It contains no mechanism to operationalize objectives and then evaluate anticipated results.

What accreditation can do is insure that the organization is anatomically sound. It will require management to see that all the vital organs and working parts are in order, but it cannot guarantee the body will move. The organization will be capable of looking, but it will not see. It will be capable of hearing, but it will not listen. It will be capable of talking, but it will not communicate. For all intents and purposes, the organization will appear to be healthy and is breathing, but in actuality it is comatose.

The challenge confronting chiefs in charge of comatose police departments is figuring out a way to revive the patient. CALEA can help these chiefs if they are willing to establish a new platform for the accreditation process. This platform must be action-oriented, focusing on performance. It will require the chief to be in touch with the community so that organizational goals will be consistent with community demands and expectations. The utility of this platform will also require a chief to have a competent management system capable of driving the organization towards the attainment of expected results.

In essence, this performance platform will require managers to examine operational linkages within the organization. It will require managers to determine if certain types of operational linkages are producing the appropriate types of results. This platform will also require managers to obtain feedback regarding the adequacy of results attained. This will be accomplished by having managers use evaluation procedures to measure the attainment of results in relationship to prevailing community expectations.

There is such a fear by CALEA that if accreditation was to assume the position of "evaluating results," it would have to withstand an overwhelming criticism of advocating "nationalism" within policing. That would be understandable if one was trying to standardize how results are attained. But that is not what is being advocated. Instead of standardizing the attainment of results, CALEA should require management to evaluate the adequacy of results in relationship to internal organizational linkages and community expectations. Let's look at the following example to emphasize the point.

In an effort to more efficiently handle a large volume of incoming calls for service, a chief may decide to implement a variety of differential police response strategies. Procedures governing call classification and prioritization, call queuing, and supervisory override can be developed and implemented. The implementation of these activities, while laudable, serve only as a means to an end, because the end result is being able to provide more time for street officers to be more responsive to demands emanating from their assigned areas. For example, if officers can spend more time conducting quality preliminary investigations, even up to the point of being able to recommend early case closures, more time could be freed up for investigative personnel. This, in turn, would provide management with an opportunity to more effectively manage investigative operations.

In this example, managers would be required to examine operational linkages (i.e. the relationship between dispatch, patrol, and investigative operations). The nature of these linkages will determine the types of results one can expect to attain. In terms of analyzing results, managers will be held accountable for expected outcomes (i.e. how the officers are using their newly found time). Are the officers properly "managing" their available resources by directing them toward the resolution of a specific type of problem; if so, what exactly are they expected to accomplish? In assessing the adequacy of results, managers must obtain community feedback. Of considerable importance is knowing if the results are consistent with community expectations. If they are not, the manager must determine why there is inconsistency. The manager must also determine what adjustments, if any, need to be implemented.

In retrospect, traditional managers prosper within organizational milieus that place a premium on administrative responsibilities. The term *management* in these organizations is probably a misnomer since the concept is operationalized through administrative compliance to written directives, policies and procedures.

What communities and police departments of tomorrow need are people who, in the truest sense of the term, are managers. They must be people who are competent in the management of work, but who are also critical thinkers capable of thriving on creativity and innovation. These managers must be obsessed with achieving qualitative results. They must realize the value of developing people within the organization as a means of attaining those results. Herein lies the opportunity for CALEA. Serious thought must be given to developing evaluation procedures that help managers attain the appropriate results for their organizations and communities.

The challenge confronting CALEA is not to standardize how things get done, but to act as a catalyst for managers to help them see that proper results are attained by virtue of what they do.

The challenge confronting CALEA is *not* to standardize how things get done, but to act as a catalyst for managers to help them see that proper results are attained by virtue of what they do. In this regard, managers need a tool that will help them analyze results from different perspectives. For example, managers should be constantly reminded to ask the following questions: 1) what should I be doing? ; 2) how is this different from what I am presently doing?; and 3) what adjustments should I make? This mind-set will require managers to understand the importance of systems integration and synergism. Since the organization to which they belong will operate as an open system, these managers will be required to develop and maintain a global community perspective. Because of their organization's strategic focus, police managers must be prepared to work with and cooperate with other city agencies and city groups. School administrations, social service agencies, health care professionals, probation and parole departments, the judiciary, churches, businesses, correctional organizations, and employment services all hold a stake in working cooperatively with police agencies. Managers in each of these organizations must be willing to be a part of a larger team effort for the betterment of the entire community.

For the police chief who perceives the department as an active partner in a community-based "Human Services System," results are defined and attained on a collaborative basis. These so-called community-based police departments, according to Bieck (1988), no longer operate independently; they function coactively within their respective cities. New, coactive partnerships are formed between the department and the other aforementioned agencies. The reason for establishing these alliances is not to soothe the public's perception of fear or safety via public relations or community relations gimmicks. To the contrary, the police and citizens work diligently together to improve upon the overall health, safety, and welfare of the entire community.

Once again, CALEA should assume a leadership role in working with community-oriented police agencies. These departments are challenging traditional values and practices. Managers working within these agencies are rethinking relationships, revising past practices, and forging new alliances. Examples include:

1. Enhancing the agency's management system by integrating functional responsibilities that are evolving within the department (i.e. patrol and investigations);
2. Developing and operationalizing new roles and responsibilities for citizens;
3. Redefining and rebuilding a team orientation within the department;
4. Establishing new performance criteria from a personnel, organizational and community perspective;
5. Building new coalitions within the community;
6. Enhancing grassroots networks and coordinating referral procedures and practices;
7. Reducing administrative dependency on policies and procedures;
8. Analyzing curriculum design and altering course content of training programs;
9. Restructuring disciplinary philosophies and implementation procedures; and
10. Describing and accounting for different types of outcomes.

Not only do these issues provide fertile ground for CALEA to establish new procedures, which they can add to their administrative foundation, but they can also work with these agencies to examine and describe new linkages that account for different types of results.

Where Do We Go From Here?

The purpose of this chapter has been to raise issues, provoke thought, and generate discussion about the accreditation process. It has been suggested that accreditation, as it is presently conceived, does provide a useful service to many organizations. It does this by establishing an administrative foundation from which the organization is able to operate on a routine basis. However, that service is of limited value to chiefs who have already established such a foundation.

It has also been suggested that even if a police department is administratively and organizationally sound, there are no assurances that an agency is adequately managed. In this regard, CALEA has an opportunity to evolve -- to develop a new platform. This platform must be performance-based and capable of requiring management to evaluate how they account for the attainment of specific types of results. By developing evaluative procedures, CALEA can facilitate professional development by challenging managers to examine their accomplishments in the context of where they are versus where they should be.

Even if a police department is administratively and organizationally sound, there are no assurances that an agency is adequately managed.

For those agencies who have adequate management systems within their departments, this instrumentation will help them insure that their organization remains an adaptive one, capable of adjusting to the changing environment of the entire community, while simultaneously preserving local control and autonomy.

Finally, it has been proposed that CALEA consider working actively with police chiefs who have undertaken the challenge of helping their department evolve into a community-based organization. As new partnerships are formed within the community, many corresponding changes will occur within the department. By working to help develop these new frontiers, CALEA will be on the leading edge of facilitating organizational development.

If accreditation is to survive the '90s, it cannot continue to be uni-dimensional. CALEA cannot continue to refine a static process which has limited value within policing. Dynamic processes must be developed whereby accreditation incorporates the ability to help managers help themselves. This can best be done by designing evaluative procedures that will allow police managers the opportunity to measure the attainment of results in relationship to prevailing community expectations.

NOTES

1.   The *Field Training Quarterly* is a publication of the Houston,
     Texas Police Department. It is a free service provided to practitioners
     of law enforcement field training. Houston started publishing the
     Quarterly in January 1987, after identifying a need for a national
     exchange of information and ideas regarding this important and
     popular program. The *Quarterly* has become one of the primary
     sources for law enforcement field training information and is
     retained by the National Criminal Justice Reference Service. It
     received the Washington Crime News Services' "Outstanding
     Publication Award" in 1988 and 1989 and was named the "Grand
     Prize Winner" in 1990.

     The *Quarterly* is currently mailed to police departments,
     sheriff departments, correctional facilities, libraries and universities
     across the nation. Agencies in Australia, Great Britain and Canada
     have also requested the magazine.

     If you are involved in law enforcement field training and
     would like to be placed on the mailing list, call or write to the editor
     at the following address: Officer Frank Webb, Field Training
     Quarterly, Houston Police Department, 17000 Aldine Westfield
     Road, Houston, TX 77073 (phone 713/230-2300).

2.   The National Association of Field Training Officers (NAFTO) is
     based in California. It was founded by Mickey Bennett, a former
     sergeant with the Long Beach, California Police Department. The
     current roster contains 141 members from eight regions in California.
     Efforts to expand to regions across the country will begin in 1992.
     For further information, contact: Mickey Bennett, Executive
     Director, NAFTO, 7220 Swale River Way, Sacramento, CA 95831
     (phone 916/424-1975).

3.   The Houston Police Department was responsible for producing
     over 50 reports and other documentation to be in compliance with
     accreditation standards. See report entitled "Accreditation Standards
     Analysis," May 1991, Houston Police Department.

REFERENCES

Behan, Neil (1984). *Law Enforcement News.* Interview of James V. Cotter, former Director of the Commission on Accreditation for Law Enforcement Agencies, by Peter Dodenhoff, Vol. X, No. 12.

Bieck, William H. (1988). The term "coactive" was shared with the author at a time when efforts were being made within the Houston Police Department to operationalize neighborhood-oriented policing (NOP) in a manner that did not dichotomize traditional patrol responsibilities from newly emerging responsibilities. The creation of a reactive, proactive and coactive continuum and associated components has helped officers and managers alike understand NOP in a nonthreatening manner.

Commission on Accreditation for Law Enforcement Agencies (1984). *Accreditation Program Overview.* Pamphlet, CALEA, Inc.

Carter, David L., Sapp, Allen D., and Stephens, Darrel W. (1991). *Survey of Contemporary Police Issues: Critical Findings.* Police Executive Research Forum.

Gates, Daryl (1985). "Law-enforcement Agencies Divided over Value of National Accreditation," by Jerry Seper and Frank Lopez, *Arizona Republic Staff* newspaper.

Goldstein, Herman (1990). *Problem-Oriented Policing.* McGraw Hill Publishing, New York.

Levitt, Theodore (1976). "Management and the Post Industrial Society," *The Public Interest,* Summer, p. 73.

Mintzberg, Henry (1983). "The Manager's Job: Folklore and Fact," in *Executive Success: Making It In Management.* Editor, Eliza G. Collins, Harvard Business Review, John Wiley and Sons, Inc., New York.

Morrison, Charles (1967). "More of State's Police Departments Seeking Accreditation," *The Hartford Courant Connecticut Newspaper,* by Steven Gield, Section B, Sunday edition.

Oettmeier, Timothy N. and Bieck, William H. (1988). *Integrating Investigative Operations Through Neighborhood Oriented Policing: Executive Session #2.* Houston Police Department, Houston, Texas.

Peters, Tom and Austin, Nancy (1985). *A Passion for Excellence: The Leadership Difference.* Random House, New York.

Peters, Tom (1988). *Thriving on Chaos: Handbook for a Management Revolution.* Alfred A. Knopf Publishers, New York.

Souryal, Sam S. (1977). *Police Administration and Management.* West Publishing Co., St. Paul, Minn.

Chapter 7

Organizing for Community Policing

The police are the public, and the public are the police. No matter how large the department, the principle must be honored or crime control is weakened.

Community policing means different things in different cities, but the anonymity of urban living works against friendly policing.

The task of organizing should begin with a clear understanding of the role of the police. Are all police officers qualified to assume the responsibilities associated with community policing?

by Patrick V. Murphy

American policing is a failure.[1] Its first responsibility is to prevent crime. Yet, the United States has the highest rates of crime and incarceration in the industrial world, although it is the wealthiest nation. Thousands of citizens who should be contributing to the economy are a drain on it, being supported by tax dollars in prison.

The police have misunderstood their role. They have attempted to accomplish their mission independently with minimal community involvement. It is a policy that reveals a fundamental misperception of the proper relationship between police and people in any democratic society. Ultimate responsibility for law observance and order rests with the community of citizens, not with the police. Every community must police itself. The function of the police is to assist parents, youths, neighbors, teachers, leaders and others to be a strong community whose eyes, ears and influence are essential in preventing crime.[2]

It is a cardinal principle of democratic societies that ultimate responsibility for peace, good order and law observance rests with the community of citizens of that society, not with an organized police force.

Although the very complexity of modern societies usually dictates that policing efforts be coordinated and directed by a force of paid professionals, their responsibility is derivative. Their role is to supplement and aid community efforts, not supplant them. And the powers permitted to these police must be carefully defined and limited.

When people have confidence in their neighborhood and their neighbors, they protect one another, are less fearful, and set behavioral standards.

A community which abandons its basic duty to police itself, to a professional police service, will soon find that the police can hope to provide no more than a bare modicum of public order and security, and this only through such repressive measures that the basic liberties of a free people are eroded, and the very democracy that the police seek to preserve is endangered. Only if the proper balance is maintained between the basic responsibility of the community and the derivative responsibility of the police can a safe and orderly society be preserved with the least burden on the individual rights and freedom.

It is unfortunate, therefore, that the history of urban policing in America in the 20th century is a consistent record of efforts by the police service to assume a disproportionate share of the responsibility for maintaining social control, and the concurrent abandonment by American communities of their portion of this duty. The result has been an increasing lawlessness which even increasingly repressive measures have been unable to curb. The delicate balance between the traditional roles of the community and the police needs to be restored. Peace-keeping must again become a joint police-community effort to stand any reasonable chance for lasting success.

The police are a small part of the total effort involved in preventing/controlling crime and drug trafficking. When people have confidence in their neighborhood and their neighbors, they protect one another, are less fearful, and set behavioral standards, especially for youths. A community is a network of people exchanging information, assisting one another, observing, cooperating with police to identify violators, but also to help minor offenders to go straight.

Neighbors and relatives supplement parents in raising children. Problem families tend to produce problem offspring. Police/citizen teamwork is important in identifying such youngsters, obtaining special support for them, and removing them from their families -- if necessary. Protecting children from physically abusive parents is a major part of crime prevention warranting police attention and community assistance. "It takes a village to raise a child."[3] The police play a critical role in making a city neighborhood function as an "urban village" for raising children, mutual protection, mutual assistance, and community empowerment.

Typically, there is only one patrol officer on duty for 5,000 people. The wise chief understands that his officers depend upon those who live and work in every neighborhood. He will appreciate the value of time spent obtaining citizen participation. Every officer hour can generate many hours of useful volunteer time. The job description for patrol officers should make clear that most of the work in reaching objectives is performed by community members rather than the officer directly. Although some tasks must be performed by an officer personally, he gets the job done principally through the volunteer efforts of those protected. The function is more that of manager than doer.

Although the national crime rate is high, the distribution of offenses varies widely by size of city and within large cities. The murder rate in one city is eight times the national average. Within another city, the murder rate in one precinct is 90 times that in another. Some parts of cities have crime rates as low as those in villages and small towns. Other parts have alarming rates. Poverty and other socioeconomic ills, which are the root causes of crime, are invariably found where crime is abundant. The middle class doesn't depend upon the police nearly as much as the poor do to protect them from criminals who live and operate in their neighborhoods. As Professor Egon Bittner has shown, policing is essentially a vocation of service to the poor.[4] Urban poverty presents especially challenging problems to officers. Large poor populations concentrated in inner cities over large areas unrelieved by any oases of middle class strength and weakened by the anonymity of urban life need police resources proportionate to their share of crime as well as creative approaches to their need for protection, partnerships with the police, and political empowerment to enable them to obtain social and economic justice.

Officers who protect the working poor need excellent training and inspired leadership to motivate and sustain them in their daily contact with so much human suffering and victimization. Their performance, for better or worse, will be strongly influenced by an attitude of compassion as contrasted with one of contempt. It is among the disadvantaged, more than the middle class or the affluent, that the police must become part of the community. It is in the low-income neighborhoods with high crime rates, and more victims, that it is most important for the police and the people to be one.

Officers who protect the working poor need excellent training and inspired leadership to motivate and sustain them in their daily contact with so much human suffering and victimization.

Hundreds of departments are changing from police-oriented to community-oriented policing; from reactive to proactive relations with the people. It entails a transition from stronger policing to friendly policing.

In order to grasp the implications of this strong trend, it is necessary to understand the proper role of the police. The police themselves have misunderstood their role, attempted to do the job without sufficiently involving the community, and have failed to organize their departments to accomplish the mission. Many departments that have been in a "community policing" mode for several years continue to be organized in a manner that impedes success in preventing crime and fostering social control. Authority and responsibility are assigned inappropriately.

American policing is uniquely local. It has not been systematized. It is a fragmented, insular non-system. There are more than 15,000 agencies. They are extremely isolated from one another. The exchange of ideas, policies and criminal intelligence are severely limited (see Behan's chapter). Careers are confined to one department almost without exception. The profession has developed although there is a clear need for a fully professional entry standard for every officer given law enforcement authority.[5] States have failed to do enough to upgrade, coordinate and set standards for local policing within their borders. Fifteen thousand local departments cannot work successfully without a comprehensive national support structure of planning, coordination, intelligence, statistics, research, experimentation, demonstrations, technical assistance, training, education, personnel exchanges and standards. The federal government fails to provide anything resembling an adequate back-up system. The entire police service suffers as a result. The American people are victimized by excessive crime, fear and drug trafficking.

Life is naturally friendlier in small towns. As a result, people and police work closely. Crime is minimal. The single-officer department provides a model for larger agencies.

Without the benefit of a body of knowledge or the resources that would be provided by an established profession, it is not surprising that individual departments are very different. Variations in policies, practices, values, goals and objectives are broad (see Behan's chapter). Yet, some common flaws in philosophy, organization and management can be identified. The problems are not found to the same extent among all kinds of departments. In fact, they are concentrated in large city departments where the highest crime rates, especially for violence, are found. Crime rates tend to be lowest in villages and sparsely populated areas. There are about 1,000 single-officer departments. They have friendly policing. Life is naturally friendlier in small towns. As a result, people and police work closely. Crime is minimal.[6]

The single-officer department provides a model for larger agencies. The friendly teamwork that occurs so naturally in a village fulfills the principle enunciated by Sir Robert Peel in London in 1829 when the "New Police" were being formed: "The police are the public, and the public are the police." No matter how large a department, the principle must be honored or crime control will be weakened. Democracy is also weakened when police and people are separated rather than united. In working poor neighborhoods, where crime rates are highest and people most dependent on the police, the failure is compounded. By not fulfilling their responsibility to be one with the public, the police actually deprive the people of their right to have a strong community for self-protection and political empowerment. In a city environment -- so unlike that in a village -- next door neighbors can be strangers rather than friends. If there are high levels of crime and fear, suspicion can alienate residents from one another. A sense of community can deteriorate to the point of collapse. Every police chief must understand that his department has a duty to assign officers to every neighborhood to become part of it. When the proper partnership is established between an officer(s) and a relatively small neighborhood population of 1,000 to 5,000 residents, a mutually supportive community develops.

Every police chief must understand that his department has a duty to assign officers to every neighborhood to become part of it.

In many cities, those who live and work in a neighborhood don't know the police officers responsible for protecting them. They are strangers. The people would be safer and officers more satisfied if they were friends. Frustration with officers because of crime and drugs, even anger because they are aloof, could change to appreciation and respect. Officers who are suspicious and cynical towards strangers could become empathetic, supportive partners to friends, even advocates for government services and programs to correct the social and economic injustices underlying the crime. The fundamental basis of policing is friendship -- an officer and the people that the officer protects knowing one another, exchanging information, assisting and supporting one another, forming partnerships, engaging in teamwork. That is how crime is prevented and social control exercised *by the people* in a democracy. The police, at least theoretically, function with the consent of the people.

Of course, in a police state -- a dictatorship -- stranger policing is the standard. Government of the people, by the people, and for the people is not the operating principle. Regrettably, many departments inadvertently follow the police state model more closely than the democratic. Officers are overbearing rather than community partners.

Even in neighborhoods with the highest crime rates, more than 90 percent of the population is law abiding. Their participation with the police is indispensable in preventing crime and exercising social control. Friendly policing is needed in such areas even more than in low crime rate sectors. Crime rate invariably correlates with poverty, under/ unemployment, and the other socioeconomic root causes of crime. A police strategy that fails to proactively build friendships with minority or poor populations is misdirected.

More than half of all police officers of all ranks are generalist patrol officers (GPOs). They wear uniforms, circulate in marked patrol cars within a beat area, and exchange information about crime, delinquency, suspicious activities and people. They interact with young people, parents, neighbors, teachers, clergy, social workers, employers, and probation/parole officers. They respond to crime scenes and emergencies.

At any time, only one GPO is on duty for approximately 5,000 residents. The people, not the police, have the largest role, by far, in preventing crime. The role of the GPO is to assist the people -- coordinate, manage, and lead. Close, active, day-to-day teamwork between every small neighborhood community and a GPO responsible for its protection is essential. A friendly relationship between the protected and *their* protector is critical. The police depend upon the information obtained from the people. The people depend upon the police to inform them about crime patterns and criminals so they can better protect themselves. Information is the lifeblood of police work.

The people depend upon the police to inform them about crime patterns and criminals so they can better protect themselves. Information is the lifeblood of police work.

The organizational structure should support friendly policing. Unfortunately, in most urban departments it produces stranger policing. Many large city departments were deliberately organized historically for stranger policing, stranger supervision, and stranger management on the theory that friendships inevitably generated corruption.[7] It was a cruel myth that has had a serious negative impact even to the present.

Community policing means different things in different cities. In some it means a relatively small community relations unit of ten officers in a department of 500. In others, each precinct has a community relations officer in addition to a central unit. Members attend community meetings and attempt to resolve grievances concerning police policies or incidents -- especially those involving minority residents.

The community policing idea is fully implemented when all patrol officers participate.

In some cities, it means little more than block watches and citizen patrols. In others, citizens volunteer as receptionists, athletic coaches, or scout leaders. In some it means assigning some officers to foot patrol. Drug Abuse Resistance Education involving officers assigned full-time to schools teaching the dangers of drug use is the major component of "community-oriented policing" in some jurisdictions. School resource officers assigned full-time to high schools and junior high schools constitute the major component in others.

Where the concept has advanced further, it is seen more as a generalist function, less as a specialized function. The patrol division participates. However, it is common for community interaction to be a specialization within the generalist patrol function. Less than 10 percent of the patrol officers in a precinct are assigned to community liaison. More than 90 percent are basically call responders oriented to handling the work that occurs during their shift, but having no continuing responsibility for solving the problem of a neighborhood by means of a community/police partnership. The community policing idea is fully implemented when all patrol officers participate. They are the generalists. There are more of them, or certainly should be, than all of the others -- supervisors, managers, and specialists. They interact more around the clock with victims, criminals, suspects, witnesses, rich, poor, powerful, powerless, homeless, mentally disturbed, injured, and all of the others across the spectrum. Although patrol officers regularly deal with a wide range of people and problems, their responsibility for prevention or follow-up varies. In some departments, the contacts and incidents are dealt with by patrol officers as isolated events, rather than pieces of a larger picture requiring a conjunctive plan of action. Their function is seen as part of rapid response -- handling, referring, and reporting incidents that occur during their on-duty shifts. They are not significantly involved in community policing.

When GPOs are fully immersed in community policing, the contacts and incidents are processed but not in isolation. They are seen as part of a larger picture. The people are informed about incidents in their area. They are mobilized to help in solving crimes, preventing violations, and working collectively for community betterment. A GPO with

Every chief is well advised to challenge the structure of his agency rather than assume it is adequate.

responsibility for liaison with a community focuses primarily on it as a collection of mutually protective and supportive families who together are more effective in partnership with a community-oriented officer than the police alone. Individual crimes and incidents are secondary considerations that should not distract from consistently strengthening the neighborhood as a community. It is the best way to reduce crime.

There is a tendency for large police departments to over-specialize. Generalist patrol officers are relieved of responsibility for certain kinds of crime or problems. It reduces the number of generalists. Each becomes responsible for the protection of more people. Specialization should be resisted. The more generalists, the smaller average population to which each will have to relate. Stronger partnerships and better community teamwork will result. Every chief is well advised to challenge the structure of his agency rather than assume it is adequate. A vigorous analysis asking the right tough questions may reveal waste, confusion, and low rates of cost-effectiveness compared with well organized departments. Police agencies are not objectively evaluated routinely. The public, news media, elected officials and police tend to accept existing organization, policies, personnel administration, and community relations as satisfactory even though a knowledgeable evaluator would find a low level of productivity. The mysteries of police work and administration are certainly beyond the grasp of the news media. They fail badly in informing the public about police budgets and effectiveness as they do concerning the crime and drug problems.

A conscientious chief introducing, or further developing, community policing will address the issues of organization, management, responsibility, authority, accountability, discretion, and community liaison.

A large city police department is a complex, decentralized bureaucracy. It functions 24 hours a day. Its officers operate with little direct supervision. They make difficult decisions, without consultation, concerning a broad range of human behaviors. It is essential that their responsibilities and authority be carefully defined if the mission of the agency is to be accomplished. They cannot operate like the single-officer village where the chief is often "available" at home rather than patrolling. Many officers may reside outside the city and commute long distances. They do not protect their own city. Community policing is most difficult to implement in a large department in a large city.

The anonymity of urban living works against friendly policing. Such a department must be organized with great care.

The function of the police is to assist every neighborhood community to exercise social control. Yet, the majority of the police, the motorized patrol officers, in many cities are principally call responders with little or no responsibility for effectively assisting people with the multi-faceted task of protecting their streets and homes. Without a responsibility for working closely with parents, students, teachers, neighbors, clergy, and the other members of a community, the officer is deprived of the opportunity to function as a friend and protector. He is under-challenged, under-fulfilled, and under-empowered to do the job an officer should do. Morale is weakened and the indispensable partnership of a small neighborhood community of about 1,000 people with an officer, who is primarily responsible for their protection, is unformed.

"The police are the public, and the public are the police." It is the most fundamental of all principles for policing a free society, formulated in 1829 in London when civilian police were created. The people and the police must work closely together exchanging information, planning, monitoring violators, intervening in troubled and violent families, and helping delinquents to go straight. A first consideration in organizing is to determine how to structure the liaison from the department to individual neighborhoods. Should call response and community policing be separated between two groups of officers, or should all officers be responsible for both?

Since the "split force" concept was tried in Wilmington, Delaware, in the 1970s, it has been replicated in many other cities. One group of officers is assigned exclusively to community policing. Another is assigned exclusively to community policing. Another is assigned exclusively to answering calls and routine patrol. The fewer the liaison officers assigned, the larger the average number of people in each area. Specialized officers, not required to respond to calls, can devote full time to liaison activities. Of course, they would have larger citizen groups to work with than would all patrol officers if they were assigned to liaison as well as responding to calls. Dividing a city into as many sub-beats as there are GPOs would result in an average population of about 1,000. A neighborhood as small as 1,000 could develop with dedicated, creative leadership from its "own" officer into a cohesive urban village capable of generating

The anonymity of urban living works against friendly policing.

many of the strengths of an isolated village including highly effective prevention of crime, disorder, and drug trafficking.

An advantage of a structure of small sub-beats, each with a single officer responsible for its protection, is that a more personal, intimate relationship is established between the officer and the people he is sworn to protect. A smaller number of people have their own officer to know and work with. The officer will identify more with his or her own people, learn more about them and the problems. Friendlier relationships will result in greater effectiveness. One officer in a community policing relationship with 1,000 people in a sub-beat is more logical than five officers assigned to a beat attempting to relate to 5,000 people. When five are responsible, often no one is responsible. When responsibility is undivided, it is unequivocally fixed.

Community policing involving all GPOs in a precinct has been experimented with intermittently in New York City since 1973. A demonstration is underway in two precincts.[8] The generalist, as contrasted with the specialist, approach has the advantage of involving all officers. It is an important consideration. Those who are not involved under the specialist model tend to remain aloof from the people. The loss of their participation is wasteful.

As policing motorized, it became possible for an officer to reach the scene of a crime or emergency more rapidly than one on foot could. Radios in patrol cars further reduced response time. New technology resulted in arrests that could not have been made previously and saved lives that would otherwise have been lost. Expectations then became unrealistic. Without the benefit of research to provide accurate information, it was assumed that rapidly responding to most calls would provide a result that more than justified the cost. The police world is not research oriented. Many policies and practices are based on myths or untested assumptions.

A first consideration in organizing is to determine how to structure the liaison from the department to individual neighborhoods.

Eventually research was done in a number of cities. It revealed that only 10 to 15 percent of requests for dispatch of a patrol car warranted a rapid response. A policy of immediate dispatch to unwarranted situations -- other than a crime in progress or life-threatening emergency -- can be costly in several ways. Accidents to police cars can result in deaths or injuries to officers or citizens, or damage to vehicles. In fact, more officers are killed in car accidents than are killed by gunfire.

Time devoted to responding to calls that don't require a dispatch or an immediate dispatch is time that is not available for community policing, solving crimes, or monitoring known criminals.

The police world is not research oriented. Many policies and practices are based on myths or untested assumptions.

Departments involved in the research and some others have developed criteria for differential police response (DPR). Alternatives to immediate dispatch include delayed dispatch, resolution by telephone by a specially trained advisor, or referrals.

All departments should use DPR. It is indispensable for a fully effective program of community-oriented policing.

Motorization generated another myth: The visibility of uniformed officers in marked police cars prevents crime. The Kansas City Preventive Patrol Experiment, designed and evaluated by the Police Foundation, found that preventive patrol had no significant impact on crime. The waste associated with so-called "preventive patrol" and unwarranted dispatches consumes enormous amounts of valuable patrol officer time which should be converted to highly productive community policing functions. The conversion from stranger to friendly policing definitely does not require additional personnel.

The challenges facing American policing are concentrated in the largest cities. Although there are more than 15,000 departments, the 200 largest cities have far more than their share of crime. Cities of over 100,000 have 25 percent of the population but 61 percent of murders.

The smaller the city, the friendlier life will be and the closer people and police. The smaller a department, the less bureaucratic and impersonal it will be. A friendlier type of policing will be practiced.

The larger a city, the more anonymous life will be. The larger a department, the more bureaucratic, impersonal and complex. It may be decentralized into precincts or districts. Organizing patrol for 24 hours a day, 7 days a week coverage while fixing responsibility for an area, at the same time that adequate supervision is provided, is a difficult problem that deserves careful analysis and periodic reevaluation.

The task of organizing should begin with a clear understanding of the role of the police. Confusion has revolved around the question of whether all officers are qualified to assume the responsibilities associated with community policing -- community organization, social work, family intervention, school liaison, making referrals, solving problems, and being a "street corner politician"[9] -- participating in the governing of an urban village. Some believe it would be premature for GPOs to be assigned such duties before a four-year college degree is an entry requirement.

A four-year degree should be required -- the sooner the better. The awesome powers and broad discretion possessed by every officer call for a baccalaureate as an entry standard. Community policing functions, however, do not involve more profound decision-making for patrol officers beyond the duty they already have -- different determinations, but not greater. Today's officers can be more effective as community partners than continuing what they are presently doing. In fact, the functions associated with community policing define the proper role of the police. Preventive patrolling monopolized by rapid response and cross dispatching is an abandonment of the indispensable role.

A patrol division, or precinct, must be organized by time, by area, and for proper supervision. Each patrol officer must be allocated according to the hours he will be scheduled for duty, by assignment to a beat or other area, in order that the particular problems can be learned and the people known. Finally, a supervisor must be responsible for the officer's performance, training and evaluation.

The tendency has been to organize patrol primarily by time of day into watches. In a city, or precinct, of 100,000 population, a typical complement would consist of 100 GPOs, 15 sergeants, 4 lieutenants, and a captain divided into three or more watches. The focus of each lieutenant watch commander tends to be on events that occur when the watch is on duty. The lieutenant's responsibility should extend to days when he is off and a sergeant member of the watch is in charge.

The sergeants and patrol officers also tend to focus on that part of the day when their group is on duty. Less attention is paid to beat problems, many of which overlap watches. Ideally, when patrol is organized primarily by time of day, each sergeant will have a zone or sector for which he will have a responsibility for community liaison, knowing the problems and people, as well as being known. Similarly, GPOs will be assigned to a beat on which they will concentrate between calls. The amount of time available for beat and sector work will depend upon how

much remains after dispatches are serviced. That, in turn, depends upon the dispatching policy. Research has found that only 10 to 15 percent of calls for an officer warrant an immediate dispatch. They are for a crime in progress or life-threatening emergency. Departments which have adopted a policy of Differential Police Response (DPR) save large portions of valuable patrol officer time which can be devoted to community-oriented policing. It results in increased productivity, crime prevention, and neighborhood community teamwork.

Of course, GPOs and sergeants will share responsibility for their beats and sectors with their counterparts from other watches. To be most effective, information should be exchanged among members of different watches assigned to the same beat or sector on a daily basis. Efforts should be coordinated. Policies and initiatives should be consistent around the clock. It is especially important that relationships between officers and those who live or work in a beat be consistent. Community-police teamwork can be seriously undercut when different watch commanders, sergeants, or GPOs adopt different policies, within their discretion, or develop different attitudes toward a community leader, school principal, or block watch team. The citizens are frustrated and confused as to why the police department cannot have a coherent approach to the problems that generate crime and disorder in their neighborhoods.

When patrol is organized primarily by time of day, there are major problems to be overcome in developing strong, productive partnerships of police and citizens at the neighborhood beat level. A motorized beat tends to be in the range of 5,000 to 10,000 residents. It is at that level that the job must be accomplished. On any larger scale, too many relationships between too many officers and too many police create confusion. Too many large police departments in seeking efficiencies of scale have forgotten that the role of the police is to assist the members of a community to police themselves. Cross-dispatching cars across beats, especially when the policy is to respond rapidly to as many calls for service as possible, can result in GPOs being out of their beat for most of a shift. It is an example of false efficiency interfering with the construction of the essential foundation of effectiveness -- community relations.

Relationships at the beat level are critical. They can be weakened when responsibility is shared as it usually is among those from different watches. Inconsistencies in policies and attitudes toward particular individuals or groups also reduce effectiveness. Are such impediments inevitable?

The conventional wisdom is that some such problems are unavoidable because patrol officers must be organized primarily by watches. Beat organization is secondary.

For community policing to yield its full potential, the conventional wisdom should be challenged. It is possible to organize patrol primarily by space and secondarily by time. A 100,000 population city, or precinct, can be divided into four zones, each headed by a lieutenant with 24-hour responsibility similar to that of a precinct captain or chief of patrol. At the next level, 10 to 20 beats can be established with populations ranging from 5,000 to 10,000. Each beat can be commanded by a sergeant who, in effect, is the "neighborhood chief of police." Between 5 and 10 patrol officers are assigned permanently to each beat. Finally, the beats are divided into sub-beats, each of which is the 24-hour responsibility of a single GPO. An officer will become the individual protector of about 1,000 people, no more than 2,000, depending upon the amount of crime measured according to a crime seriousness index.

Just as a chief of police, chief of patrol, or precinct captain has 24-hour responsibility, so would GPOs, sergeants and lieutenants. It provides for consistency in the liaison of the department with communities at the sub-beat, beat, and sector levels. It eliminates the divided responsibility among members of different watches. At the sub-beat level, the officer is able to know his or her people well since they are a relatively small number. The people will be able to relate on a friendly, personal basis to their *own* officer. A different, much stronger rapport will develop between protector and protected. The officer who had seen the work in an impersonal way, dealing with strangers who were little more than numbers, will now feel an attachment to the families and individuals who have become familiar friends.

For community policing to yield its full potential, the conventional wisdom should be challenged.

Organizing patrol primarily by space requires that it be organized secondarily by time. Patrol officers, sergeants, and lieutenants must be scheduled to provide round-the-clock coverage. Each lieutenant-sector commander would receive a schedule in advance delineating the sector's responsibility for providing a watch commander, sector supervisors, and beat patrol officers for its share of shifts during a month. Patrol officers when "in-service" for dispatch would normally cover their own

beats, except that during the low activity watch -- approximately midnight to 8:00 a.m. -- a car should cover two or more beats. Three 8-hour shifts beginning at midnight typically require strength ratios of 1:3. Calls for service and other workload factors generally follow that pattern. Also, very few opportunities for community interaction are available while a city sleeps. Community policing occurs principally on day and evening watches.

Organizing patrol primarily by space requires that it be organized secondarily by time.

Beyond providing personnel for watch duty, sergeant-beat commanders should have flexibility in scheduling their officers to best meet the needs of the beat and the sub-beats. Approximately five officers are required to cover a position continuously, allowing for days off, court time, training, vacation and sick leave. However, on a midnight shift, one officer can cover two or three beats. The saving permits the use of extra officers for other necessary beat work -- crime analysis, problem solving, criminal intelligence, coordination with probation/parole, preventing drugs in schools, etc. during day or evening hours. By placing all GPOs under the flexible control of beat sergeants, their time can be put to best use.

A majority of police are patrol officers. Where most crime is found, their valuable time is misused in "chasing calls" where they are not needed. The best use of their time is leveraging the eyes, ears, influence and networking of a small neighborhood community which can accomplish more than police in preventing crime. Patrol should be organized primarily by space, rather than time -- sector, beat and sub-beat managers replacing watch commanders, watch sergeants, and call responders.

Community policing is the friendly kind. It is found in small towns. They enjoy low crime rates. To bring it to cities, departments must be organized to facilitate community partnerships at the sub-beat and beat levels. The people of every small neighborhood community and their officer must become one. The poor are the most dependent on the police for protection and mutual improvement. Every patrol officer, not just some, should be a community officer.

NOTES

1. Pierce, Neal R. *Baltimore Sun*, January 13, 1992.
2. Statement of Mission. Lincoln, Nebraska Police Department.
3. African proverb.
4. Bittner, Egon. *Local Government Police Management.* Washington, D.C.: International City Management Association, 1982, p. 8.
5. *President's Crime Commission Report.* Washington, D.C.: Government Printing Office, 1967.
6. *Uniform Crime Reports 1990.* Washington, D.C.: Federal Bureau of Investigation.
7. Wilson, O.W. *Police Administration.* New York: McGraw-Hill, 1950, p. 471.
8. Press Release, New York Police Department, December 13, 1990.
9. Muir, William Ker, Jr. *Police* (Streetcorner Politicians). Chicago: University of Chicago Press, 1977.

Chapter 8

Controlling Police Wrongdoing

Undertaking anything as dramatic as reform - which involves not only harsh measures, but radical change - involves a keen understanding of the environment as well as the issues. Too many police executives have foundered on the shoals of irrelevancy.

by: **Anthony V. Bouza**
Lawrence W. Sherman

The need for reform is usually announced in blaring headlines:

"Ring of cops accused of drug thefts, murder."

"As many as 10% of the force reportedly involved in an investigation of corruption."

"Black citizens decry latest police shooting: accuse department of brutality."

"Investigation reveals wide involvement of police with drugs."

"Management Analysis calls for Sweeping Reforms in the PD."

"Citizen wins huge suit alleging police inaction."

"Union assails Chief's attempts at changes."

"Widening Police Scandal said to involve political figures."

"FBI entering investigation into police wrongdoing."

We've all seen them. Every city has had its share. Insiders decry conditions and call for reforms. The agenda is full and busy.

Despite the obvious needs, there are many obstacles to change and inducements to inaction. The path of reform involves activism, risks, and costs.

The police chief functions in a world of tremendous complexity, great opportunity, and real power. He is frequently at the center of meaningful action, with a real chance to make a difference in the lives of the people. Decisions made will shape the form of the agency's response, frequently making the difference between safety or injury, or even life and death. The power to affect people's lives is one of the enduring enticements of public life.

The police, as guardians and protectors of the public safety, wield enormous power; and this power, for good or ill, is directed by the chief. Most police agencies continue to observe the military model of hierarchical structure and approach to orders and communication, which tends to create a rigid centralized system that is generally responsive to the director's will.

The chief functions in a world of competing interests and shifting alliances -- a world of concrete reality, ideals and abstractions. He may be responding to a mayoral concern or a council-manic action, while considering the impact of the response on the people's more amorphous, but not less real, interests.

Usually, there is the Mayor who hired the chief and with whom a delicate relationship must be maintained. The Mayor is a politician whose foremost interest, frequently, is to get elected. Good government is the best politics, but it is usually tempting to apply the short-term solution, since long-term reforms frequently bring pain and difficulty in their initial stages. It isn't always easy to see the soaring approach to the sound barrier. The instinct, at that point, is to let up on the throttle. Reform is like that -- manholing maximum opposition as the point of breakthrough nears.

Developing a functioning relationship, where the Mayor offers policy direction, where agreement is reached as to goals, and where the chief attends to the daily internal workings and adjustments of the police department, is easier to describe than to apply. The temptation to tinker sometimes proves irresistible.

The City Council constitutes another body with which the chief must deal. Each is different, yet they are all alike in the sense of being comprised of ambitious politicians fighting for air space and scarce resources.

Civil Service, once the vehicle for sweeping reforms, has, in many places, calcified into the captive of unions and other bureaucracies, preserving the status quo and protecting the interests of the constituencies its reforms created. This, thus, becomes one of the ironies of reform -- that it enables an excluded group to prosper, and thereby tempts it to protect its preserve and exclude others. This, of course, suggests that the key to reform is constant self-examination, frequent change, and almost perennial strife.

Police unions have become powerful players in this civic drama. Once fraternal organizations that buried comrades and eased widows' sufferings, they grew, through de facto union shop realities and dues checkoffs into arbiters of policy and direction and, sometimes, into vetoers of police chief candidates. Their money and political power have created leverage over the political masters of the police, often enabling them to do an end-run around the cop's chief executive.

Then there is the media -- the feared and loathed press. There is no institution in our society that is more powerful or frightening to us. How sensitive we are to criticism. Never is it sharper than when it is etched in ink. The hostility toward and suspicion of the press, by such self-protecting institutions as the police, fatefully guide policies in disastrous directions. The hostility fuels the flames of press suspicion and resentment, justifying their most critical approaches.

There is another side to this press issue, though, that is even more important yet, while paid lip service, is rarely embraced: the public's right to know. A democracy requires an informed electorate, and the people get their information from the press. This simple syllogism ought to suggest to bureaucrats that it is their simple duty to keep the public informed, through open and accessible channels. The press is the key channel.

An argument might easily be made that the overwhelming preponderance of secrets are thinly veiled attempts to keep the public from discovering the human frailties of the officials. Legitimate concern for secrecy, in an open society based on the rule of law, applies to a very limited area of municipal government operations. As the conduit feeding the public's need for insights and information, the press can become the most important ally for reform.

In addition to dealing with elected and appointed officials, the union and the press, the chief is, of course, a major player in the criminal justice system. This system is a delicate organism that needs to function

The chief is a balloon, in a room full of other balloons, labeled "Police Union" or "Civil Service" or "Mayor" or "Council" or "Judge" or such, all unstably rubbing against each other, in no discernible pattern, with occasional explosions.

cooperatively, yet it is frequently riven by factional concerns. Each player is driven to fight for his turf, usually through the annual budget process. Additionally, the pressures created by occasional failures, and the public's resultant outcry of outrage, often leads the players to succumb to finger pointing. Thus, an organism whose functionings need to be characterized by an oily smooth meshing of organizational gears is often reduced to tortured grindings, as the principals scurry for cover as the public's ire tempts them to throw sand at each other.

Besides having to function in a world of sheriffs, prosecutors, judges, defense lawyers, probation and parole officials, and jailers of all sorts and descriptions, the chief is frequently, in this litigious age, sucked into the dark world of civil processes where suits, arbitrations and mediations become the fodder of daily experience, and where referees and other creatures spawned by this busy labyrinth abound.

Then, of course, there are the people. The public is spoken of as if it were one monolithic body; but it is, in fact, many groupings, with divergent interests. One need only look at the Black, Native American, Gay, Hispanic, or White communities to immediately identify many issues that might separate any one group from the rest. Gender, of course, lends an additional, and weighty, factor to the equation.

Thus, there are many publics, many constituencies, many divergent interests at work. If one had to conjure an image that best illustrated the process, it might be that the chief is a balloon, in a room full of other balloons, labeled "Police Union" or "Civil Service" or "Mayor" or "Council" or "Judge" or such, all unstably rubbing against each other, in no discernible pattern, with occasional explosions.

Practically everyone who moves from the private to the public sector is struck by the complexity of the process, the number of players and their variety, and the need for understanding the forces at work and their possible effect on the project at hand. Parvenus to politics -- and every act of government (including the chief's) is a political act -- almost invariably remark on the complexity of the world they've entered. This intricate environment may well, when combined with the importance of the questions, explain, at least partly, the fascination of public life.

Undertaking anything as dramatic as reform -- which involves not only harsh measures, usually, but radical change -- involves a keen understanding of the environment as well as the issues. The issues must be chosen carefully lest credit be dissipated on frivolous pursuits. There is a finite amount of credit and energy to be spent and directed, and too many executives have foundered on the shoals of the status quo.

The players and organizations named are traditionally described as partners, whose cooperation is essential to any reform; but the truth is that they can frequently be the obstacles to change as they represent entrenched, powerful interests whose profit lies in the maintenance of the status quo.

Machiavelli remarked on how reform inspires the fury of the interest endangered, while those to be benefited see, at best, a misty possibility of gain and cannot be relied on to take great risks on behalf of amorphous prospects.

In adopting a style for overcoming obstacles to reform, one needs to consider the options. Mindless, slavish adherence to a strategy that once worked will, in altering circumstances, come a cropper. Subtlety and flexibility are needed. No one approach will be best in all circumstances, and sometimes the best possible approach may be beyond the practitioner's 'ken, forcing a roll-back to the next best tactic. There is little point in asking an executive to do what he cannot perform. One has to focus on the strengths and marry these to the most suitable approaches.

Thus one might consider the direct approach; a frontal assault; a gradual, evolutionary process; the conciliatory method; a search for consensus; even retreat -- or whatever else may seem appropriate to the circumstances. An essential guide to the process is that, whatever strategy is adopted, it conform to the rule of law very strictly. It is also wise to consider change when the adopted path doesn't seem to be leading anywhere.

Setting the Agenda for Reform

Every police organization is both alike and different: alike in the sense of mission, structure, problems, approaches and daily workings; different in the sense that it is a product of its peculiar urban culture and political history and experience. Cities are, after all, much alike, yet markedly different, because of the chemical mix of the players over the decades. Police organizations mirror both the similarities and the differences.

Police organizations mirror both the similarities and the differences of their communities.

When discussing police reforms, then, we must first acknowledge that the problems requiring such correction may be very different.

Where the cops meet the poor is where the rubber of oppression meets the road of brutality.

One department may have serious problems with the Black, Gay or Hispanic communities while another may be seriously involved with the criminal element. The problems might, for purposes of convenience, be described under the rubrics of brutality or corruption.

An organization, as the label implies, is an organism, with many parts. Messages are transmitted both subtly and in the clear. A system of values has been shaped by, and is reflected in, these messages. Dissonances are instinctively recognized and resisted. A value system pervades even the most corrupt, cynical, or brutal police agency, and it is essential that its elements be recognized and evaluated (see Behan's chapter). Tilting at the wrong windmill exhausts a lot of energy, in futile pursuits.

Perquisites, privileges, and small accommodations accrue, like barnacles, on police agencies, pointing the way to possible sources of problems. If the higher-ups are getting theirs, however subtly, the troops will find ways to translate their actions to obtain the equivalents.

Some organizations get mired in alcohol control issues that can take many shapes, such as after-hours clubs, notorious bars, selling to minors, or even bootlegging -- a not-quite-forgotten art. Others might have drifted into the demi-monde of vice, where connections involving sex become the temptation to twist the law. Others have stumbled over gambling issues, and lately others have gotten mired in drugs and the sick, profligate culture they have spawned.

Where the cops meet the poor is where the rubber of oppression meets the road of brutality. This is most clearly illustrated by incidents -- between cops and Blacks, for example -- that sparked riots. These "aberrations" are more usually reflective of the police agency's organizational culture and underlying attitude. The same might be said for any encounter between the police and those they regard as "assholes." In recent years, the growing population of the homeless has forced increasingly sophisticated and sensitive police agencies to undertake the sort of actions that frequently inspire charges of repression or worse.

Brutality and corruption relate directly to the interaction between cops and their clientele. In these areas, we see the external relations of the police world at work, but these are frequently foisted by internal problems that, for lack of reform, have festered and grown, giving a kind of internal impetus to external abuses.

Internal Problems

Organizations are shaped by the incidents that have dotted their histories, and by the players who directed their fortunes. Because these differ from place to place, each organization develops its own unique culture.

Where New York City, in the '50s and '60s, had a department that experienced widespread use of brutality and corruption, other cities experienced other problems. In New York, for example, brutality encompassed abuse of Blacks, under the guise of controlling a dangerous element, as well as heavy-handed responses to not-very-disorderly demonstrations and frequent resort to third-degree methods. Until *Mapp v. Ohio* in 1960, search warrants concerned only the scholars, not the investigators who, on minimal provocation, "hit the flat" of suspects without fear or concern for constitutional niceties.

In New York, for example, corruption centered on bars and gambling -- pads and scores. Drugs were then frowned upon as dirty. There was a definite value hierarchy in play. The rituals were well-known: if you wanted to keep your hands clean, you eschewed assignment in plain-clothes units enforcing what were called "public morals." This meant alcohol, gambling and prostitution.

In other cities, the sources of the sort of corruption that drained police energies from the task of serving the people took other forms. Frequently, these involved internal approaches such as promotions, favorable assignments, lucrative pensions, salary increases, or such inefficiencies as feather-bedding or privileges.

In Minneapolis, for example, the citizens, alarmed by municipal unrest, embraced the offered solution and elected the police union head to the Mayoralty. Those who had helped him prospered. Those who had opposed him suffered the fate of the losers -- demotions, transfers, or unattractive assignments. As the two-year Mayoral cycle played out, an unfortunate tandem rhythm was set in motion, with *ins* alternating with *outs* in controlling the city. A decade of this reduced the police into organizational crisis. This ushered in a period of reform, just as the abuses of a generation earlier had forced New York to confront the brutality problem in 1966, in the form of a debate on a Civilian Review Board, which actually masked the struggle to promote accountability raging just beneath the surface. Six years later, under the impetus of the

Knapp Commission's disclosures of corruption, they'd take on this problem too. The vote for a Civilian Review Board lost, but the mechanisms with which to eliminate systemic, protected, widely accepted brutalities were set in place.

By 1980, for example, Minneapolis had a sworn force that was swollen with over 40 percent supervisors, creating the absurd ratio of almost one boss to every worker. There were six precincts where four, at most, were needed, and all two-person patrols which, in times of scarce resources, constituted expensive feather-bedding. Women and minorities had been excluded. The thumpers -- those ham-handed dispensers of street justice -- could expect to be protected, and they were. Six permanent chiefs and two acting chiefs guided the agency over the decade of the '70s.

The tremendous struggle to get cops to wear name tags, in the '80s, became a symbol of the issue of accountability, as the union fought furiously to resist the notion of identifying public servants.

Every election saw enormous shifts of personnel, reflecting the spoils of victory and the realities of political defeat. In such a world, merit and performance did not count as much as whose side one was on when the ballots were counted.

Before the counting, however, the faithful had to be enlisted in the lawn-sign-pounding, leaflet distributing, calling, and other organizational chores necessary to insure the triumph of one's champion. Rarely had a police agency been as nakedly, or as thoroughly, politicized.

New York, in contrast, could not have been said to have had its department tainted by partisan political struggles. These were mostly left to the union. The agency itself, however, was shot through with abuses that came from the combination of wielding grant power and not being held accountable for its use. The literature is full of references to the problems faced periodically by other jurisdictions.

The tremendous struggle to get cops to wear name tags, in the '80s, became a symbol of the issue of accountability.

Whether in Kansas City or St. Louis (where the municipal controls are still wielded at the state-house level rather than City Hall because of corruption problems everyone has long since forgotten) or in Chicago, Philadelphia or Boston (which have seen their own share of municipal difficulties, occasioned by cupidity or cruelty), American cities have, periodically, been hosts to abuses of power that ultimately required heavy reforms. They did not, however, always come.

Identifying Targets for Reform

There are many ways of identifying targets for reform. In New York, for example, the need for better relations between police and minorities, or police and students or demonstrators, could not have been more obvious in the '60s. Similarly, the scandals erupting over pads, shake-downs, flaking and scores finally created a climate for reform. In Minneapolis, the imperative need was to take the police out of partisan politics.

Frequently, there have been reports, studies or commissions to point the way. In Philadelphia, a report not only served as a guide to the reforms of the mid-'80s but also as a rallying point around which a consensus and scale of priorities could be built. In a short while, the abuses were forgotten, the report was shelved, and the reform chief departed. As with most such neglects, this one caused no furor. The dust settled and everyone returned to business as usual.

Sometimes it makes good sense to create an investigative body to analyze the problems and recommend reforms. This carries the added weights of objectivity and disinterest. In order for such efforts to succeed, they must identify real and serious problems, suggest workable solutions, and be prestigious documents that secure the public's support and which are embraced by the administrators responsible for following its mandates. This is a delicate process, since failure in any area will cause the effort to collapse. The bureaucratic woods are full of studies that were, for one reason or another, never harkened to, if they were ever read. The Knapp Commission's report, in New York City, was a good example of a successful undertaking. Philadelphia represents Brand X. The Warren Christopher Commission's report on the LAPD remains a question mark.

The chief police administrator, functioning in a complex world of fiercely competing interests, must be careful to choose targets carefully. Too many defeats will cause an unhealthy public odor that will see support go elsewhere. Trivial or superficial issues, not seen as tied to providing higher levels of safety, will be perceived by the public as mere exertions of will -- that do not rise much above ego satisfaction.

Chances are that not more than two or three issues can be taken on in any given year. Assuming a reasonable tenure of half a decade, it becomes clearer that the chief will have 10 to 15 windmills at which to tilt. It is important that the right ones be chosen.

The chief, as the head of the agency and the administrator responsible for its actions, must sift through the evidence and choose the direction. Although he reports to the Mayor and is given policy direction by his civilian masters, the fact is that the chief is usually the only official with the knowledge or experience to make the key decisions.

The sources of information are many and varied. There is, of course, the press. There will be articles, editorials, series and commentaries. There are the cops, at all levels. Enough questions will probably result in repeated surfacing of the real problems. There are the other players in the system, who have to deal with the police agency every day. There are frequently scholarly studies or reports. There are internal reports and results of investigations. Finally, and foremost, there is the public.

Chances are that not more than two or three issues can be taken on in any given year. Assuming a reasonable tenure of half a decade, it becomes clearer that the chief will have 10 to 15 windmills at which to tilt. It is important that the right ones be chosen.

The police are public servants, responsible for the public's safety, as well as for the people's untrammeled exercise of rights. The clients are often in the best position to enunciate their needs or to identify errors or problems.

The public writes, calls and visits -- offering a continuous flood of information as to how the agency is doing. Access is critical. The chief must be in direct contact in order to feel what the people feel. This means reading the letters, taking the calls (without screening), and seeing all visitors. It also means going out into the community and not only delivering hard, factual reports, but listening to the questions and complaints. Direct contact with the touchstone of reality is both difficult and important. It is a lot easier and more comfortable to allow the little insulations to prosper.

There is a constant sifting process as the chief absorbs and processes the flow of data. Gradually, patterns will begin to emerge. The wheat of real problems will be separated from the chaff of private pleadings. The intervention of any filter, however, will affect the quality of the information received.

As the chief assimilates the data, the problems will become clearer. What is not said is, for example, as important as what is. In Minneapolis, for example, prisoners frequently complained of being thumped but rarely alleged that any property or money had been taken. Even the violence possessed a pattern. At first, they reported blows, kicks, clubbings, or the use of sap gloves. As a few cops were disciplined, the complaints shifted to handcuffs being pressed too tightly or being treated roughly in the search or frisk positions, where a certain amount of handling became inevitable. As these activities gained official attention, the reports shifted to verbal abuse or brusque, officious mannerisms. The shifting commentaries very likely reflected changing patterns of police response. Review of Internal Affairs reports or statistics will never convey the flavor of encountering the letter, the voice, or the person directly.

Seizing Opportunities for Reform

Reform is drastic corrective action. If undertaken in a vacuum, the forces affected will work and coalesce to defeat the effort. The importance of strategy, tactics and planning are paramount. This means seizing available opportunities, as well as creating a climate receptive to reform.

As with any other form of human endeavor, the opportunities exist side-by-side with camouflage intended to conceal their whereabouts. Thus, while every age offers manifold chances for reaping wealth, these become obvious, to the vast majority, in retrospect, when they've been exploited and drained by the very few prescient enough to have seen new changes and to have taken them.

A severe budget crisis, for example, might well become the vehicle for effective prunings, rather than a mechanical separation of the youngest and most energetic. Coupling such a crisis to a call for managerial reforms will have an almost instant appeal to a public eager for better service, but reluctant to fund it.

An investigation, an arrest, or an incident can also become the impetus for reforms. Such events possess dramatic properties that automatically focus public attention on the event. If displayed as symbols of widespread, underlying problems, they might easily be the rallying points for generating public interest and support for attacking the conditions that created the problem. Obviously, the cases must be chosen with care. If they are not true paradigms, then a dead-end will be struck and the public's energy will deflate, with painful consequences for future efforts. Success builds on success, and failure promotes more of the same.

The press ought to be viewed as the most important partner in any reform effort, whether as reporter of developments or initiator of the expose. Fear of investigative series or resourceful reportorial efforts drives the thinking of too many police executives. Such enterprises ought to be welcomed as another part to reform -- another investigative and corrective tool with which to attach wrongdoing in the ranks. Police executives are altogether too defensive, even hostile, to outside discovery of malfeasance within the ranks. The better path is to go after the problems energetically, and to welcome any outside help, from whatever source, as long as it is legal.

The efforts of other outside agencies -- such as Grand Juries, the FBI, prosecutors, special investigative bodies, or boards of inquiry -- should be warmly embraced and supported. The public's interest lies in cleansing the agency, thereby freeing it to operate more efficiently. All too often the chief's response is to cover flanks and adopt defensive measures. If the purpose is reform, the agency help will be accepted, gladly, from all fronts. If the purpose is to protect one's own ego and persona, then all but the most credit-reflecting actions will be resented.

Civilian Review Boards

Egregious acts of police brutality will frequently spark demands for the creation of a Civilian Review Board. Again we are confronted with a complex reality, behind the simplistic rhetoric that so frequently attends such debates. It is another battle for control.

The question, of course, is how much power, and of what sort, is to be granted to this body. Our system is predicated on outside review, civilian control and representative government, but this is quite different from ceding the power to govern an agency.

The press ought to be viewed as the most important partner in any reform effort.

The chief is responsible for the government and administration of the department. The power to investigate and hold accountable is probably the keystone of the process. The creation of a body that has the power to investigate and discipline fatally weakens the chief's ability to run the agency.

Civilian Review Boards are, almost by necessity, staffed with people unfamiliar with the special world of the police. They are rarely able to distinguish between honest, good faith errors and bad faith acts of wrongdoing. The chief, on the other hand, brings a world of knowledge and experience to such judgments. Civilians are frequently co-opted by canny maneuvers which would be less likely to gull an experienced executive.

Civilian Review Boards are rarely able to distinguish between honest, good faith errors and bad faith acts of wrongdoing.

Civilian Review Boards can be vehicles for reform to the degree that they can provide a public window into the internal workings of a police agency and report to the people on their observations. They are also in a position to call for official investigations such as the FBI or the local prosecutor or a special state investigative body or even a Grand Jury. This hortatory power is frequently dismissed as trivial, but it can be a strong weapon in manholing public opinion and support for needed changes. To cede to these bodies, the chief's responsibility for governing the department is to create organizational confusion and to divert the chief executive of his most important weapon in administering the agency -- the power to discipline.

Court Decisions

Court decisions, for example, have, since *Mapp v. Ohio* in 1960 and moving forward with *Escobedo v. Illinois, Miranda v. Arizona,* and *Gardner v. Tennessee,* to name only a few, inspired the most vituperative reactions from police executives when they should have been hailed as the inspirers of terribly needed, long overdue reforms. It would be difficult to think of influencers of comparable worth in eliminating such police abuses as baseless searches and seizures, third degree methods, and even the employment of unjustified deadly force.

Supreme Court decisions have probably moved the police more rapidly along the road toward the Holy Grail of professionalization than any other single factor in this century. In fact, it could be argued that one of the great police reforms of this century, *Gardner v. Tennessee,* where the Supreme Court held it unconstitutional to use deadly force on an un-armed, un-dangerous, un-violent felon, was made possible by the intervention of police executives who joined in an amicus curiae brief that must have had a powerful impact on the Justices. This surprising development illustrates quite clearly the many divergent paths possible for the generation of police reforms.

The point is that police chiefs have both the duty and the responsibility for moving the police toward cleaner, more legal, more effective levels of performance. This area is rich with promise for generalizing the people's support for reforms of all descriptions.

Techniques

Once the problems have been identified, sorted out, and prioritized, and a corrective strategy adopted, it is important that the public's support be enlisted. This has been said so often that we may no longer truly recognize the importance of this alliance but, absent citizen involvement -- such as calls to radio shows, letters to the editor, calls to political leaders, etc. -- the reformer can be easily isolated and defeated by the array of forces inevitably stirred to opposition.

The press, as the conduit of the public's right to know, becomes the most important tool in any strategy of reform. They are not the only one, however. Public bodies, such as Citizens Leagues, or Leagues of Women Voters, are natural allies in a struggle for reforms. It is important to enlist such allies in the struggle. Their constituencies are frequently influential, intelligent and interested.

Executives abhor intrusions, yet it may be the soundest practice to invite an inquiry, examination, or audit. The first message this conveys is a lack of fear that one will be embarrassed or compromised, and the second is that one has a genuine interest in reform and is willing to risk outsiders' examinations to bring it about. In such undertakings as reforms, there is both form and substance. Both must be pursued in tandem. Symbols do matter. In an age of image-bombardment, it is important to get through and convey the message. How the problem is attacked becomes the substance of the enterprise.

It is very important that, in terms of form and substance, the chief be able to distinguish between the issues that impact on performance -- hence the public's welfare and safety -- and those that constitute the mere trappings of office. Too many administrators have spent too much energy securing compliance for the sake of ego satisfaction rather than worrying about how any given breach may affect the public interest. Command is not an ego trip, nor an assertion of will to show them who is boss. Command is granted to facilitate the high tasks of public service.

The martinet imposes his will, inflates his persona, and feeds his ego. The public servant focuses on the people's needs. Thus, it becomes clear that reform is not just a program of action, but one that must frequently be preceded and invariably accompanied by education. The public must understand the need for reform and see, clearly, how it ties in to improved service and protection.

Organizational Messages

The internal life of a police agency would appear to be a pretty straightforward business. Orders are transmitted and carried out. Policies are enunciated and pursued. The chief speaks and the troops listen and obey.

In reality, few things could be further from the truth. Organizations respond to the real messages. How did the administration respond to this problem? What are the administration's real values, notwithstanding the party line the times require them to utter? What values are transmitted in the behavior of the administration?

The administration of a police agency probably transmits its values and priorities far more clearly in its actions than in its memos, yet the real world seems to function as if the reverse were true.

The administration of a police agency probably transmits its values and priorities far more clearly in its actions than in its memos, yet the real world seems to function as if the reverse were true.

The thumpers and thieves within the ranks, referred to as the "meat eaters" in the Knapp Investigation (as opposed to the tamer mass of grass eaters" going along with the herd), frequently set the organizational tone. They are, many times, the leaders -- the most energetic, daring and admired. The genre has even been given a name by the title of a famous film, "Dirty Harry." The chief is frequently locked in a battle for control of the agency with these leaders, within the ranks, who are usually pursuing some nihilistic private agenda that has little relationship to legitimate organizational purposes, however much Hollywood may strive to anoint their efforts.

The integrity and character of the chief are, then, critical. To order one thing and do another is not, as is often thought, to convey a mixed message, but rather to clearly indicate that it is from the actions that others take their cue.

The process of selecting the chief should, then, be very carefully pursued. The anointment of a favorite insider conveys one message; the selection (after a tortured, public search) of another conveys another.

The chief's behavior in the post will be much more closely observed than the orders emanating from his office. There must be integrity, consistency and character reflected in the action. Such personal qualities are the most important factors in the effectiveness of the leadership brought to the agency.

In attacking the unfit and weeding out the unsuitable employee, an inordinate amount of time and energy must be spent. In a sense, everyone's attention is riveted there anyway, since they represent the lowest level of conduct found acceptable by the agency. When a miscreant is fired, then, the message is that the conduct is no longer acceptable. This dismissal of number 10, for example, should have a salutory effect on the next marginal worker, number 9. Numbers 1 and 2 will work hard whoever is in charge and whatever the policies, and the others in increasing intensity as they get nearer the brink will be watching. The point is that concentrating the effort on the last ranked one is not necessarily neglecting the other nine. The other point is that the employment of terror (a negative force such as dismissal) is as legitimate as the use of positive motivational forces.

Cops have enormous power. It is frequently labeled *discretion* because they can pick and choose from among a cornucopia of ordinances, laws and regulations. They are also experienced in manipulating situations into unintended breaches that offer the opportunity for official response. Policing is one of the very few professions where the most important decisions -- vis a vis their clientele -- are taken at the lowest rank level of the organization.

The "attitude test" is a good illustration. Cops size up situations and people in shorthand fashion. They don't have a lot of time and frequently resort to stereotyping. If you are labeled a jerk, you will very likely wind up in a lot more trouble than if the cop believes you're okay and properly respectful. Cops do not respond well to attacks on their person or challenges to their authority.

Much of the work of the police reformer lies in the areas of limiting and redirecting this discretion, away from the exercise of personal pique and toward pursuing wider organizational objectives. Requiring, for example, cops to always report any use of force will, like the earlier reform requiring an investigation of every shooting by the police, result in more circumspect behavior. The behavior of cops can be changed, through administrative fiat, if the change is rational and sound, and if transgressions are dealt with reasonably harshly.

The police world is *sui generis*. It is insular and sealed. Its secrets are kept faithfully by its acolytes. Cops soon discover that the world neither appreciates their efforts to produce order nor understands their explanations for the necessity of their actions. After an initial euphoric desire to share with others, cops are usually reduced to speaking only to each other, in the accepted argot. They deal with the dark underbelly of the human beast. This usually causes them to be either cynical or baleful observers of their fellow man.

A close sense of fraternity envelops the practitioners. They become intensely loyal. There is a sense of *us and them*. The cops are the good guys, fighting the bad. Why doesn't the world understand? Fort Apache. The Alamo. Their precincts sometimes reflect their view of beleaguered outposts in the midst of hostiles. The loyalty gets expressed in fierce common protectionism. A code of silence, stronger than Omerta, rules the responses of cops caught up in investigations of wrongdoing. All of this could be seen at work in the beating of Rodney King, Jr. on March 3, 1991, by the L.A.P.D.

After the initial euphoric desire to share with others, cops are usually reduced to speaking only to each other, in the accepted argot.

The socialization of recruits starts early and proceeds mercilessly. No cop can escape it. The search for psychological screens that will weed out the brutes will founder on the shoals of the realization that these wrongdoers were shaped by agency forces, not recruited.

These factors are challenges to administrators who believe their agency must engage in true partnership with the communities they serve.

Training must be extensive, relevant and continuous. The officer must be sensitized to the issues he will confront. The complexity of contemporary American society requires a sophistication hitherto undreamed of. This will require the attraction of suitably educated recruits, drawn in to the profession purposefully and early. The Peace Officer Standards and Training process, requiring two years of specialized college education, followed by a basic training curriculum and a licensing test, holds the promise of providing prepared and motivated recruits (see Dodenhoff's chapter). When this is followed by a rigorous background investigation and thorough training, in formal classrooms and by Field Training Officers during a year's probation, the hope of producing a competent professional police officer is greatly enhanced.

The messages must be simple, and constant. Serve the people. Perform your job and you'll be supported. Make a good faith mistake, and we'll try to help. Break the law or make a bad faith act, and the organization will go for your throat.

Such messages hold the promise of shifting behavior into the desired forms. Changing attitudes is a much more difficult process, involving a lot of training and organizational reinforcement.

Doing it Yourself

The most important element in any reform of a police agency is public awareness and support. If the people do not agree that a reform is needed, they will withhold their support. That will usually tilt the battle in favor of the entrenched interests anxious to preserve their status.

The messages must be simple, and constant. Serve the people. Perform your job and you'll be supported. Make a good faith mistake, and we'll try to help. Break the law or make a bad faith act, and the organization will go for your throat.

Educating the public to the urgent need of change is one of the key responsibilities of the police chief. His role as educator is a real one. His tools are the forums available to his use -- the press, public meetings and, not unimportantly but frequently overlooked, his own ability to weigh in with an editorial or Op-Ed piece.

The chief, to be effective, must be an effective communicator, both within and without the agency. This means not only speaking clearly and effectively, but listening, reading and writing as well. This is probably the most important skill a police CEO can develop.

Issues are best and most clearly illustrated through real cases that embody the major questions. It is important that an in-house capability be developed to research, analyze, and develop solutions for problems that arise. This speaks more to a socratic capability than it does to the routine Research and Planning Unit so many agencies adopt, but which frequently are unworthy of the name.

If, for example, the chief routinely accepts every invitation to speak, to any group, constituencies for reforms will be identified and enlisted. This sort of high-profile effort may make politicians restive, but an anonymous chief whose policies are not widely known will not be able to wield the power necessary to undertake serious reforms.

Everything to its season. While Everett could speak for hours, before Lincoln's talk at Gettysburg, today's reality is that each of us, in public life, is afforded seconds to communicate our views. This means the distillation of complex issues and programs into a few sound bytes that, at once, both convey the message with utter clarity and are gripping enough to capture flighty attentions. This, too, imposes the need for developing new skills. It requires a lot of thought to first decide the issues, settle on an answer, and then edit and condense that reply into some catchy, sexy language.

An anonymous chief whose policies are most widely known will not be able to wield the power necessary to undertake serious reforms.

Madison Avenue and public relations specialists have taught us the importance of quick, punchy, effective communication. In eradicating a particularly egregious abuse, for example, the most powerful educational weapon to arouse the citizenry to action might well be a slogan. Ideally, this should capture the essence of the problem and emblazon the issue indelibly in the public consciousness.

Within the organization, safety valves have to be created to allow workers to seek the alternatives of treatment as they accept the realities, or inevitability, of reform. Stress and Wellness programs, which encompass a panoply of approaches from counseling to therapy, to Alcoholics or Gamblers Anonymous or whatever, to physical fitness have to be provided. Since cops normally only confide in other cops, these will probably have to be staffed by cops.

Stress and Wellness programs constitute a message from the organization: get help. The other side of the message is that if you're found out, it is too late to claim you're ill and need assistance.

Random testing for drugs and alertness to the abuse of alcohol will inhibit the spread of broad difficulties that sometimes, inexplicably, overcome police agencies. The search for abusers transmits a crystal-clear organizational message about tolerated and not tolerated behavior.

The Supreme Court has held that random drug testing is a permissible intrusion in safety-sensitive and law enforcement jobs.

Again, the stick must be employed with the carrot. An open-door policy and total accessibility will offer the prospect of contact with decision-makers who can offer guidance. Running a police agency requires use of both positive and negative factors.

The Mechanics of Reform

Reform is nothing more than the cleansing of the police body from within. It is a way of insuring that cops become the servants of the law, not its masters.

There is never a propitious or appropriate time to undertake radical change for the better. The cautious will always raise frightening objections. It will be summer, or an election may be in the offing, or a contract is being negotiated, or a court decision is being awaited, or any of a hundred excuses for postponement will be raised. Obviously, there can exist legitimate impediments to action, but the chief must be alert to the prospects and weigh the circumstances carefully. Real obstacles ought to be clear enough and, even here, determination can be displayed through preparation and the fixing of a time-table for the adoption of reforms. Momentum and expectation are important elements in the process. Once it is perceived that the glow of action might be dimmed by cautious counsel, the pendulum begins to swing toward the resisters of reform.

Reform is nothing more than the cleansing of the police body from within. It is a way of insuring that cops become the servants of the law, not its masters. Reforms may be undertaken with lightning swiftness, when circumstances serendipitously deliver a target of opportunity, or they may be tortuous organizational shifts involving months of planning and preparation.

Institutionalizing reforms involves weaving organizational change into the body of the agency. This might be done through the creation of inspection or auditing units or the development of a strong Internal Affairs unit, the employment of internal spies, and the adoption of aggressive techniques.

Reforms need to be tied to the adoption of a system of organizational values that are consistent, clear, and widely known and accepted. The adoption of a formal statement, enunciating these values, can be a solid foundation for reform.

The police have much to learn from the corporate world -- things like polling, independent audits, surprise inspections, and other techniques for verifying what is really taking place. The police world over-relies on self-reporting and its own routine, predictable, up-the-chain-of-command processes. The chief has to develop tools that provide outside verification. Soliciting letters, directly, to the chief through, for example, a post office box or calls to a publicized number will speed the flow of information.

Some will be cranks or kooks, but many will be legitimate and convey a real sense of the true problems.

The use of police spies -- a terrifically unpopular practice within the ranks -- reached the apex of its experience following the disclosures of widespread corruption in the New York City Police Department by the Knapp Commission. Public outrage and demand for reform overcame the internal organizational resistance (focused, organized, and led by the union -- the Patrolman's Benevolent Association) and strengthened the hand of a determined police chief. In time, hundreds of cops were secretly reporting acts of serious wrongdoing to their headquarters monitors. Unremitting resistance and hostility gradually wore down the enthusiasm of subsequent administrators for this unpopular practice.

The use of self-initiating integrity tests, where, for example, a "found wallet" containing cash would be turned over to a cop, to see if he'd turn it in and report it, created quite a furor. The sending of hippie-looking people into precincts, to inquire how a complaint of police brutality might be made against an officer revealed that compliance with regulations was anything but uniform. Commanders lost their posts when the testers were unceremoniously thrown out of the precinct. The rest got the message. All of these tactics, and others, were made possible by a climate-for-reform created by the Knapp Commission and the resultant public demand for action. The strategies are limited only by the confines of the human imagination and the requirements of law. This is an important area for daring and inventiveness.

The point is to test and verify the true organizational responses through inside and outside looks at the agency's workings. The creation of a strong Internal Affairs unit is essential to the development of an effective program of reform. Assignment to the unit should be seen as one of the essentials of progressing in the organization.

Reform is a result, an objective. Many roads can lead to this end. The executive must be aware of the myriad of possible strategies. Some have been wrought through simple administrative fiat, the issuance of an order -- others through court orders or litigation. Some required attacking language in the labor contract. Others necessitated deep and complicated criminal investigations. Flexibility and daring are essentials to the process. Determined follow-through, in terms of arrests, discipline, etc., becomes a more eloquent testimonial of the administration's determination than the most elaborate exhortation.

Reform is a broad term. It connotes correcting flaws. It can go from attacking serious and systemic acts of police brutality or corruption to issues relating to waste, mismanagement, or administrative abuses. The organizational message must be clear and consistent. The agency is guided by clearly defined legal and moral principles.

In conducting aggressive investigations of wrongdoing, the surest guide is the law. Securing court orders for wiretaps, buggings, or searches invests the process with the protective cloak of the law. Internal processes, however, do not lend themselves that easily to legal directions. In assignments, transfers, promotions, demotions, or other personnel or organizational decisions, the legal strictures will afford little guidance. Here, ethics come more clearly into play, and nowhere is the organizational message more closely observed.

If such decisions are taken with a decent and obvious regard for honest judgments, then the internal message connects harmoniously with the agency's internal actions. If the administration is seen to accommodate its comfort, whim or convenience, or if perquisites and privileges are seen to attach to high office, then those at the lower rungs will adapt their behavior accordingly. A shirking of principles at the top will result in the troops translating the action into a warrant for their own wrongdoing. Nothing, in recent years, so eroded the public's confidence in their Congress than the revelation that its members had banking privileges that routinely overlooked overdrafts.

Internal Concerns

The limits of span of control clearly indicate the parameters of possible action by any single individual. Whether one likes it or not, organizations are run by many people, arranged in a pyramidal structure. Thus, the chief must select the best and the brightest as his associates. This has become such a bromide that it is hardly worth repeating. Why, then, bother? Because too many top executives are insecure and threatened by talented subordinates and, giving in to these feelings, surround themselves with compliant toadies instead.

The importance of bringing the ablest forward cannot be over-stressed. Besides communicating the soundest message, it enables the creation of the strongest team, while insuring the agency's future, as well as preserving whatever hope there may be for projecting the reforms beyond the life of the current administration.

The methods employed in selecting or assigning personnel ought to be objective, relevant, and clear to all. Having them in writing enables everyone to know and evaluate the standards employed.

Actions ought to be predicated on reasonable factors, and these factors should be formally articulated, and signed, so that all may see the grounds on which any decision was made. Boiler-plate phrases should not be adopted. Every important decision should be based on articulable grounds, and those grounds have to be articulated.

The pressure to perform, so frequently absent in governmental operations, must be there. Obviously mistakes will occur, but there must be accountability. It is not enough to say that the purposes of government are too noble to be measured. Commanders must be held responsible for the state of their commands. Theirs is not an insurer's responsibility, where they are held liable for every act, but rather a steward's, where they must be accountable for conditions they should have known about and corrected. This distinction is critical to the effective running of an organization. It distinguishes between the draconian response of the panicked martinet and the reasoned judgment of an executive who considers what was known, what should have been known, when should it have been known, and what was done about it.

The pursuit of accreditation will insure that the agency is complying with minimal standards, in a series of police operations that were, in the experience and study of many organizations, essential to its proper functioning.

The Union

Dealing with powerful, determined, fast-growing police unions has become one of the very complex challenges to contemporary chiefs. Here, as with the press, attitude must be examined since it will ultimately, if not always in direct or obvious ways, guide actions.

The laborer is worthy of his hire. Thus does the Bible remind us of the importance of preserving the worker's dignity. The worker has a right to join others for self-protection against management's power and possible abuse. The two most important factors in the elevation of the American worker in this century have been education and unionization. The police executive must see the union as essential to the worker's well being and work with it, in a constructive, adversarial relationship that clearly calls for understanding each other's role.

The union is there to secure protection, salaries and benefits for the worker. The chief is there to manage the enterprise. The accretion of power, such as what police unions have experienced in developing the financial and political power to influence elections and appointments, will lead inevitably to a temptation to abuse it. Unions have developed powerful allies in all political councils. They frequently control Civil Service Commissions. They take a deep interest in the careers of arbitrators, judges and referees. They have frozen requirements that impede effective management of the agency by insisting on their entrance into the labor contract. Many managerial obligations have been traded away by city negotiators anxious to save dollars. Seniority often appears as the arbiter of assignment decisions. Promotions and assignments have also been written into the contract's language. Unions have become very adept at solidifying power in various repositories, including the law. They have become increasingly comfortable in the corridors of power.

Poor management doesn't usually result in a dramatic collapse, but rather produces subtle, long-term changes that ultimately develop into genuine crises.

Police unionism, like its twin in the corporate sector, grew in response to the abuses of management, visited on individual workers who, feeling helpless and exploited, banded together for self-protection.

Chiefs routinely forced cops to work extra hours without compensation; switched tours arbitrarily; punished, changed assignments, or delivered difficult transfers on little more than whim; played favorites and took over critical actions on the basis of personal, often performance-irrelevant factors that finally convinced the cops to join together to curb such abuses of administrative power through the countervailing weight of united action.

The key significance of the development of police unions lies in the pervasive, continuing and hidden costs of mismanagement -- which may, even today, be policing's greatest problem.

Poor management doesn't usually result in a dramatic collapse, but rather produces subtle, long-term changes that ultimately develop into genuine crises. By then, it is too far down the road to identify a poor administrator or an egregiously flawed administrative decision as the culprit.

It may not be too much to say that the deep and universal economic problems of America's cities might most effectively be addressed by implementing hard-headed managerial and administrative reforms to bloated and inefficient police agencies.

It cannot be said that unions, anywhere, promote brutality, corruption, or any other act of police wrongdoing. Yet, because of legal responsibility to represent the accused, their identification with the worker, and the need to maximize his protection, unions frequently become the greatest obstacles to reform.

In taking on such a powerful body, in a battle to control the agency, the strongest ally becomes the public. Securing their support requires that the people be informed (through the press) and that they see their interests tied clearly to the proposed reform.

Thus, in taking on the union, the chief must make his support for the institution clear, as he identifies the areas of contention and illustrates how the abuses harm the people and how reform will help.

The rhythm and flow of organizational life functions on momentum. Stagnation, labor unrest, poor performance, inadequate leadership, and the toleration of wrongs will drag morale to the depths. Reforms, conversely, create an opposite momentum. Their motion generates activism and enlists, in the battle, some who, in other circumstances, might have been content to remain onlookers. These converts will also bring their own agendas, ideas and targets, thereby spreading the radial effects of reform and greatly increasing the number of problems that can be attacked. A reform mode thus becomes established. It will force interaction with other improvements, thereby providing further momentum.

The morale of an agency is really its spirit, and it is to be judged not by what is said about it but through the surer evidence of actions. An agency in reform, with purposeful, proved workers, will evidence its morale in the elan with which it tackles its challenges. Contradictory organizational messages from above short circuit the process and sow confusion in the ranks.

Reforms cannot be undertaken with precisely equal zeal. Some wrongs are more serious than others. There has to be a sense of proportion and a clear set of priorities. Each reform will engender resistance, and the laws of physics will remind us about creating immovable objects.

Changing the behavior of tough cops will not occur through exhortations, speeches or eloquent or even threatening orders. Cops respond to actions.

Change threatens the status quo and all who profit from it. Those to be benefited will not risk much for speculative gains. There is a limit to the number of opponents one can take on at one time.

Reform must be like correcting one's children, i.e. undertaken with determination and energy, and undergirded by love. It must be clearly enunciated that the motivation is to strengthen the organization so that it will serve the people better.

The people are bombarded, daily, with hundreds of messages. Their interests must be made clear to them if yours is to be heard above the clamor. It is not public apathy that stalls reforms, but rather lack of public awareness. That is the chief's task.

The effort must be attended by reasonableness, proportion, objectivity and integrity.

Alcohol abuse is different from marijuana use which, in itself, is different from cocaine sniffing. Taking a free cup of coffee is wrong, but not as serious as stealing a drug dealer's money. There are gradations of wrong, and a sense of proportion is critical. All wrongs are not equal, even if they are all wrongs.

Changing the behavior of tough cops will not occur through exhortations, speeches, or eloquent or even threatening orders. Cops respond to actions. They live in a world where one focuses on what one does. The threat of discipline will not faze them. The sequence must include a clear, consistent message -- conveyed in every conceivable way, not just in words or memos -- followed by swift, decisive actions. Maximillian Robespierre said, "Virtue, without terror, is powerless."

A police agency exists to serve the people. When a chief is appointed, the first and most crucial decision he can make is whether to promote the comfort and convenience of his colleagues, with whom he identifies and with whom he grew up in the agency, or serve the interests of the people. While the ideas are, in practice, virtually irreconcilable, choosing the second course will produce a vigorous, healthy, effective police department, and its members will respond to that reality.

Chapter 9

Police Leadership and the Management of Liability: A Systemic Approach

The only certain cure for liability is arranging for an unlisted telephone number for the police agency, the elimination of guns, cars and cuffs, a total prohibition against the use of police cars, and finally a ban on making any arrests or searches.

by J. Patrick Gallagher

Not that they really needed it, but law enforcement executives have in the past decade acclimated themselves to the almost daily threat of lawsuits stemming from the activities of their officers and by the alleged deficiencies of their organization's training and policies.

By acclimation, I mean not an accommodation with this source of financial loss or major distraction from their admittedly more important commitment to the maintenance of the quality of life in our communities by the protection of the public and the provision of quality service to their communities. Already hard pressed executives have merely grown accustomed to the civil repercussions to the activities of their officers which seem to generate a steady flow of litigation based on highly repetitive approaches devised by the plaintiff's bar. Organizations which excel in analytical and investigative skills fail to examine the hackneyed M.O. of their opponents in the civil arena or what one observer has called the "mean streets in the land of civil." Failing to analyze the tactics of their opponents, I also feel that police organizations have failed to look critically at their own shortcomings, and consequently have neglected to place their emphasis in areas which would generate the highest payoffs.

Executives themselves have certainly found themselves the direct focus of this litigation as the plaintiffs have targeted the agency's policies, procedures, customs, usages or practices as either being unconstitutional or have claimed that the policymakers were deliberately indifferent to the adequate training of the officers in the light of the tasks assigned. The post-*Canton* era has undoubtedly made it easier for these suits to go forward because of some actual and perceived deficiencies in the inner management of our law enforcement agencies.

Liability just will not disappear. I have facetiously remarked that the only certain cure for liability is arranging for an unlisted telephone number for the police agency, the elimination of guns, cars, and cuffs, a total prohibition against the use of police cars, and finally a ban on making any arrests or searches. Sure, the effects will be dramatic; and while lawsuits will plummet in number, so will any indication of police efficiency, effectiveness, and quality of service. Law enforcement officers will of necessity continue to provide service and perform a variety of tasks that society actually needs them to perform, and most of them involve some degree of risk which cannot be eliminated.

A number of basic policies involving the leadership and management of agencies must be questioned and drastically revised.

But I feel that the problem has been exacerbated not only by the failure to analyze the opponents' strategies which are admittedly an open book, coupled with a delinquency in stressing the improvement in the most critical areas of the police organization, but also by an ongoing commitment to certain policies whose effects set up a framework which almost makes for an impossible task in combatting litigation or even in managing it satisfactorily.

The Folly of Certain Policy Commitments

The problems with police and the onslaught of liability, to my mind, will never be resolved until there is a comprehensive reevaluation of some basic assumptions at the very core of our strategies to deal with both the challenge of more effective, efficient and quality-driven service to the public and the simultaneous control of, and decrease in, the amount of liability.

What must precede any other steps is the realization that leadership with vision and values (see Behan's chapter), good management, and quality supervision are essential to the attainment of both of the above objectives. Furthermore, to me it appears that a number of basic policies involving the leadership and management of agencies must be questioned and drastically revised.

Barbara Tuchman in her book *The March of Folly* defines a policy as folly "if pursued contrary to the self-interest of the group. Self-interest is whatever conduces to the welfare or advantage of the body being governed; folly is a policy that in these terms is counter-productive." The law enforcement profession has developed in this country haphazardly with a tremendous spurt in improvement in the past decade or so (ironically driven more by the results of civil litigation than by pure appeals to higher levels of professionalism).

Ongoing commitments to policies detrimental to the attainment of desirable goals have stymied law enforcement since on one hand it faces increased and more serious needs for its services while on the other it now finds it is operating in a broader plain sown liberally with the deadly mines of litigation. Tuchman makes a strong case for certain policies being considered folly or counter-productive when her threefold test is applied. According to Tuchman, policy is folly when:

1. It is perceived as counter-productive in the present time, and not just in retrospect.

2. There is a feasible alternative course of action available.

3. It is the policy of a group, a broad representation of one profession, and not just that of an individual executive.

It is my contention that the law enforcement profession is consciously or unconsciously committed to certain policies which are innately detrimental or, as Tuchman would say, "counter-productive" to the self-interest, the welfare, or the advantage of the group, especially in relationship to the dual objective of greater effectiveness and higher quality service with a corresponding decrease in liability.

Tuchman in *The March of Folly* examines in minute detail four examples in history that show decisively the disastrous results of commitment to counter-productive policies. She clearly proves to me at least her contention in her analysis of the Greeks and the Fall of Troy, the Renaissance Popes, the British and their treatment of the American colonies, and the United States' involvement in Vietnam. Every single example can be related to the law enforcement profession and speak directly to the possible solution of the problems that it is facing.

Questioning Law Enforcement Policies

In analyzing the management and direction of the law enforcement system and applying Tuchman's criteria to parts of it, here are the policies which must be reexamined because, as accepted and operationalized, they can only be considered as folly.

1. *The profession can continue to see the necessary presence of policy as essential to establishing restrictions on officers rather than on establishing a liberating force to heighten and improve performance while it makes little effort to realize the degree of effort necessary to change an organization's life-style, which is actually the rationale for policy in the first place.*

    Policy for the most part is seen as a destructive "gotcha" process, and not one that frees the officer to operate more efficiently and effectively. On the contrary, policies must be developed and taught in the sense that they are to channelize (or to "canalize" as one recent U.S. Supreme Court decision states) police activities and discretion. Policies must be present to improve and focus performance and not merely to spotlight those who do not meet those performance standards.

2. *The profession can offer inadequate training to its police officers at most levels, for most tasks, and for critical policies and somehow expect positive results and the attainment of the desired objectives.*

    Training has been for too long the stepchild of the profession and is rarely integrated, qualitative, contextual, validated, proficiency-based, and extended enough to provide the law enforcement personnel with the solid base for the tasks which they are called on to perform. The training necessary to meet the expectations that the profession has for its officers, supervisors and executives is frankly lacking.

3. *The profession can get by with preparation of supervisors that falls far short of the expectations for those positions. Supervisors can pick up their responsibilities by a form of osmosis and then perform at the desirable*

Policy for the most part is seen as a destructive "gotcha" process, and not one that frees the officer to operate more efficiently and effectively.

levels. The expectation is present that leadership can be developed without an incremental effort at every level in the organization.

Supervision at every level has never produced anything close to the leadership necessary to improve performance; neither has supervision exerted the quality control essential to a continuous raise in the level of service. The overwhelming and universal neglect of the preparation of every level of supervisors, especially those at the first-line, to meet the demanding expectations that the profession has for its upper level personnel (sergeants and above) has continuously retarded the performance of entire departments, and consequently made it easier for litigation to be successful against police. Furthermore, as a result, supervision in its active mode operates like policy in a "gotcha" attitude, rather than as a promoter of high-level performance in subordinates. There is a failure to produce first-line supervisors who are leaders. Since few sergeants are developed who can lead six or eight, we have few lieutenants or captains who can lead 40 or 50, and hence few chiefs who can lead 100.

4. *The profession can continue to have discipline operate in its most negative form, the ultimate "gotcha," and can consistently neglect efforts to support and encourage excellent performance as an ordinary course of action.*

In combination with the negative orientation of both policy and supervision, discipline contributes mightily to reduced performance. Or on the other hand, supervisors shy away from discipline, hence corrections to inadequate performance are seldom made. On the contrary, the emphasis must be placed on performance management which is initiated with performance planning and followed by evaluation. When corrective action is taken, it must be in the sense of raising that level of performance to that which is expected, constantly asking what can be done to better performance, to reach the level of what Ken Blanchard calls "legendary service" and what should be called for police "heroic service" -- the doing of all ordinary things extraordinarily well.

5. *The profession can continue to ignore the compilation of data, the subsequent analysis, and the remedial and corrective actions indicated along with the constant scanning of the environment so necessary to identify problems in their earliest stages and to keep abreast of relevant issues.*

It might be said of us if we were running businesses that we never examined our own spreadsheets. Generally, the records which are kept are not utilized to make management decisions that will, in turn, reduce problems. Usually the data in complaints, lawsuits, I.A. investigations, the indications of chronic offenders, and much of the newest research and writings in the profession are not regularly reviewed and acted upon. Furthermore, since the first step is lacking, the subsequent revision of training, policies and procedures is absent.

6. *The profession can operate effectively without available, aggressive, experienced, competent legal training, legal counsel, and legal updates. Police officers are seen as able to be effective without really knowing the law.*

In an environment seething with legalities, in a litigious society, with constantly new and progressively demanding case law and new statutes, the police have been exceedingly slow to get access to legal counsel and systemic legal updates in a continuous manner. Given the importance of this component, there is little wonder that law enforcement is out-gunned; law enforcement officers never reach the position of acting with total assurance and confidence in the legal arena, which in fact represents most of the enforcement actions which they take.

Can Liability be a Positive Force?

But if we think of it, in the past ten years what has contributed more to the increase in the quality of police service? Given two alternatives -- appeals for greater professionalism or liability and litigation -- undoubtedly the answer would be the latter. Liability has gotten the attention of executives individually and the law enforcement profession corporately. Dramatic changes have taken place and at a pace remarkably accelerated in contrast to the glacial speed with which newer thinking and transformations have affected policing in the pre-litigation era arbitrarily defined as prior to 1975.

In the period after Rodney King, events on the liability front will not get any easier. The forecast is for a tremendously increased scrutiny especially on the use of force, the quality of supervision, and the departmental response to chronic use of force offenders. It is important to acknowledge that while police might bemoan the judgments, the facts in the cases clearly show serious shortcomings in police performance, supervision, training, discipline, and ultimately police leadership itself.

Once members of the police profession begin to think positively, then the question of liability is put into a different perspective.

But it makes no sense to merely rant and rave against these forces without eventually directing our analytical ability to determine what will lessen the burden. Once members of the police profession begin to think positively, then the question of liability is put into a different perspective. The odds against winning are not insurmountable if certain efforts can be put into place to lead and manage our agencies more effectively. But it will also mean the eschewing of the policies whose adherence can only be considered as folly.

Early on in reviewing the problem of liability, it is easy to come to this conclusion: Liability management is nothing but leadership with vision and values, good management, and quality supervision, for no step taken to curtail or diminish liability should not already have been taken by the good leader, manager or supervisor.

For the past decade, I have had the opportunity to assist law enforcement agencies in every single state in dealing with the question of liability. To accomplish this objective, I have conducted extensive training for every level of public and police officials, have developed a wide range of liability assessment formats, have reviewed and revised hundreds of policies, have provided expert witnesses testimony and case consultations, have conducted many management or quality assurance studies, have organized computerized legal lessons and legal updates, and have devised customized action plans for law enforcement agencies.

After these ten years, I can say with a certain degree of authority that the liability burden shouldered by our executives and by our law enforcement agencies is for the most part a result of the commitment to the aforementioned policies. Continued adherence will only prolong the difficulty of managing liability and achieving a higher degree of effectiveness and quality of service. Contrariwise, a prolonged and studied commitment to the opposite positions will more than ameliorate our position; it will radically improve it.

Police officers and top-level officials for the most part do not understand what the exposures are, how the civil liability game is played, and what must be done to be more successful at combatting liability.

This involvement over that period has brought me to certain inescapable conclusions about the weaknesses in our protective system against liability. These weaknesses are those which Tuchman in *The March of Folly* would call "counter-productive policy" since these arrangements are so obviously contrary to the self interest and advantage of the profession.

Efforts to counter liability without confronting the systemic weaknesses will result in little change, ongoing legal problems, and inefficient and ineffective law enforcement agencies. When carefully analyzed, it is hard to explain the managerial myopia that has kept us so much on the defensive with little solid progress. We can start with the principle that police can only beat a system that they understand. Police officers and top-level officials for the most part do not understand what the exposures are, how the civil liability game is played, and what must be done to be more successful at combatting liability. To me, they have not made the linkage between effective leadership, good management and quality supervision, and the subsequent and simultaneous reduction of potential liability.

The Six-Layered Liability Protection System

My ongoing analysis has led to the development of the *Six-Layered Liability Protection System* where the interplay of all six components accomplished these objectives: It actually improves the quality of the management of the department, it places the department in the strongest position possible to defend itself against lawsuits, and it develops a proactive posture for the decrease of future lawsuits. The presence of all six components, with a high degree of quality, combined with an equally high degree of interaction and mutual support among all six, presents a formidable obstacle against lawsuits. This in reality represents a rethinking and reevaluation of some long overlooked approaches to the manner in which police activities and services have been effected in the past.

The Six-Layered Liability Protection System has been developed from the uniformity of the responses of police executives around the country to the six basic policy statements posed above, and to the analysis of why the profession eventually has a problem of such magnitude with liability.

Starting with good leadership, the basic premises of the Six-Layered Liability Protection System are:

> *policy* seen in a positive mode based on the foreseeability principle of providing necessary direction for anticipated activities of officers,

> contextual proficiency-based *training* in all aspects of the regulated tasks and in the high risk/critical task policies,

> quality *supervision* that emphasizes "looking over" rather than "overlooking," and Ken Blanchard's orientation for supervision that it is going around trying to catch people doing something *right*,

> *discipline* that emphasizes personnel management and every manner of positive reinforcement of excellent or heroic service,

> continuous *review* and *revision* of everything in the law enforcement environment, and

> ongoing *legal support* and *legal updates* to include timely and relevant legal training.

The System places a great deal of emphasis on the proactive and active components: policy, training, supervision, review and revision, and legal support and updates. The System requires that all six components interact with each other. The System takes into consideration the solid principles on quality service now influencing so strongly all aspects of the public and private sector. These principles paraphrased from Philip Crosby in his *Quality Without Tears* are:

1. The *definition* of quality policing is conformance to requirements.

2. The *system* of quality policing is prevention, not appraisal.

3. The *standard* of quality policing is zero defects, not "That's good enough."

Failure comes about when the principles that generate on one hand quality service and on the other ineffective policing and liability are overlooked, when each component is not put in place and does not interact with each other, and when leadership does not establish a supportive environment for improvement to take place.

The Plaintiff's Five-Point Plan of Attack

Failure to accept these principles while simultaneously oblivious to the very obvious plaintiff's plan of attack doom police agencies' efforts at improvement and avoidance of liability. The plaintiff will undoubtedly evaluate the facts in the case involving the officers at the scene, and then attempt to reach beyond the officer into the department by attacking policy, training, supervision and discipline.

This initial probe effected by discovery methods will be geared to establishing a total of five points of attack. During this process, the initial incident and the original facts in the case might be overshadowed by the gaping deficiencies identified through the discovery process and eventually the trial itself. (Many agencies, feeling that the facts in the case are not that seriously weighted against them, nevertheless settle because of the potential damage which might be uncovered when policy, training, supervision and disciplinary records are scrutinized.)

It remains for the police executives to so improve the factors over which they have control (policy, training, supervision and discipline) that they will withstand any attack, thereby forcing the plaintiff to concentrate on the facts in the case which might not be overwhelmingly against the officer.

While this strategy is forthright and feasible, it fails frequently because of the inherent weaknesses in the components over which the department supposedly has control. Policy is inadequate, not timely, nor comprehensive enough, or worse still replaced by custom, usage and practice. Training does not take place for the major policies, and there is little state-of-the-art training documented for a wide range of skills, attitude improvement, values, and knowledge. Supervision is not supportive, is reactive (often monitoring but not controlling), and is not seen as an extension of management and the attainment of its goals. Discipline is inconsistent, seldom used, and not documented sufficiently.

The agency thus loses the case not on the facts of the incident but more so because of the failure of the department to have their policy, training, supervision and discipline components at or above the appropriate standard.

This corporate failure to appreciate the comparative benefits of the quality control of these four elements lays bare the agency's defenses and only exacerbates the problem of liability. At this juncture, it might be forced to settle when, with foresight and due diligence in attending to the leadership and management responsibilities of the agency, the damage could never be accomplished.

But many agencies will feel that they do have their act together at the department level with these four components. However, I hold that while the development of police has improved appreciably in the past few years, it is a failure to realize some of the dynamics of policy, a failure to appreciate the efforts which must go into training officers in policies, and a failure to develop first-line supervision into the key bulwark and support of quality performance that eventually does the agency in.

Now we have gone full circle, and this results from the *March of Folly Syndrome* and the commitment to policies which do not serve the self interest or advantage of the department.

The Organizational Dynamics of Policy

The dynamics of policy within an organization must be recognized when we see that policy is in effect "a course of action chosen from among alternatives," or a "policy statement, ordinance, regulation, or decision that is officially adopted and promulgated by the municipality's lawmaking officers, or by an official to whom the lawmakers have delegated policymaking authority or persistent widespread practice of city officials which, although not officially adopted and promulgated policy, is so common and well settled as to constitute a custom that fairly represents municipal policy."

This leads us to see that in actuality, there are three types of policy within an organization. There is the *formal* issued by the chief executive, the *informal* which is the formal translated by supervisors, and the *operational* which is the one followed by officers and possibly for which the agency will be held responsible. But when asked "Is it easier to have the formal or the informal made operational?", chief executives have unanimously responded that it is easier for the informal, the one controlled and initiated by first-line supervisors for the most part, to become operational. This same group would admit that the first-line supervisor is in reality a more effective policymaker than the chief executive. Is it or is it not folly, as defined by Tuchman, to accept so readily this policy which makes the department leadership so impotent and actually constitute an abdication of leadership.

The chief executive has the responsibility to change organizational life-style by means of policies, buttressed by training, supervision, and discipline.

Unfortunately, while this is a ready admission, there is little if anything done to remedy this situation. Furthermore, this oversight is compounded by the fact that this same group will also admit that if you give a copy of one policy to 30 first-line supervisors, there will be 30 interpretations. But despite the acknowledgment of these problems, nothing is done to reduce their negative impact.

The chief executive has the responsibility to change organizational life-style by means of policies, buttressed by training, supervision, and discipline. General George C. Patton said: "Issuing an order is only ten percent; the remaining ninety percent consists in making sure that the order is rigorously and effectively executed." Once the formal policy has been issued, it is the daunting challenge of the ninety percent of effort that is lacking since the full impact of the training system, the input of quality supervision and the appropriate discipline do little to change the organizational life-style. The sad conclusion is that formal policy does little to become operationalized, and in reality is twisted and reinterpreted through every level in the organization.

Systemic Approaches to Training in Policies

Once there is a realization that a high degree of effort is necessary to train personnel in the policies, there are a number of additional steps which can be taken to make the efforts more effective. Let's be practical. The first step is to realize that there are usually only about ten or so "high risk/ critical task" policies that give rise to about 80 to 90 percent of the operational and liability problems. The concentration must therefore be on this small number of policies because this will give the highest return for the effort.

Secondly, a practical follow-up suggestion: Place all these high risk/ critical task policies on colored paper to distinguish them from the others. Thirdly, recognize the reality of the situation and actually designate these high risk/critical task policies as "need to know" policies; all the others will then be categorized as "need to reference." All the efforts will concentrate on the former.

The executive could follow this approach. With the next major policy issues, make sure that supervisors are trained, from the top down, before the ranks below them. Start with the command staff (in agencies large enough) or all of the supervisors in smaller agencies. Present the policy to them (they should be familiar with it because of the policy development process which the executive has employed), and ideally show a videotape (three to five minutes in length) of the executive enunciating the major points in the policy. Then have the command staff or supervisors take the new policy and apply a series of hypotheticals to it. The chief executive should then give guidance as to the correctness of each application of the policy to the situation outlined in the hypothetical, guiding the command staff to assure a more consistent interpretation of the policy through this form of consensus training. Command personnel or supervisors should repeat the process down through the ranks.

With this method, there is a greater chance for a more uniform interpretation of the policy, a greater chance for the formal policy to become operational, and increased likelihood of greater accountability since the excuses for non-enforcement have been stripped away.

With the new policy, establish a multi-level review for all incident reports dealing with this category. For example, with a new domestic violence policy, require that all domestic violence incident reports be reviewed and approved by not only sergeants, but also lieutenants and captains for a sufficient period of time to have made sure that all the information is being recorded and that all procedures are being followed.

Having identified the high risk/critical task policies, initiate a special form of roll-call training which would feature a three- to five-minute videotape of the chief executive emphasizing the major points in the policy while simultaneously handing out a one-page summary of the same policy. This training would be done for one policy for one solid week. Then the process would be repeated for the second policy, and the third in the high risk/critical task group. At the end of ten weeks, conceivably all ten of these policies would have been the subject of roll-call training, there would be a videotape on file along with a written summary, the department could rightly claim that it had devoted one week of roll-call training to each of their major policies, the training would be uniform, and probably all the officers would have been at roll calls during that period. Finally, in addition, require that all policies that relate to any type of in-service training be treated during the course of that training.

Require occasional post-incident reviews and "critiques to learn, not critiques to blame." This critical process can be the subject of inexpensive, timely, and relevant in-service training that, with the direction of a skilled and experienced supervisor, can become invaluable training to raise the level of performance with special emphasis on the more difficult tasks. Directed in the spirit of "What could we have done to better handle this incident?", the training can be brief but very much to the point in an extremely positive manner -- for, as the Zen proverb says, we "learn in order to do better that which we already do well."

Checklists might be developed for a Supervisor's Field Manual to include training material, policies and procedures for the many occasional but extremely stressful incidents which a supervisor might have to handle. In training situations, I have repeatedly asked groups of supervisors to draw up a checklist, say, for a barricaded subject or for an officer-involved shooting or a Hazmat incident. Without any stress, six to eight supervisors given 15 minutes will come up with a list of items that admittedly is deficient in listing the tasks that should really be accomplished at the scene. Yet, the field supervisor is expected in a much shorter period of time, under heavy stress, to recall all of the varied tasks required at that type of incident.

The manual approach incorporates simple checklists on a variety of high risk/critical tasks and is meant to be propped on the hood of a car and used for ready reference to make sure that every sub-task is taken care of. If the manual allows a field supervisor to correctly accomplish one more of the expected and necessary duties, it would be worthwhile.

Improving the Quality of Supervision

The improvement of the quality of supervision is dependent on the realization that the training of future supervisors starts on an officer's first day on the job. His/her first exposure to a supervisor in those impressionable first months could be crucial to the attitudes held toward supervision for the rest of their careers. Executives readily admit their perplexity in trying to improve the quality of first-line supervision, but for the most part they remain remarkably inattentive to the degree of effort necessary to develop and present contextual training given the criticality of the first-line supervisor's contributions to the overall effectiveness of the agency. High-quality supervisory performance will only enhance the executive's evaluation in his position, for nothing will make an executive look good as much as quality, responsible supervisors.

Nothing will make an executive look good as much as quality, responsible supervisors.

Supervisory training is too important to be provided after the fact when supervisory responsibility has already been assumed. Additionally, supervisory training cannot be provided to just a few supervisors at a time. This error is frequently committed when some supervisors are able to go off for a couple of weeks of supervisory training. When they return, they are an anomaly -- for, if the training is effective, there is little of a supportive environment existing for change in supervisory styles. The Japanese have a proverb: "Only the nail that stands up is hammered."

So too with these supervisors who want to implement their new found skills and ideas. They are hammered by those above them who are probably non-supportive, they are hammered by their peers who are being shown up, and they are hammered by their subordinates who cannot understand and even less accept the change in style. In a brief period of time, they revert to the previous style of supervision, and there is little lasting benefit to the individual and the department.

Second-line supervision is notoriously lax in actually providing positive supervision for first-line supervisors. These upper-level supervisors are not held responsible for the performance of first-line supervisors under them. Another vital support for improvement in supervision is lost, and the inadequate training level for the next round of second-level supervisors is repeated.

But the oft-repeated twofold objective is that this cycle can and must be broken. Some approaches to this objective could be the establishment of a Field Training Supervisor program patterned on the FTO but concentrating on new first-line supervisors assigned under the guidance and mentorship of an experienced supervisor for a set period of time. This could, in effect, even make the probationary period a lot more meaningful.

If we continue to do business the way we have, then we will continue to pay the price of doing business this way.

So set up the system that the second-line supervisors are actually involved in providing direct and active supervision to those below them, while providing regular contextual training in supervision and leadership for all first-line supervisors. Train supervisors so that they maintain the proper focus at all incidents -- neither getting too involved and thereby becoming participants nor removing themselves too far and becoming spectators. In either of these cases, the department has lost the presence of real supervision. Make sure that all supervisors know all the high risk/critical task policies and can apply them with assurance and confidence.

Some Conclusions

Our policing system must be examined critically for those policies which fall under Tuchman's definition of "policy as folly." These policies must be eliminated, and in their stead ones must be initiated that emphasize the positive aspects of policy and discipline, the repeated comprehensiveness of training, and the force of positive supervisors coupled with continuous review and revision and large doses of legal support and training.

Here I have concentrated more so on positing of the six "folly policies" and some ideas on improvements in our anticipation of the plaintiff's approach and our realignment of priorities to focus on policy, training and supervision.

There is no need to continue to have our best efforts stymied by ineffective strategies and increasing litigation when every quarter calls for the need to buttress the quality of life in our communities by improvement of police services. If we continue to do business the way we have, then we will continue to pay the price of doing business this way. If we no longer want to pay that price -- ineffective organizations, harried officers and executives, and constant litigation -- then we must change the way we do business. That conclusion to me is inescapable and can only make life a lot easier.

Chapter 10

A Critical and Constructive Look at the Defensibility of Police Pursuit Training

Police officers and agencies are frequent targets of litigation and claims of excessive force including unreasonable pursuit, the most frequent. Settlements and judgments in these cases have reached extreme levels.

Where should police pursuit training be headed?

by:　William C. Smith
　　　Geoffrey P. Alpert

Actuarial statisticians and safety engineers have estimated the extent and costs of accidents, injuries and deaths for many activities and occupations for more than a century. While their facts and figures may deter some organizations and individuals from participating in high-risk endeavors, others continue to take risks and enjoy the challenge.

A classic example of a cost-benefit analysis in the construction industry is the planning, insuring and building of the Bay Bridge from Oakland to San Francisco, California. The dangers of building an unprecedented suspension bridge, including job tasks, types and levels of risk, error, among others were analyzed and computed. The nature and extent of accidents, injuries and deaths were estimated, and costs associated with those values were added to the construction costs. Obviously, the policy-makers calculated that the benefits of building the bridge were worth the expected foreseeable human and financial risks.

The concept of calculated risk refers to the ratio of costs and benefits. The critical issue is to identify and measure accurately the costs and benefits. When the potential or anticipated benefits outweigh the risks, then a planned course of action will be acceptable (see Glines, 1980). Risk analysis includes risk assessment and risk management, and risk is best understood as "... the likelihood of injury, harm, damage or loss multiplied by its potential magnitude" (Grose, 1987: 25).

In order to understand risk, the organizational contexts in which they exist must be understood. In the construction industry, the bottom line is (hopefully) the quality of the product and the financial profit. Other organizational contexts are more complicated. For example, police work includes many high-risk activities which move beyond financial considerations and include the balance of law enforcement and public safety (see Alpert and Dunham, 1990). Police administrators and policy-makers must accept, attempt to reduce or avoid physical risk and transfer financial risk. Too often these two types of risk are managed as separate entities, with the former controlled by administrators and the latter in the domain of an insurance carrier.

Police Pursuit Training

It is an axiomatic principle of law enforcement driver training programs that the driver of the police vehicle is one point of an interactive triangle, which has at its remaining corners the police vehicle and the environment (IADLEST, 1990). A great deal of emphasis is placed upon the fact that only one-third of the interactive arrangement, the police driver, is subject to control during the course of police emergency or pursuit response. Accordingly, the officer must become aware of personal capabilities and take into account environment and mechanical occurrences which may affect the ability to accomplish the mission of police -- to protect lives.

In its pure, clinical configuration, the interactive triangle would generate little controversy. Few would disagree that an officer is better able to control personal actions, reactions and communication than changing the weather, road conditions, population density, or the abilities of the police cruiser.

A non-clinical setting, however, requires an adjustment, or at least a redefinition of one element of the triangle. Many law enforcement driving programs view their mission as one of skill development, and emphasize exercises designed to hone the trainee's mechanical skill to control the multi-ton guided weapon known as the police cruiser. The unfortunate reality is that much less effort is devoted to training *when* to use those acquired skills. Comparatively, a pursuit is as dangerous to the public as the use of a firearm (Alpert and Fridell, 1992). The potential for physical and human injury becomes frightening where the kinetic energy of a 3,500-pound projectile is unleashed. Similarly, the danger of pursuit is multiplied with each vehicle encountered, and frequent assessment of the risk of continuation is paramount (Alpert and Dunham, 1990; Alpert and Fridell, 1992).

Three factors are traditionally identified as comprising the police-driving triangle, and it is clear that only one can be subject to control in the heat of the pursuit. Therefore, the police driver is the focus of effective pursuit policy and risk management.

Identifying the Problem

Legal Considerations

Police officers and agencies are frequent targets of litigation and claims of excessive force including unreasonable pursuit which are the most frequent (Alpert and Fridell, 1992). Settlements and judgments in these cases have reached extreme levels (see, e.g., *Maday v. City of San Diego*, 1989).

Sources of Pursuit Claims. Injuries which have been suffered by an innocent third party (either driver, passenger, or pedestrian) result in a suit against agencies and individual officers. These claims are worded to reflect the interest of the plaintiff which has been violated. As will be developed later, an injured suspect's claim for violation of Fourth Amendment interests will bear little similarity to a third-party claim alleging a Fourteenth Amendment substantive due process injury. The importance of these two types of claims becomes self-evident in Section 1983 litigation brought against the police (see Urbonya, 1991). As a large number of pursuit cases are brought solely as state tort claims, these actions are equally important to pursuit litigation. The significance of Section 1983 theories of recovery rests in the extension of claims beyond the concept of "negligence" into the realms of such concepts as "egregious conduct" or "seizure." By looking at this expanded litigation base, proactive law enforcement administrators can protect their officers and, more important, the public they serve, by identifying the legal dangers inherent in pursuit activities and taking active steps to safeguard against them (Zevitz, 1987).

The "Due Care" Dilemma and Establishment of Negligence. As a general proposition, most police pursuit claims hinge on the conduct of the officers involved, which is alleged to be negligent, grossly negligent, reckless, or some variation thereof (see, e.g., *Wood v. Ostrander*, 1991, for a different look at the threshold requirement). In effect, the plaintiff is attempting to establish that the pursuing officer's conduct violated a standard of "due care" or was, in some fashion, unreasonable under the circumstances. One good example of the issues which must be considered comes from *Brown v. City of Pinellas Park*, 1990: 475-476 (citations omitted):

> This case involves two societal values which conflict: (1) that of encouraging motor vehicle pursuits of lawbreakers by law enforcement officers, thereby encouraging apprehensions of lawbreakers, and (2) that of discouraging injury or death to innocent bystanders resulting from motor vehicle pursuits of lawbreakers by law enforcement officers. Our decision to reverse in effect assigns to the value reflected in (2) more weight than to that in (1) under the alleged circumstances of this case. Our reversal therefore is to the effect that the protection of innocent bystanders from what may be considered under the alleged circumstances as being likely, or at least foreseeable and readily avoidable, injury or death outweighs the importance of the pursuit and possible apprehension of the lawbreaker in this case who had run a red light. This result is consistent with what has been called "the modern tendency ... against the rule of non-liability of government units for the acts of their policemen ..."

Establishment of this breach of duty of due care to the plaintiff may be premised upon the officer's violation of a state statute governing pursuit activities, departmental pursuit policy, or some accepted standard, local ordinance regulating, for example, traffic movements, or a determination by a jury that the pursuing officer's conduct was unreasonable under the circumstances.

Many states have incorporated into their State Emergency Vehicle statutes the language of the Model Vehicle Code. The mandate given the driver of the emergency vehicle, in addition to operation of audible and visual warning signals, is to exercise "due care," which is defined in *Black's Law Dictionary* (1979: 448) as follows:

Just, proper, and sufficient care, so far as the circumstances demand it; the absence of negligence. That care
which an ordinarily prudent person would have
exercised under the same or similar circumstances.
"Due care" is care proportioned to any given situation,
its surroundings, peculiarities, and hazards. It may and
often does require extraordinary care. "Due care,"
"reasonable care," and "ordinary care" are often used
as convertible terms.

This term, as usually understood in cases where the gist
of the action is the defendant's negligence, implies not
only that a party has not been negligent or careless, but
that he has been guilty of no violation of law in relation
to the subject-matter or transaction which constitutes
the cause of action.

While this direction, as a legal concept, is capable of ready recitation, its
implementation is fraught with difficulty. What can be said to constitute
"due care" is an extremely subjective call in the adrenaline-charged
atmosphere of the pursuit. Unfortunately, many departments are content
to leave the determination to the officer's discretion altogether or advise
in general terms only (Kroeker and McCoy, 1989). Typically, the advice
is that pursuit should be terminated "when the danger to the public is
significantly increased by the pursuit's continuation" or when "the need
to apprehend the suspect is outweighed by the danger to the public."

With this admonition instilled in the mind of the patrol officer, many
departments feel themselves shielded from the institutional law
enforcement threat known as the civil liability action. The apparent
logic of such an approach is that the officer behind the wheel will
properly assess risks and make intelligent, proper and legally defensible
decisions based upon the departmental mandate to use "due care" and,
in doing so, will protect both himself and the department. Unfortunately,
In a very practical sense, this scheme places the protection of the public secondary to avoiding
negligence is the absence of liability. As a result, the emphasis upon "due care" is mere lip service
due care. to a statutory mandate.

The flip side of the concept of "due care" is that of "negligence." In a
very practical sense, negligence is the absence of due care. *Black's Law
Dictionary* (1979: 930-931) defines the concept as follows:

> ... the failure to use such care as a reasonably prudent
> and careful person would use under similar circum-
> stances; it is the doing of some act which a person of
> ordinary prudence would not have done under similar
> circumstances or failure to do what a person of ordinary
> prudence would have done under similar circumstances.

Thus, a suit premised upon officer "negligence" attacks the officer's
failure to exercise "due care" during the course of the police pursuit.

A number of considerations impact on the availability of negligence as
a viable basis for pursuit litigation. Important ones include the U.S.
Supreme Court decisions in *Davidson v. Cannon* (1986) and *Daniels v.
Williams* (1986), in which the court held mere negligence insufficient to
support a Fourteenth Amendment due process claim under 42 U.S.C.
1983. While the absolute contours of the *Davidson-Daniels* line of
reasoning remain to be developed in the courts, the emergent view
appears to be that mere negligence will not ultimately be a sufficient
basis for Section 1983 liability. At least one court has extended the
apparent prohibition to gross negligence and recklessness in Section
1983 actions, holding "deliberate indifference" to be the threshold
requirement (see *Wood v. Ostrander*, 1991). While this may not impact
directly the availability of a state tort claim for injury based on police
negligence in a vehicular pursuit, the presence of state tort claims
legislation or state "immunity" statute may shield both the individual
officer and department from liability for pursuit activities (Alpert and
Smith, 1991).

What remains to be resolved is the impact of such legislation on
corresponding state emergency vehicle statutes which require the use of
emergency warning equipment on a vehicle responding to an emergency
or engaging in pursuit where violation of traffic regulations may occur.
An apparent conflict is that the statutory mandate to use "due care" may
be rendered meaningless under some Tort Claims Acts where the failure
to comply is classed as simple negligence. In instances of gross negligence or recklessness, apparently, a state court tort claim would be
meritorious. Also, the interpretation of an "immunity" statute, such as
the one now in effect in California, may hold that existence of a policy
meeting specified statutory criteria may be sufficient to confer immunity
even where the conduct of the police in the pursuit may *not* have

complied with the policy (see *Kishida v. State of California*, 1991, and *Weiner v. City of San Diego*, 1991).

The significance of these issues to pursuit policy development and training must bring closure to the concepts of "negligence" and "due care" in emergency vehicle operations. As noted earlier, an admonition to exercise "due care" or not to drive in a "negligent" fashion means little in a cognitive or judicial sense. A defensible training program will be premised upon a policy which incorporates applicable state statute and local ordinance requirements and translates them into meaningful terms. To attempt to protect officer and public alike, it is incumbent upon the department to provide, through training, a real world understanding of appropriate pursuit behavior. As will be developed later in this chapter, training in the assessment of risk and behavior modification programs can help accomplish this goal.

The Availability of Section 1983

Section 1983 states:

> Every person who, under color of any statute, ordinance, regulation, custom, or usage, of any State or Territory, subjects, or causes to be subjected, any citizen of the United States or other person within the jurisdiction thereof to the deprivation of any rights, privileges, or immunities secured by the Constitution and laws, shall be liable to the party injured in an action at law, suit in equity, or other proper proceeding for redress.

In general terms, a violation of Section 1983 requires that a person acting "under color of" state law violate the constitutional rights of another which are protected by the U.S. Constitution "and laws."

To attempt to protect officer and public alike, it is incumbent upon the department to provide, through training, a real world understanding of appropriate pursuit behavior.

While Section 1983 creates no right, in and of itself, it does provide a vehicle for relief for the violation of established rights. The relief is available in both federal and state court. Section 1983 becomes of critical importance where police pursuit activity involves violation of a "constitutional right." Quick scrutiny of the U.S. Constitution and the factual underpinnings to pursuit shows that the violations most likely to occur are those involving the Fourth Amendment's prohibition against "unreasonable seizures," or the Fourteenth Amendment's "due process" provision.

Police Pursuits as "Seizures. " While the Supreme Court has in at least one case recognized that a seizure by use of deadly force can occur in pursuit activities, the parameters of "what" precisely constitutes a "seizure" for pursuit purposes are very ambiguous.

The Supreme Court has in at least one case recognized that a seizure by use of deadly force can occur in pursuit activities.

In *Brower v. Inyo County* (1989), the Court was faced with a high-speed pursuit of a stolen car which was terminated when the suspect collided with an 18-wheel tractor-trailer which had been placed across a two-lane highway behind a curve by the police. Additionally, a police car, with its headlights on, had been positioned to blind the suspect and conceal the fact of the roadblock.

In holding that a "seizure" had occurred, the court noted that "government termination of freedom of movement *through means intentionally applied"* (*Brower v. Inyo County*, 1989: 597, emphasis in original) is the critical requirement. In a gratuitous comment, the court noted that in a hypothetical situation where a "... pursuing police car sought to stop the suspect only by the show of authority represented by flashing lights and continuing pursuit ...," no seizure would occur, but that if "... the police cruiser had pulled alongside the fleeing car and sideswiped it ...," then a seizure would have occurred (1989: 597). The *Brower* court's statement of the "intentional" government intervention requirement must be balanced against other Supreme Court pronouncements which erode somewhat the "clarity" of the *Brower* definition of seizure.

In *Michigan v. Chesternut* (1988), the Court took the opportunity to analyze "when" a seizure could be said to occur. The conclusion was that "only if, in view of all the circumstances surrounding the incident, a reasonable person would have believed that he was not free to leave," then a seizure had occurred. In noting that the record in *Chesternut* did not reflect that the police "activated a siren or flashers or that they commanded respondent to halt or displayed any weapons; or that they *operated the car in an aggressive manner to block respondent's course or otherwise control the direction or speed of his movement* (1988: 575), the court concluded that no seizure had occurred." However, in footnote 9 (575-576), the court further noted:

> We ... leave for another day the determination of the circumstances in which police pursuit could amount to a seizure under the Fourth Amendment.

The linchpin of *Brower* is that seizure occurs only where there is governmental *termination of freedom of movement* through means intentionally applied.

Implicit is the requirement that there must be a complete lack of freedom of movement which has been occasioned by the intentional government intervention. *Chesternut*, however, leads to an analysis based upon whether, under all the circumstances, a reasonable person would have concluded that he is not free to go. Read in conjunction, one might conclude that a seizure occurs where a reasonable person, under all the circumstances, would conclude that his freedom of movement has been terminated, and such termination occurs by intentional government means.

The application of this hybrid *Brower-Chesternut* definition to police pursuits is a thorny issue. Clearly, a pursued suspect *might* conclude by an officer's show of flashing lights and activation of a siren that he is not free to go and that the officer is attempting to terminate the suspect's freedom of movement by aggressive behavior, which may fall short of actual physical contact with the suspect's vehicle.

But does a "seizure" occur if the suspect continues flight, effectively avoiding "termination" of freedom of movement? Is the critical viewpoint the intent of the officer or the behavior of the suspect? Does "termination" of the suspect's freedom of movement require complete control of the suspect's course? These questions have been brought into sharp focus by the court in yet a third case which, again, explores the parameters of a Fourth Amendment seizure.

In *California v. Hodari D.* (1991), the court categorized seizures into those effected by application of physical force and those effected by show of authority. The Court held that seizure occurs where there is "... *either* the application of physical force, however slight, *or*, where that is absent, sub to an officer's 'show of authority' to restrain the subject's liberty."

While the first prong of the *Hodari D.* definition may cause few problems, the second opens a Pandora's Box as far as police pursuits are concerned.

Although it seemed somewhat clear after *Chesternut*, and even *Brower*, that an officer's intentional signaling to a suspect that he is not free to leave would merely require a "totality of circumstances" analysis before it could be deemed a seizure, *Hodari D.* would seem to indicate that, absent compliance with such a signal or the use of physical force to effect a stop, no seizure occurs.

Taking the liberty of extension of the *Hodari D.* reasoning, one must ask, then, whether the occurrence of a seizure in non-physical force pursuits is contingent upon the behavior of the police or the suspect? Inasmuch as the Fourth Amendment is a restraint on governmental authority, should a suspect's "sub" to a show of government authority be a factor in determining the reasonableness of police pursuit behavior?

Of course, the issue is not whether police pursuits must be judged as implicating the Fourth Amendment or, for that matter, the Fourteenth Amendment, in Section 1983 actions. The foremost issue is the reasonableness of police pursuit activity as it may impact the safety of the public.

Prior to the *Hodari D.* decision, at least one interesting interpretation of the police pursuit *qua* seizure had occurred.

In *Wright v. District of Columbia* (1990), a particularly egregious vehicular pursuit by plain-clothes vice officers of the District of Columbia Metropolitan Police Department in an unmarked police car of an alleged traffic offender was held to constitute a "seizure" for purposes of Section 1983 jurisdiction even though no physical acquisition of control of the fleeing vehicle occurred and there was no compliance with the police request to stop. The *Wright* court's decision rests heavily on the Supreme Court ruling in *Chesternut* and specifically points out that while under the acts of *Chesternut* the Supreme Court had found no seizure to have occurred, that determination hinged on the fact that "... there was no evidence that anything occurred to communicate to the defendant that he was at liberty to ignore the police presence and go about his business" (see *Wright v. District of Columbia*, 1990:9).

Further, the *Wright* court noted that Justices Kennedy and Scalia, who concurred in *Chesternut* because they felt that "neither 'chase' nor 'investigative pursuit' need be included in the lexicon of the Fourth Amendment" (*Wright v. District of Columbia*, 1990:9, quoting *Michigan v. Chesternut*, 1988: 576-577), had not barred inquiry into "hot pursuit."

Interestingly, the same court noted that (*Michigan v. Chesternut*, 1988: 577):

> It is at least plausible to say that whether or not the officers' conduct communicates to a person a reasonable belief that they intend to apprehend him, such conduct does not implicate Fourth Amendment protections until it achieves a restraining effect.

The *Wright* court noted that "... when the police operate the chasing vehicle in an aggressive manner to block a fleeing vehicle or otherwise control its speed or direction ..., their actions might communicate to a reasonable person an attempt to capture or otherwise intrude upon the person's freedom of movement and thus be a seizure" (see *Wright v. District of Columbia*, 1990: 8).

Wright is important for the lip service the opinion pays to the mind-set of the pursued suspect as it impacts on the reasonableness of the seizure which was deemed to have occurred. This is engaging because it appears after *Hodari D.*, mind-set becomes relevant only if it produces compliance with the police "show of authority." Whether the U.S. Supreme Court ever defines the contours of "seizure by pursuit" is not the ultimate legal issue. It is, however, a matter of significant concern to law enforcement executives and risk managers who must proactively speculate on the policy and training issues most likely to impact on daily operations.

Police Pursuits as Due Process Violations. Although pursuit "seizure" claims under Section 1983 provide ripe material for controversy, the fact remains that they are typically limited to situations in which a pursued *suspect* has suffered injury.

By and large, the greater tragedy of police pursuit operations occurs where an innocent third party is injured by pursuit activity. Section 1983 is available to these parties where the police pursuit conduct can be shown to violate the due process provisions of the Fourteenth Amendment, which states, in part, "No state shall ... deprive any person of life [or] liberty ... without due process of law."

As a succinct proposition, violation of substantive due process requires a showing that a state's action constitute "egregious conduct" (Urbonya, 1991). In the context of pursuit cases, an injured third party must show that the police conduct in the course of the pursuit was egregious under the circumstances. Recalling briefly the earlier reference in this chapter to the U.S. Supreme Court decisions in *Daniels v. Williams* and *Davidson v. Cannon*, the conduct in question must arise to a level greater than simple negligence.

In evaluating whether a police pursuit which results in third-party injury violated substantive due process, a court must balance the injured party's interest in the security of his or her life or freedom against the police need to immediately apprehend. Factors which weigh into the balance are numerous, but include the seriousness of the offense for which the suspect was being pursued, traffic and weather conditions, population density, and a host of others. Of interest also is a court's determination of what duty, if any, was owed to the motoring public by the pursuing officer.

All of these factors, likewise, must be weighed in the balance by the officer behind the wheel who engages a suspected violator in pursuit. In addition, as in an analysis of negligence, the pursuing officer's conduct will be gauged against applicable statutes and ordinances in a determination of whether it was "egregious" so as to support a plaintiff's claim under Section 1983. By and large, Section 1983 claims based on "due process" violations will likely occur more frequently than those based on "seizures" (see *Frye v. Town of Akron*, 1991, and *Rivas v. Freeman*, 1991).

The Implications for Pursuit Training

Whether or not the U.S. Supreme Court ever makes a final categorical determination that *all* police pursuits constitute seizures, or are *per se* unreasonable, its discussion of scenarios such as those involved in *Brower* and the possibility that "grossly negligent" police pursuits may be actionable as "substantive due process" violations ought to compel law enforcement executives and risk managers into a critical evaluation of present policies and programs. The U.S. Supreme Court's decision in *City of Canton v. Harris* has made abundantly clear that a failure to train in critical law enforcement functions is an invitation to municipal liability. *Brower*, likewise, has spelled out that a "dead man's" roadblock and other physical contacts which may occur in the course of a pursuit may constitute "seizures" within the meaning of the Fourth Amendment.

Irrespective of their multi-faceted response require-ments, the primary duty of the police is to protect lives.

In *Garner v. Tennessee* (471 U.S. 1 1985), the Supreme Court advised that seizures, especially those by deadly force, must be evaluated in a "balancing test" which considers the extent of the governmental intrusion against the affected individual's Fourth Amendment "freedom" interests. *Daniels v. Williams* (1986) and *Davidson v. Cannon* (1986) and their lower federal and state court progeny have left open the current availability of substantive due process claims for police pursuit activities which go beyond simple negligence. The recent decisions of the U.S. Supreme Court and lower federal and state courts stress an increasing degree of accountability for police pursuit operations.

The ability for police to pursue offenders is a critical function and should no more be eliminated than removal of a police officer's firearm. However, the use of a pursuit must be controlled in a similar fashion (Alpert and Dunham, 1990).

Where Should Pursuit Training be Heading?

Devotion of the majority of a police pursuit training course, or Emergency Vehicle Operation course (EVOC) as it is more generically known to the mechanics of handling the police cruiser in pursuit, is an ill-fated decision. Since police driving is the only controllable variable of the police driver triangle, it must be constantly developed. However, it is secondary to another skill which must be instilled in officers new and seasoned: Risk Assessment.

Risk Assessment and Protection of the Public. Irrespective of their multi-faceted response requirements, the primary duty of the police is to protect lives (Alpert and Dunham, 1988). Considering the extensive amount of time spent by an officer driving, the police cruiser has become a critical part of achieving that mission. It is at least as important as his firearm. In *City of Canton v. Harris* (1989), the U.S. Supreme Court's now-famous footnote 10 posits that failure to train an officer in the use of deadly force could be seen as "deliberate indifference" on the part of municipal policy-makers. Statistically, police policy-makers must ask themselves whether their officers are more likely to pursue a suspect vehicle or discharge their weapons at a suspect (Alpert and Fridell, 1992, and Alpert, 1989). The answer is clear. Yet, the time devoted to training an officer "when and when not" to pursue is significantly less than the effort devoted to training for target acquisition and firearm proficiency.

Indeed, and unfortunately, in some agencies a philosophy of "run 'em 'till the wheels fall off" prevails. In many instances, officers allow the act of the pursuit to become a personal vendetta with the pursued -- concerns for public safety thrown to the side, the underlying offense for which pursuit was initiated irrelevant. The prolonged adrenaline-charged course of the pursuit is unmatched in its discharge of a firearm at a fleeing dangerous felon (Alpert and Fridell, 1992). An emphasis on risk assessment must be integrated into police pursuit training programs.

Developing the Risk Assessment Program. Pursuit risk assessment is tied to a clearly defined policy. Once the policy is distributed to the officers, training must be developed to ensure a real world understanding of its principles. Once the training is conducted, the department must supervise, control, and hold accountable the officers involved to ensure that the principles embodied in the policy are followed (Alpert and Dunham, 1990). Law enforcement executives and risk managers share a mutual interest in ensuring that pursuit policy and practices reflect realistically the philosophy of the police agency and the needs of the community.

Pursuit Risk Management:
The Nuts and Bolts of Police Development

A policy's *first* principle is that an officer's primary responsibility is to protect lives. Because pursuits are all "potentially" dangerous and because officers are likely to react to the heat of the moment, an overall statement must be included as a first element and as a reminder. *Second*, as the aim is to protect lives, a statement concerning the rationale of pursuit driving should follow. And this must include the need to immediately apprehend a suspect balanced against the danger created by the pursuit. This point must be stressed repeatedly.

Third, a definition of pursuit should follow the stated rationale. For example, a pursuit can be characterized as a situation where the driver of a vehicle is aware that an officer driving a police vehicle with emergency lights and siren is attempting to apprehend him and the driver of this vehicle attempts to avoid apprehension by increasing speed or taking other evasive actions or refuses to stop.

Fourth, there should be some statement concerning the specific tactical limitations permitted in pursuits. These limitations may be influenced by one or more of the following factors:

Unfortunately, in some agencies a philosophy of "run 'em 'till the wheels fall off" prevails. In many instances, officers allow the act of the pursuit to become a personal vendetta with the pursued -- concerns for public safety thrown to the side, the underlying offense for which pursuit was initiated irrelevant.

1. *Officers' background and preparation:*

    a. tactical preparation (training, experience and familiarity with area (including escape routes); and
    b. type of vehicle (condition, equipment, etc.).

2. *Knowledge of incident, area, and conditions:*

    a. traffic conditions (density, speed, etc.);
    b. pedestrian traffic;
    c. road conditions (width, lanes, fitness, surface);
    d. geographic area (hills, sidewalks, curb breaks, etc.);
    e. weather visibility;
    f. location of pursuit (residential, commercial, freeway, school zones, etc.); and
    g. time of day.

3. *Information pertaining to offender:*

    a. the offense committed by the offender;
    b. likelihood of successful apprehension (identification of offender and address), probability of apprehending offender at a later time, and extent to which offender will go to avoid capture);
    c. age or maturity of offender;
    d. effect of officer's driving on offender's driving; and
    e. whether the officer's action is a moving force of the offender's recklessness.

An example would be the number of vehicles authorized to become involved in a pursuit -- and their role in the pursuit. These vehicles must operate in an emergency mode, with lights and siren. A limited number of back-up vehicles can position themselves at strategic locations and can parallel the route. This number and their specific function must be determined by policy, and the vehicles must be assigned and controlled by a supervisor. It is important that officers recognize the impact of their decisions during a pursuit and that they are not engaged merely in a contest to win. Officers must continually reevaluate the situation to determine the need to immediately apprehend a suspect balanced against the danger created by the pursuit. For example, if there is no realistic way to apprehend or capture the suspect, there must exist some reason or justification to take risks. Also, as officers may be caught up in the moment, it is important that the supervisor take control of the pursuit. But the supervisor must rely upon the information provided by the lead officer in order to make proper decisions. This requires that sufficient information be provided by the pursuing officer. Communication at a minimum includes:

1. the crime for which the suspect is wanted;
2. what is known about the suspect, and his actions;
3. location and direction;
4. environment in which the pursuit is taking place, including vehicular or pedestrian traffic -- likelihood of traffic increasing;
5. speed of both vehicles;
6. driving behavior of the pursued; and
7. any description of vehicle and passenger.

It is essential to stress that officers can *not* assume that an individual observed for a traffic violation *must* be involved in something more serious because he is fleeing. Officers must rely on what they know, not what they think or sense. Increasing risks during a pursuit can only be justified by what is known (Alpert and Smith, 1991).

One way to help officers balance their decision is to have them apply the same standards as in weighing alternatives to firing a weapon in a situation where innocent bystanders may be endangered.

The purpose of pursuit is to apprehend a suspect. Within the responsibility of police, to protect lives, this purpose must be kept in mind at all times, and all tactics or activities undertaken must be with safety and apprehension in mind. It is necessary for officers and supervisors to ask themselves: if this pursuit results in an injury or death, or even property damage, would a reasonable person understand why the pursuit occurred, why it was continued, or why it was necessary? This question will ultimately be asked, and it is appropriate to have it in the guidelines.

One way to help officers balance their decision is to have them apply the same standards as in weighing alternatives to firing a weapon in a situation where innocent bystanders may be endangered. Whenever the officer fires a weapon, he must be concerned that the bullet may accidentally hit an unintended target. By comparison, in a pursuit, the officer has not only his vehicle to worry about but he also must consider the pursued vehicle creating dangerous situations and other vehicles creating danger by attempting to get out of the way. An officer would probably want to take some of these risks if he were chasing an individual who just robbed the convenience store and killed two clerks. If trained to do so, he may even choose to use a roadblock, shoot at the car, or take some other drastic action which will be considered use of deadly force (Alpert and Fridell, 1992).

But for a traffic violator, a juvenile, or a suspected property offender, what risks are reasonable? A policy should include the warning that the officers' behavior will likely be reviewed and analyzed by a "common man" mentality. Will the officer be able to convince a group of non-police that his behavior and the risks he took were reasonable under the conditions?

Termination of the Pursuit

The need to immediately apprehend a suspect must be balanced against the danger created by the pursuit. When the dangers or risks of a pursuit, or the foreseeability or likelihood of a collision outweigh the need to immediately apprehend the suspect, the lead officer or his supervisor must terminate it. This is usually dictated by the nature of the offense for which the law violator is wanted and the recklessness of his driving. Other considerations, however, are also important:

1. an analysis of whether speed dangerously exceeds the normal flow of traffic;
2. the type of vehicle being pursued (i.e. motorcycle or muscle-car);
3. the likelihood and extent of pedestrians or vehicular traffic;
4. the danger of erratic maneuvering by the violator such as driving the wrong way on a one-way street, driving without lights, driving over curbs or through private property;
5. the distance between the officer and the offender;
6. the danger of exceptional speed;
7. the identification of the suspect as a juvenile;
8. whether a clear and unreasonable hazard exists to the officer, law violator, or members of the public; and
9. the totality of the hazards created during a pursuit.

There are many other questions which must be addressed by policy including the use of offensive tactics, passing and the spacing of vehicles, the use of roadblocks and ramming, among others. The specific responsibilities of the supervisor and the possibilities of an interjurisdictional pursuit must be considered and addressed in a policy (Alpert and Dunham, 1990).

The Weaker the Policy, the Greater Need for Training and Accountability.

There is a strong relationship between a policy and the training necessary to support it. The more vague a policy, the more decisions an officer can make about risk. This requires significant training, supervision, control and accountability. It is unacceptable merely to hope that an offender will stop voluntarily, become involved in a collision, or run out of gas. There must be some plan to take the person into custody, or the foreseeability of a collision increases as the chase takes on the characteristics of a drag race.

At the heart of defensible pursuit training is instruction in risk identification and assessment.

It is necessary to hold accountable any officer who has been involved in a pursuit. Collecting proper data and writing an analytical critique is the first step. Accountability serves several purposes: first, the information contained in a critique can help determine if the pursuit was necessary and within the prescribed guidelines; second, a critique will help determine if training needs should be considered; third, a critique will help determine if a change in policy is needed; and fourth, over a period of time, the data included from these reports will reveal trends and demonstrate specific risk factors (Alpert and Dunham, 1990).

The policy, its incorporation into training, and its application all become questions which relate to departmental or municipal liability. If the policy, custom or practice of the department can be seen as the "moving force" behind an officer's action and can be tied to the plaintiff's injury, then municipal liability is a relative certainty. Above all, the policy must be in compliance with the law (Alpert and Smith, 1991).

If a department's pursuit policy and training incorporates the ideas presented above and its practices conform with the recommendations, accidents and injury will be reduced and liability will be minimized. To provide further protection, one excellent strategy is to deny officers who have not received specific training in pursuit from chasing law violators.

Unnecessary risk to the public violates the nature of the police mission.

This idea was introduced by the British Association of Chief Police Officers, and it has been adopted by several American departments. Specifically, such a policy informs its officers who have not passed an approved course in the risk of pursuit driving that they are not authorized to become involved in a chase.

Defensible Training: Translating Policy into Practice

Pursuit training must provide more than mere lip service to the principles embodied in the policy. Similarly, departmental disciplinary actions must reflect any differences in the actions taken in pursuit with the policy, even if no accident or injury results. Any officer who violates policy must be disciplined and must receive further training and education. Results of current police litigation stress that courts look not only to the existence of training but to its sufficiency. The holdings in cases such as *City of Canton v. Harris* (1989), *David v. Mason County* (1991), *Frye v. Town of Akron* (1991), and *Rivas v. Freeman* (1991) demonstrates that management of police pursuit risks requires an in-depth analysis of the elements of the pursuit. That is, tactics authorized by the agency for its officers must be a critical and integral part of the training process as well as policy. For example, to authorize by policy, the use of roadblocks or "ramming" techniques without corresponding training is a grievous invitation to a "deliberate indifference" claim if injury to a suspect, or for that matter officer, should occur,

At the heart of defensible pursuit training is instruction in risk identification and assessment. The training must not be delivered from a purely theoretical standpoint but must integrate practical illustrations of risks which are unacceptable under agency policy. It must also be understood by the risk manager that the restrictiveness of the policy will help determine the degree of risks which will be taken. Officers must, by second nature, come to recognize which offender and environmental factors should trigger a decision to terminate a chase.

The training must integrate all departmental responsibilities, even those which may be mandated under directives or policies other than the pursuit policy. Obvious examples are departmental communications directives and deadly force policies (Alpert and Fridell, 1992).

Finally, training must address the need to modify unacceptable pursuit behavior and to create awareness of the needs and expectations of the public. It is an axiomatic truth that policing is a balance of law enforcement and public safety. Unnecessary risk to the public violates the nature of the police mission. Training can help control the adrenaline-created disregard for public safety that, in some instances, accompanies the pursuit and the frenetic overreaction that is exhibited in its culmination when a suspect is taken into custody (Alpert and Smith, 1991).

Defensible pursuit training programs must include steps to remedy deficiencies in pursuit practices. As one observer has wryly noted, "It is better to build a fence at the top of the cliff than to park an ambulance underneath."

A Concluding Observation

There is no doubt that Pursuit Risk Management Programs must be the collaborative effort of law enforcement executives and risk managers. While no amount of training nor even the most thorough of policies can prevent pursuit claims, the critical question should never resolve itself into one of prevention of claims. The ultimate goal should be to reduce bad pursuits, accidents and injuries.

"It is better to build a fence at the top of the cliff than to park an ambulance underneath."

The safety of the public must be foremost in the minds of law enforcement executives and risk managers so that the motto "To Protect and Serve" does not become a glib shibboleth, and the well-being of law enforcement's constituency is not rendered secondary to liability prevention.

REFERENCES

Alpert, Geoffrey P. "Police Use of Deadly Force: The Miami Experience," in Dunham, Roger D. and Alpert, Geoffrey P. (Eds.), *Critical Issues in Policing: Contemporary Readings*. Prospect Heights, IL: Waveland Press, 1989, pp. 480-495.

Alpert, Geoffrey P. and Dunham, Roger G. *Police Pursuit Driving: Controlling Responses to Emergency Situations*. Westport, CT: Greenwood Press, 1990.

Alpert, Geoffrey P. and Dunham, Roger G. *Policing Urban America*. Prospect Heights: Waveland Press, 1988.

Alpert, Geoffrey P. and Fridell, Lorie. *Police Vehicles and Firearms: Instruments of Deadly Force*. Prospect Heights: Waveland Press, 1992.

Alpert, Geoffrey P. and Smith, William. *Beyond City Limits and Into the Wood(s): A Brief Look at the Policy Implications of City of Canton v. Harris and Wood v. Ostrander.* American Journal of Police 10: 19-40 (1991).

Black's Law Dictionary, 5th edition. West Publishing Co. (1979).

California Highway Patrol. *Pursuit Study*. Sacramento: California Highway Patrol, 1983.

Glines, Carroll. *Jimmy Doolittle: Master of the Calculated Risk*. New York: Van Nostrand Reinhold Co., 1980.

Grose, Vernon. *Managing Risk: Systematic Loss Prevention for Executives*. Englewood Cliffs, NJ: Prentice-Hall, 1987.

International Association of Chiefs of Police and United States Department of Transportation. *A Manual of Police Traffic Services: Polices and Procedures*. IACP and U.S. Department of Transportation, 1986.

International Association of Directors of Law Enforcement Standards and Training. *National Law Enforcement Driver Training Reference Guide*. D. Green Publishers (1990).

Kroeker, Mark and McCoy, Candice. "Establishing and Implementing Department Policies," in Fyfe, James J. (Ed.), *Police Practice in the '90s: Key Management Issues*. Washington, DC: International City Management Association, 1989, pp. 107-113.

Prosser, W. Page and Keeton, Robert, et al. Torts (5th ed.). West Publishing Co. (1984).

Urbonya, Kathryn. *The Constitutionality of High-Speed Pursuits Under the Fourth and Fourteenth Amendments.* St. Louis Law Review 35: 205-288 (1991).

Zevitz, Richard. *Police Civil Liability and the Law of High Speed Pursuit.* Marquette Law Review 70: 237-284 (1987).

CASES

Bevis v. City of Indianapolis, 565 N.E.2d 772 (Ind. App. 4th Dist. 1991).

Brower v. Inyo County, 489 U.S. 593 (1989).

Brown v. City of Pinellas Park, 15 FLW DD468 (Feb. 23, 1990).

California v. Hodari D., ___ U.S. ___, 111 S.Ct. 1547 (1991).

California v. Martinez, 444 U.S. 277 (1980).

City of Canton v. Harris, 109 S.Ct. 1197 (1989).

Daniels v. Williams, 474 U.S. 327 (1986).

Davidson v. Cannon 474 U.S. 344 (1986).

Davis v. Mason County, 927 F.2d 1473 (9th Cir. 1991).

Frye v. Town of Akron, 759 F.Supp. 1320 (N.D. Ind. 1991).

Garner v. Tennessee, 471 U.S. 1 (1985).

Kishida v. State of California, 229 Cal. App. 3d 329 (1991).

Maday v. City of San Diego, Unreported (1989).

Michigan v. Chesternut, 486 U.S. 567 (1988).

Rivas v. Freeman, N. 88-5377 (11th Cir. Sept. 9, 1991).

Rochin v. California, 342 U.S. 165 (1952).

Travis v. City of Mesquite, In the Supreme Court of Texas No. C-85-76 (Dec. 31, 1990).

Weiner v. City of San Diego, 229 Cal. App. 3d 1203 (1991).

Wood v. Ostrander, 851 F.2d 1212 (9th Cir. 1988) (modified on rehearing in No. 87-3924, June 27, 1989).

Wright v. District of Columbia (U.S. District Court for the District of Columbia, Civil Action No. 87-2157 (RCL); Memorandum Opinion filed June 21, 1990).

Chapter 11

Changing the Police Response to Domestic Violence: The Continuing Controversy

Clearly, there has been a broadening of the perceived role of police in domestic violence cases. Increased support exists for formal organizational change emphasizing proactive policing.

Can the classic patterns of police behavior and attitudes change too? What barriers linger between police and victim advocates?

by: **Eve S. Buzawa**
      Carl G. Buzawa

T *he cops don't care whether we live or die, just as long as we do it quietly.*

Anonymous

I just don't understand these women; they want us to throw out their man and then they invite him back in. No matter what we do, it really is useless.

Detroit police officer

Feminist demands for more law and order function at a symbolic rather than an instrumental level. Feminists argue that it is the absence of law, the lack of application of the law, or the selective enforcement of law which has created a cultural climate in which particular behaviors, including violence against women, is condoned. The law then serves symbolically to support a climate of violence against women and sets the scene for that climate.

Susan Edwards, 1990

The above statements from the victim and police officer (considerably cleaned up) were given by interviewees in a field study in Detroit, Michigan. They, along with Susan Edwards, illustrate the extent of perceived miscommunication and hostility among the victim, the police, and many academics over domestic violence and the proper police response.

This chapter advances the theory that conflicts over domestic violence policy formation and implementation are profound and likely to continue despite good faith efforts of many to bridge the gaps between parties. Such conflict might initially have been based upon historical practices (as examined in the next section of this chapter). However, as described later, competing priorities for the police mission with respect to the role of arrests, the trend toward "community policing," and growing budgetary restrictions, tend to continue sources of friction. Finally, competing agendas among the police department, victims, and victim advocates appear to make conflict endemic.

Despite enactment of new statutes and promulgation of "modern" policies, many police agencies have not dramatically changed "street level" justice.

What was Reality?

Why study the "classic" police reaction to domestic violence if it has changed? We should if only to measure the degree of evolution among police departments. In addition, despite enactment of new statutes and promulgation of "modern" policies, many police agencies have not dramatically changed "street level" justice. Finally, to the extent perceptions may influence reality, they *are* reality.

The classic police response has three characteristics: Few domestic violence cases were formally addressed by the police, the majority being "screened out"; the police did not desire to intervene in "family disputes"; and there was a strong, sometimes overwhelming bias against making arrests.

Case screening.

Virtually all researchers concur that only a small minority of intimate assaults result in actual dispatch of police officers (see particularly Pierce, 1992; Manning, 1992). Under-reporting was partially due to screening by victims and bystanders. Estimates of calls to the police as a percentage of actual domestic violence incidents ranged from 2 percent (Dobash and Dobash, 1979) to just under 50 percent (Langan and Innes, 1986). The best estimates confirmed that less than 10 percent of such incidents were reported. In one of the largest studies conducted, a 1985 sample of over 6,000 households determined that only 6.7 percent of all spousal assaults were reported (Kantor and Straus, 1987; see also Dutton, 1988).

Bystander calls were also screened on the basis of marital status. Non-marital incidents were more likely to be observed than those involving married or currently cohabitating adults. When disputes in a family were observed, they were often relegated to "problem family" or "disturbance" status and/or simply viewed as an expected neighborhood occurrence. Neither was likely to elicit a call to the police as would a threat to the public order or a "breach of the peace."

Furthermore, decisions to call the police in domestic violence cases were differentially screened in meaningful and disturbing manners (Berk, Berk, Newton and Loseke, 1984). It has long been known that there is a far greater percentage of under-reported violent crimes among the middle and upper classes. Hence, the police predominantly see domestic violence in the lower socioeconomic groups (Parnas, 1967; Westley, 1970; Black, 1980).

Many explanations for this phenomenon have been advanced. Black (1976, 1980) believes this was primarily attributable to the economic dependency of middle-class women. This was in sharp contrast to the relative economic independence of lower-class women whose direct earnings and/or welfare payments often were the family's economic mainstay. Similarly, Parnas (1967) and Westley (1970) noted that while domestic violence existed in all classes, violence in the middle-upper classes were more likely to be diverted to doctors, the clergy, or other family members. These victims preferred to bring their problems to social equals. Their concerns over confidentiality, particularly in small communities, still appear to inhibit middle-class reporting.

Of equal significance, police have also improperly excluded cases through express call screening by dispatchers, and the facially neutral technology of call prioritization. Thus, many assaults, even those constituting a felony by anyone's definition, were re-categorized as minor "family trouble calls."

In such calls, the person was discouraged from demanding a police response and diverted out of the system. They were referred to social service agencies or told that no one could provide assistance for "marital conflicts." If police intervention was still requested, dispatch would occur only when time permitted (Manning, 1988; Norton, 1979; Bannon, 1974). One study found that in a sample of cases, over two-thirds of cases were "solved" by dispatchers. While formally condemned, this practice was unofficially accepted and well-documented.

While domestic violence existed in all classes, violence in the middle-upper classes were more likely to be diverted to doctors, the clergy, or other family members.

Evidence is inconclusive as to whether severity of violence was related to the probability of police calls and/or dispatch. Kantor and Straus (1988) reported that 14.4 percent of incidents involving major violence were reported to police compared to 3.2 percent of minor violence. However, Pierce (1992) based a study on comparative police and emergency room data and found that the most severe cases of violence resulted in medical rather than police referrals. These cases were not customarily reported to the police. Walker (1979) had earlier reported that only 10 percent of cases involving serious injury were ever reported to police. The net effect was that police-citizen encounters were a rarity and relegated to a small minority of potentially reportable incidents.

The police did not desire to intervene.

Research exploring police attitudes has consistently shown that most police officers, regardless of individual or department characteristics, historically (and to a lesser extent to this date) express strong dislike for responding to "family" troubles. Reasons may be typologized into four categories: organizational impediments, lack of sufficient/sophisticated training, cynicism that such calls were not "real" policing and could not be helped, and finally excessive worries over safety.

Until a wave of reform legislation was enacted (between 1976 and early 1991), virtually all states imposed major common law limitations upon police authority. Unless police actually witnessed an incident, they could only make warrantless arrests for felonies, not misdemeanors. In contrast, misdemeanors required prior issuance of an arrest warrant.

This limited police action. Domestic violence assaults are often termed misdemeanors, regardless of severity, absent homicide or life-threatening injury (Langan and Innes, 1986). Due to the restrictions on misdemeanor response, few arrests and little effective action could be taken even if desired. After all, most offenders retained enough self-control not to repeat an assault in an officer's presence. As a result, many police believed that their role was peripheral -- restricted to a perfunctory or service-oriented call to separate the parties.

A study on comparative police and emergency room data found that the most severe cases of violence resulted in medical rather than police referrals.

Another major impediment to effective action, prevalent in large departments, was that information could not advise a responding officer of prior related offenses. Because misdemeanor records were not well-organized nor computerized, large departments were often unable to differentiate between first offenders and hard-core recidivists -- unlike the "rap sheets" distributed for repeat offenders for many offenses. As a result, the system tended to treat such offenses as isolated occurrences (Pierce and Deutsch, 1989).

Researchers have noted that police have a profound ignorance of the proper methods to handle domestic violence.

Finally, the number and distribution of the calls posed significant challenges to police resources. Apart from traffic and code enforcement actions, domestic violence calls constituted the single largest category of calls in many cities (Bannon, 1974). Even worse, domestic violence typically occurred during the weekend or evenings when other calls, including drunk driving, altercations, loud parties, etc., put greatest organizational demands on the police. A 1986 study of incident reports revealed that a majority of domestic incidents reported to the police occurred Friday through Sunday, most frequently between 6:00 p.m. and 2:00 a.m., hours when police typically have minimal staffing and many competing calls (Brosan, et al., 1987).

Police also were not well equipped to cope with domestic violence. Many researchers have noted that police have a profound ignorance of the proper methods to handle domestic violence (Bannon, 1974; Loving and Quirk, 1982). In fact, Ford (1987) reported in one sample that over 50 percent of the officers did not know probable cause requirements for domestic violence related assaults.

Poor training certainly contributed to this lack of understanding. In a 1970s survey of most large police departments, Buzawa (1976) reported that the average police department devoted only a total of four to eight hours of training to all disturbances. These included handling a "disturbed person," restraining drunks, and "domestics." The quality of instruction was also problematic. As an economy measure, many departments used in-house instructors, usually senior-line personnel or limited-duty officers (those who, due to injury/age, could not be assigned patrol duties). At risk of over-generalizing, their bias was toward the "old school" -- that domestic violence was a waste of time, and dangerous. Instructions were to restore and maintain control and then leave as soon as possible. As such, training often reinforced old prejudices and did not teach new methods of problem-solving.

Police officer attitudes have compounded some problems. It has been a truism that police are cynical toward the public and their problems, particularly in "domestic" related calls (Manning, 1979; Punch, 1985;

While arresting an offender on a domestic assault charge might theoretically reify law enforcement images, domestic violence was never considered a serious crime nor part of the crime-fighter image.

Radford, 1989). Cynicism is especially distinctive in domestic violence cases; however, traditional law enforcement and code violations work demands conformance to established SOPs. In contrast, handling dynamic and volatile interventions among intimates requires skill and a willingness to expend considerable effort. Neither are likely if the officer cynically believes no positive outcome is likely.

Issues of class reinforce cynicism. When police confront members of the lower economic classes and minorities, they often act in a bureaucratic, impersonal fashion, being quite authoritarian and unlikely to show compassion (Black, 1980). To some extent, this is due to racist and classicist assumptions about the lives and mores of the citizenry. For example, many officers that were interviewed stated that violence is a normal part of the lives of the lower class. Implicitly, domestic problems are a logical outgrowth of this environment. Being "normal," many officers were unwilling to intervene and more inclined to "manage" the dispute by avoiding public branches of peace. This was seen as preferable to futile efforts to resolve conflicts or undertaking a confrontational arrest.

General cynicism is compounded by specific feelings of police toward domestic violence. Risking over-generalization, they tend to believe that such cases were not one of their proper responsibilities. They tend to be uncomfortable with social work type tasks and prefer instead law enforcement (Bard and Zacker, 1974).

In this context, the police subculture values a "good pinch" (Van Maanen, 1978). While arresting an offender on a domestic assault charge might theoretically reify law enforcement images, domestic violence was never considered a serious crime (Stanko, 1989) nor part of the crime-fighter image. Also, diffusing a potential crisis was of little value to an officer's self image or his career (Stanko, 1989). Instead, the officer would rely upon acts of heroism and/or "significant arrests" to achieve distinction. This contradicted the reality of their work in which non-law enforcement tasks predominated (Berk and Loseke, 1980; Reiss, 1971; Van Maanen, 1974).

Police also tended to view domestic violence cases as being particularly dangerous. Anecdotal evidence of unprovoked attacks by offenders and "unappreciative" victims are legion among almost all groups of officers. This is explainable: almost no other source of injury is as unpredictable or as personally outrageous as being assaulted when responding to a "domestic" case. Officers often recount how the victim then "turned" against them when they attempted an arrest.

For many years, the FBI reinforced such beliefs by publishing an annual report of the source of police officer deaths purporting to show that "disturbance calls" were among the most common sources of officer death.

Recent research has cast doubt on such fears. A report sponsored by the National Institute of Justice found that rates of injury were overstated by three times in FBI reports due to the practice of lumping together all disturbance calls including domestics with gang fights, bar brawls, etc. (Garner and Clemner, 1986). Analysis of data from 1974 to 1983 showed that responses to *domestic* disturbances just ranked eighth as a source of officer deaths -- the danger of such calls being greatly exaggerated (Ellis, 1987).

However, research has not entirely resolved how dangerous responding to domestic violence is. Uchida, Brooks and Kioer (1988) questioned the conclusion of Garner and Clemner and found that the domestic calls were one of the highest sources of injury among the 11 indexed crime categories, while robbery was near bottom in danger rank. However, this study only examined danger on the basis of frequency at risk rather than time spent.

Despite controversy in the research published for the past several years, most officers *still* believe that domestic violence is an extraordinarily dangerous crime. It is unclear why beliefs among officers have not yet changed. This may partially be because social science research rarely "penetrates" to the consciousness of the line personnel. An alternative, if cynical, explanation is that excessive fears of danger serve a useful function. It justifies ambiguity toward domestic violence and otherwise unjustifiable policies. For example, some police organizations require two officers to respond to domestics and, if only one arrives, he is instructed to wait for the arrival of a back-up unit. This, of course, often delays intervention, perhaps endangering a victim.

Despite controversy in the research published for the past several years, most officers still believe that domestic violence is an extraordinarily dangerous crime. It is unclear why beliefs among officers have not yet changed.

The police did not desire to make arrests.

Viewed in isolation and without knowledge of past practices, one might suppose high rates of arrest for domestic assault. After all, there is a known victim, usually with apparent injury. Since the offender is known, apprehension is usually straightforward. This, of course, is not the case. Historically, the closer the relationship between victim and offender, the less the likelihood of arrest (Black, 1980; Bell, 1984). Buzawa and Buzawa (1991) in a review of different studies found that estimates of arrests as a percentage of police/citizen encounters vary widely between 3 and 21 percent, depending on department characteristics and policies. The highest was a relatively recent study by Dutton (1987) showing 21 percent.[1]

There are varied reasons for officer reluctance to arrest. The police department may discourage arrests when these force the department to divert scarce resources to processing an arrest. There is also an additional cost to the officer in terms of time and paperwork. From his perspective, this is unjustified for a low-status misdemeanor with relatively poor changes of conviction (Buzawa, 1990). The physical risks to the officer also are perceived as dramatically increasing when an arrest is made. Most officer assaults on officers occur when their official neutrality is abandoned; and a finding, however tentative, of criminal conduct coupled with an arrest concomitant restraint on the assailant's freedom. Many cynical officers also inappropriately generalize that an arrest risks changing the victim's attitude, making her supportive of "her man" against the outsider.

Some argue that failure to arrest in domestic violence cases simply validates the observation that police did not care about victim rights. While this partially may be true, it ignores the inherent difficulties faced by individual officers and the police organization in allocation of limited resources. Police organizations are being confronted by increasing demands to respond formally to a variety of newly rediscovered offenses including drugs, drunk driving, and street crime.

Furthermore, it is unclear that police departments disproportionately failed to make domestic violence arrests. In a review of the literature, Elliott (1989) found that arrest rates for non-family assaults were significantly greater than for domestic assaults. Value judgments not withstanding, arrest is simply not an option exercised by the police with great frequency in any assault absent other factors such as a need to maintain officer control, disrespect, etc. This is in line with the body of

---

[1] It is unclear the extent to which higher figures indicate an upward trend due to the sweeping police changes, or is instead different baselines in divergent departments.

police literature that has found that in routine police work, arrests are simply not that commonly used as a sanction (Skolnick, 1966; Parnas, 1967; Wilson, 1968; Bittner, 1970, 1974; Black, 1971; summarized in Elliott, 1989).

When have arrests occurred?

When arrests are made, they are made in conformance with expected legal criteria. Some research reports very little correlation between injury to the victim and arrest (Buzawa, 1991).[2]

Instead, in common with other offenses that police viewed as a relatively minor arrest, data suggests that situation-specific factors predominate the decision to arrest. These may be grouped into three categories: police-offender interaction, police-victim interaction, and police organizational issues.

The primary influence of the offender on the officer's decision is what he does *after* the officer arrives. If he displays disrespect, this potentially justifies arrest. Violence in the officer's presence implies a threat to the officer's ability to control the situation (Ferraro, 1989; Dolan, et al., 1986) or that the suspect is personally hostile to the police (Bayley, 1986). Thus viewed, arrest is a mechanism of asserting authority rather than to protect the victim. Many police officials would view such a discriminator as entirely proper; loss of situational control is highly predictive of the threat of officer injury.

The primary influence of the offender on the officer's decision is what he does after the officer arrives. If he displays disrespect, this potentially justifies arrest.

Interaction between the victim and the police is also very important in the arrest decision. Victim preference is critical since the victim is in the best position to know how her rights should be vindicated, and her cooperation is usually essential to a successful prosecution. Some studies have shown that victim preference was a de facto prerequisite to an arrest (Bell, 1984) or at least greatly increased the chances of arrest (Berk and Loseke, 1980-81; Worden and Pollitz, 1984).

The problem with the "classic" police approach is that a victim's desire was usually *insufficient* alone to justify arrest without some legally extraneous factor such as the offender being disrespectful to the officer.

---

[2] However, see Kantor and Straus (1987) showing at least some correlation between severity and arrest.

A victim's preference for arrest was, often inappropriately, not followed. Moreover, one forthcoming study (Buzawa, et al., 1992) found that while victim preferences were very important in Detroit, Michigan, in other departments (in the state of Massachusetts), this was not a factor. In the Massachusetts departments surveyed, approximately 75 percent of the responding officers could not even *report* what the victims' preferences were, let alone follow them.

The victim-police interaction also effected arrest rates in a more troublesome fashion. It has long been known that police regularly judge the conduct of the citizens with whom they interact. This is actually necessary for them to respond in often ambiguous and potentially dangerous environments and to appropriately exercise discretion. However, in the context of domestic violence, many police have judged victims' conduct to be inappropriate and hence unworthy of an arrest. For example, if the victim and offender were married and still cohabitating, arrests were far less frequent. The police viewed the victim's conduct as inappropriate and limited the probability of prosecution. Similarly, Buzawa, et al. (1992) found that when the victim was disruptive, drunk, or verbally abusive toward the officers, her views were virtually ignored. Arrests were also unlikely if the victim acted in a manner which in some way offended the officers. Hence, if she was an 'unfaithful spouse," arrest was uncommon (Saunders and Size, 1986). If a pattern of the "victim" battling the offender emerged, officers appeared unwilling or unable to determine who was criminally responsible, and arrest was uncommon (Buzawa, et al., 1992). Conversely, if the victim was rational, undemanding and deferential, the police accorded her preferences more consideration in arrest decisions (Ford, 1983).

Finally, although not subject to extensive empirical examination, organizational factors appear to affect arrest rates. Hence, if the call occurred during a particularly busy period or at the end of an officer shift, it was far less likely to result in arrest (Ferraro, 1989; Worden and Pollitz, 1984).

Why Change Has Occurred

> *Every several years, the police as a social and political institution are reformed.*
>
> Preface
> *Community Policing: Rhetoric or Reality*
> edited by Jack Greene and Stephen Mastrofski

Policy change has clearly been dramatic.

Commencing with Pennsylvania in 1976, virtually all states passed statutes reforming the criminal justice response to domestic violence. These statutes established policies encouraging proactive police response within a concerted effort to curb domestic violence. Arrests were to be made when officers responded to violations of existing assault statutes, new statutory "domestic violence laws," and violations of protective or restraining orders. Of even greater importance, for the first time most statutes allowed warrantless arrests for un-witnessed domestic violence related assaults. Virtually all states had such statutes by 1990 (Buzawa and Buzawa, 1990). In conformity with this statutory direction, most departments have changed their policies (Chapman and Pence, 1988; Pleck, 1989).

It would be simplistic to assert that any particular factor accounts for the sudden shift in official policies. In part, this change was a logical extension of overall trends to criminalize conduct. While nominally illegal, for many years domestic violence, along with other misdemeanor offenses, had been tacitly tolerated by failure to rigorously enforce existing laws. By the 1970s, there was an increasing trend toward more rigorously applying criminal sanctions. This has been applied to "resurrect" previously unenforced laws, increase criminal penalties, or create new crimes.

The sudden shift in official policies was a logical extension of overall trends to criminalize conduct.

As a consequence, the previous trend to attempt reform of offenders has been de-emphasized while more punitive solutions predominate (Walker, 1985). Thus, drug offender rehabilitation and youthful offender programs were dropped or not adequately funded in favor of trying addicts as criminals and juveniles as adult offenders, child abusers were arrested while rehabilitation became of secondary importance, and drunk drivers were treated far more harshly.

In this context, many interest groups, policy-makers, and domestic violence researchers have emphasized the criminality of an assault. They deride mediation of conflicts as inappropriate, or alternately restrict this exclusively to situations where violence has not yet occurred (Lerman, 1984). In this climate, it is not surprising that service/ treatment focused policing such as specialized crisis intervention units -- first used in the 1970s in New York City and subsequently copied in many cities (Bard, 1973; Liebman and Schwartz, 1973) -- were quietly abandoned in favor of arrest-oriented policing.

The ability of the police to "shame" the offender or hold him to public scorn by arrest is seen as useful to modify aberrant behavior and deter others.

The orientation toward punishment may also be seen as a function of the greater penetration of economics-derived insights to crime prevention. Such a perspective favorably considers deterrence obtained through police actions apart from any realistic hope of conviction. Hence, the ability of the police to "shame" the offender or hold him to public scorn by arrest is seen as useful to modify aberrant behavior and deter others. This logic has been expressly applied to the control of domestic violence independent of conviction (Sherman and Berk, 1984; Dutton, 1987).

It is interesting that academics and feminists, usually liberal in other contexts, fail to find anything distressing about using police in this manner. While the police as an institution are often deeply mistrusted by these same people, they have largely endorsed changes that increase police involvement in intimate disputes and family violence. This is true despite some evidence that police more often use such statutes against minority and disadvantaged males than other offenders, not the middle class "respectful" or "respectable" white males. The implications this poses are apparently either ignored or simply overridden by desperation about effecting any change in the police response to domestic violence by other means.

Due to past clear failures to adequately handle domestic violence, political pressure on the police has become a major factor speeding adoption of more proactive practices (Chapman and Pence, 1988) as have lawsuits addressing more egregious failures of police conduct (Pleck, 1989; Hathaway, 1986). Until recently at least, this trend appeared to be rapidly accelerating (Cohn and Sherman, 1987). In fact, the "clarity" of a mandatory arrest policy and its resultant ability to justify in a court setting may, at least partially, explain why police officials have so eagerly embraced mandatory arrest policies.

While increased criminalization of offenses, political pressure, and fear of lawsuits undoubtedly set the stage of change, the rapidity thereof has been startling. In our opinion, the catalyst for such rapid change was the Minneapolis study, first published by Sherman and Berk in 1984. This study used an experimental research design to "prove" that an arrest was far more effective to deter future violence than more separation or even mediation.

Despite the lack of consensus over the effects of arrest, the Sherman and Berk study clearly had a singular influence in the direction toward emphasizing arrests. Part of this was due to the extraordinary efforts of the authors to publicize the research (Meeker and Binder, 1990; Cohn and Sherman, 1990).

Sherman and Berk's heavily publicized Minneapolis study was followed by numerous articles by Sherman, et al. that emphasized the importance of arrest as part of a strategy to deter violence and to uphold the rights of the victim.[3]

The proper role of arrest is still being debated in the context of ongoing replications of the earlier study. Tentative evidence from the first released replication study in Omaha, Nebraska, indicates that Sherman and Berk's earlier embrace of pro-arrest policies may have been premature. The latter study has, as of this date, failed to find major differences in recidivism rates among the various police responses (Dunford, Hurzinga and Elliott, 1990). Lack of support has also been seen in the Charlotte replication, and tentative supportive conclusions from the Milwaukee replication study have been challenged.

In response to this new data, Larry Sherman has dramatically changed his position. Now he appears to conclude that arrest may only provide initial deterrence (Sherman, et al., 1991). Since an arrest has the effect of increasing anger as well as fear, he posits that as time passes, the fear component decreases and the arrested party becomes angry at the indignities of an arrest, making an arrest "criminogenic."

Based on past history, we may therefore expect to see numerous well publicized articles questioning the use of arrest. We also expect that the

---

[3] A rigorous analysis of the Minneapolis study is clearly beyond the scope of this paper. Instead, the reader is directed to the lively and stinging analysis of Meeker and Binder, 1990, 1992, and the spirited rejoinder of Cohn and Sherman, 1990.

In their research, Sherman and Berk really did not provide an analysis for why mandatory arrest would deter future abuse, and as a result it became quite controversial among academics. This undoubtedly helped to push the National Institute of Justice to fund a series of replication studies. Further, researchers from other areas began to note the incongruity of their results with findings from general criminology and juvenile delinquency (Elliott, 1991, cited in Gelles, 1991).

Increased criminalization of offenses, political pressure, and fear of lawsuits undoubtedly set the stage of change.

earlier role of well publicized research encouraging arrest will not be heavily emphasized. Much as we earlier criticized the largely un-critical acceptance of the very limited Minneapolis study, we must now strongly caution against trumpeting of a new "revisionist" orthodoxy that too broadly challenges the use of arrest. At a minimum, any such review should be prepared to examine not only relatively earlier quantifiable measures of specific deterrence (deterring repeat crime of the offender arrested) but also the effects of a publicized arrest upon potential offenders (general deterrence). Similarly, to have any degree of external validity, research designs should be prepared to discuss and account not only for characteristics of the arrest itself (such as duration of confinement, manner of arrest, etc.) but what happened afterward, e.g. the systemic component. An arrest, after all, brings the offender into the criminal justice system. What happens then? Not surprisingly, different outcomes may occur depending on the subject's processing -- to conviction and the resultant sanction, plea bargain, or merely a rapid case dismissal.

In fact, mere replication of the same research design is likely to produce ambiguous or self-limiting data. In contrast, other researchers have attempted to show a more sophisticated correlation between arrest and deterrence. These suggest that arrest by itself may not be the key factor in modifying future deviant conduct. Instead, the act of bringing the offender into the purview of criminal justice system by whatever means (warrantless arrest by the police, arrest subsequent to a warrant, or a summons to appear before a court official) may have some long-term effect in recidivism. The possible key may be the criminal justice system's ability to mandate long-term rehabilitation (Ford, 1991).[4]

Hence, learning anger control and substance abuse therapy may account for recidivism differences seen in some but not all studies.

---

[4] Even here controversy exists. Some new research has tentatively found that behavioral modification techniques may themselves have adverse consequences. It found that some offenders in short-term programs became *more* likely to be violent, probably due to unintended self-reinforcing aspects of some group training programs (Urban Institute, 1991). If this report is subsequently confirmed in other contexts, it would provide a very discouraging predictor of future attempts to treat assailants. It may also mean that affects of arrest as well as other efforts to reform or deter an offender may depend on characteristics of the assailant as well as the particular treatment modality used.

The change in training.

One area of profound change has been the training given to new officers and in-service personnel. Departments throughout the country have rapidly shifted from materials that had emphasized the futility and danger of intervention and focused upon mediation. Now many stress the role of the police in a coordinated program to handle domestic violence through pro-arrest strategies.

Through the National Institute of Justice, the federal government has clearly promoted the research and conclusions of the Minneapolis study implicitly favoring mandatory arrest. Although we might be overly cynical, what is in favor by the federal government gets funded -- what get funded gains adherents, and over time is seen as intrinsically good.

The training industry certainly has grown with the encouragement of federal funds. For example, one project supervised by the U.S. Department of Justice was designed to train higher level supervisors in local law enforcement. It conducted 18 seminars and trained 882 supervisors and victim advocates (National Organization of Black Law Enforcement Executives, 1990). Participant evaluations suggested that attitudinal change had indeed occurred. Many trainees displayed a willingness to confront the problem of poor performance in their departments. Not surprisingly, there were many requests that information on police liability be provided.

One area of profound change has been the training given to new officers and in-service personnel. Departments throughout the country have rapidly shifted from materials that had emphasized the futility and danger of intervention and focused upon mediation.

Similarly, comprehensive training materials have been developed by the U.S. Department of Justice, Office of Crime, National Victims Resources Center (1990), and in a Training Handbook from the Victim Services Agency (1989). While difficult to generalize, these materials favor an activist police response to domestic violence and use of arrest powers far more frequently than in the past. In addition, many other seminars have been conducted on the state level, including one in Michigan which one of the authors helped develop and implement.

While little empirical research exists, there is some conformation that real attitudinal change is taking place among those officers exposed to these materials. One experiment involved a simulation of how trained officers and a control group handled incidents. The trained officers performed far more competently at handling incidents and diffusing emotional intensity (Bundy, Buchanan and Pino, 1986).

Other authors have, however, despaired about effecting *long-term* attitudinal change. Stanko (1989) wrote that training would ultimately make little difference due to male attitudes that condoned "moderate" domestic violence, the paramilitary organizational structure of the police, and the retrograde information "training" that new officers receive from their cynical hardened peers. Further, Scargzi (1991) reported that in the case of Massachusetts recruits who were given training, there was no attitudinal change in male recruits while reporting significant change in the fewer numbers of female recruits.

It should also be stressed that behavioral change may occur even independently of a new progressive attitude toward domestic violence. Certainly, in many cases, trained supervisors have demanded their subordinates change behavior despite their personal reservations for fear of subjecting their police department to significant liability.[5]

Policing on the street: has it changed?

Clearly, there has been a broadening of the perceived role of police in domestic violence cases. Increased support exists for formal organizational changes emphasizing proactive policing. Training is evident at the national, state, and local levels.

---

[5] Although many liability actions have been commenced against police departments for failure to protect the rights of victims, a recent article published in the FBI Law Enforcement Bulletin (1991) claims that few such challenges succeed, at least in Federal Court, in claiming violation of substantive and procedural Due Process and Equal Protection guaranteed by the 14th and 13th Amendments.

The FBI may not, however, be a totally unbiased source. Another article recently published (Forrell, 1990-91) suggests that police departments *will* be exposed to such liability if their conduct improperly fails to protect women.

Similarly, many fact situations may lend themselves not only to claims of violation of federal and state laws, but also to claims of negligence. In any event, to limit liability, even the FBI suggests that police departments promulgate (and adhere to) written policies in handling domestic violence calls. They also strongly suggest conducting and documenting appropriate training and making certain that officer bias does not cause disparity in arrest rates.

What is more problematic is the actual change in "street level" justice. Most research either has examined classic patterns of police behavior or, if more recently conducted, the "new" policing. While potentially instructive, the latter studies have not yet focused on the extent or the process of change. It is therefore difficult to ascertain the impact on street-level practices.

Even without empirical data, a pattern may be emerging. Most high-level police officials now appear to willingly embrace pro-arrest policies. This has encountered far greater resistance from line personnel. Police administrators often tend to be more progressive than line personnel. Manning (1977) has observed that policy in police departments is often incorrectly assumed to originate with the chief. In fact, most discretion is with the officers who can obstruct implementation of any policy (Manning, 1977).

Unless trained, many, if not most, patrol officers remain equivocal about the proper police role in this field. While higher percentages than in the past may acknowledge that a crime has been committed, they are frustrated by the failure of intervention to lead to immediate change. This often feeds cynicism and a desire to circumvent policies placing the police in such a role.

> *Policy in police departments is often incorrectly assumed to originate with the chief. In fact, most discretion is with the officers who can obstruct implementation of any policy.*

Police literature suggests that in such cases, actual change is problematic. Rank and file police retain an unusual degree of discretion. Official rules, no matter how strict, are difficult to enforce when the usual measure of output, decisions to arrest/not arrest, depend upon an officer's judgment as to proof of injury, probable cause, and defenses (such as self-defense). This makes implementation uncertain and fraught with unexpected consequences.

For example, Ferraro (1989) found that when the Phoenix Police Department tried to enforce a new presumptive arrest policy, the policies were ignored, circumvented, or changed almost beyond recognition. The increased threat of arrest was used *against* the victim as in "if we receive another call from this house, *both* of you will be arrested." This is not an idle threat. A study of Oregon's mandatory arrest law found that (at least initially) dual arrests were very common.

Martin (1991) reported in Connecticut that roughly 20 percent of arrests for family violence were "dual arrest" incidents; and if non-intimate family violence were omitted, about 35 percent of adult intimate violence involved dual arrests. This is especially troubling since for women it was usually the first arrest, even though 43 percent of the women arrested were previously identified in police reports *as victims* (Martin, 1991).

Not surprisingly, dual arrests significantly decreased chances of prosecution as victims were effectively coerced to "reconcile" and drop complaints. There was considerable departmental variation within Connecticut. However, Martin (1991) found departments with few arrests were more likely to have high rates of dual arrest. For example, she reported that one department had five arrests, four of which were dual. This infers organizational resistance and the use of an arrest procedure to "silence" women victims. Martin (1991) also reported that the State Police had the highest rate of dual arrests, despite the fact they had the highest level of domestic violence training.

The actual data on incidents of arrest is ambiguous. Connecticut reported that 10,751 family violence incidents led to arrests within a six-month period, a figure startling high -- at least as compared to past practices (Connecticut State Police, 1990).

In other jurisdictions, few encounters result in arrest despite statutory broadening of police powers, ostensible support from administration, and heavy political and legal pressure from women's advocates (Buzawa and Buzawa, 1991).

Has the nature of conflict changed?

To some extent, increasing criminalization in the police response to domestic violence has resulted in a shifting of conflicts from the dominant motif of the police being criticized by victims and victim advocates to a more complex pattern of police conflict within the police organization and within the police department's political environment. Until recently, the only significant conflict was external to the organization -- that between the largely unified and somewhat apathetic police and the victim and her advocates. Police, both command officials and the rank and file, perceived that their proper role in domestic violence was limited. Consequently, services provided to victims rarely met the latter's expectations.

Recent policy changes have shattered police cohesion, both among elite policy-makers and between these officials and their rank and file officers. Police commanders have been presented with several policy dilemmas dealing with the ideology of their mission and obtaining required resources.

One of the most recent and highly regarded new approaches to policing is encompassed by the generic term "community policing." While this topic is discussed elsewhere in this chapter, suffice to state that key tenets are as follows: (1) the police should, wherever possible, operate with consensus in a service community; (2) the police should listen to citizens' concerns -- not just when responding to a law enforcement call; (3) the police should consider how citizens define problems even when these definitions differ from those of the police; and (4) the police force and citizens should work together to solve problems.[6]

These are said to facilitate improved attitudes of the citizenry toward the police *and* vice versa, and provide for more effective use of police services as defined both by the police and the community. Numerous methods to achieve the above are being widely employed or at least experimented with, such as newsletters, victim re-contacts, police community relations, citizen contact patrols, etc. *Many*, if not most, such measures rely explicitly or implicitly upon increasing the rank and file police officer discretion. Such discretion is needed to respond to charging circumstances, "humanize" the police role, and shift their police image from one of rote law enforcer to a valued community service.

Police commanders have been presented with several policy dilemmas dealing with the ideology of their mission and obtaining required resources.

These tenets are in stark contrast with the strict law enforcement orientation of today. Conflicts arise primarily over the latter's emphasis on arrest. In a law enforcement mode, to establish evidence of a crime and to justify arrest, the police must ask specific questions and are in a role inherently more threatening than the community policing model suggests.

---

[6] For an excellent discussion of these precepts, see Wycoff in Greene and Mastrofski (1990).

Similarly, the emphasis on arrest as an ultimate organizational goal de-emphasizes and at times trivializes a victim's goals. Her desires may be to immediately end abuse, establish that she was "wronged," "reform" the offender, and/or implicitly change the power balance of an existing relationship. A police-generated arrest strongly implies that the victim is irrational and must have a higher authority make her decisions. Although the case disposition may be the same, this type of arrest is in stark contrast to an arrest model where the victim desires to press charges after being informed of her rights.

Similarly, the reality is that most arrests will likely continue to be made in poor crime-best urban neighborhoods. This is likely to result in disproportionate arrests of poor and/or minority offenders. Images of police making large numbers of arrests of emotionally upset men may significantly disrupt the non-law enforcement image being cultivated by community policing. Finally, simply adopting an official policy promoting arrests, no matter how justified, tends to undermine rank and file police officer discretion, one of the key tenets of community policing.

As might be expected, the inherent conflict between community policing and aggressive policing of domestic violence is markedly worse in a mandatory arrest jurisdiction. The police role becomes inherently threatening when subjects become aware that the officer *must* arrest if he finds requisite conduct. Victims' goals are not only trivialized but are made expressly irrelevant in the key decision -- the decision to arrest. There is a heightened probability of conflict between the officer and the offender and even the victim when the victim does not want arrest. This is, of course, especially true in the disturbing pattern of dual arrests now being reported in many such jurisdictions. Finally, police officer discretion is not only limited in theory, it is expressly removed in this area.

Images of police making large numbers of arrests of emotionally upset men may significantly disrupt the non-law enforcement image being cultivated by community policing.

In addition to divergent ideologies over the role and function of the police, present police administrators are faced with extraordinary budgetary pressures. We should acknowledge the reality that aggressive policing of domestic violence may "soak up" scarce resources. Significant police and court personnel must be added. When coupled with mandatory arrest, this presents administrators with an implicit dilemma -- re-prioritizing resources away from other tasks or controlling demand for domestic violence resources.

This dilemma is sharpened by the trend cited by Manning that "one of the most important trends in policing in the last 25 years is the rising demand for police services in the financial context of shrinking resources." Manning reports that there is a resultant increased tendency for police to control or manage demand through technology. Hence, the 911 calling system, initially designed for quicker responses, becomes a tacit or even explicit mechanism for controlling demand by allocating scarce resources, e.g. police patrols.

"One of the most important trends in policing in the last 25 years is the rising demand for police services in the financial context of shrinking resources."

If aggressive enforcement of domestic violence statutes becomes the policy of most police departments -- without a concomitant increase in resources -- paradoxical pressure may arise to screen out cases at earlier phases. While this may be controlled by threat of legal action, the real problems posed, police management should be acknowledged.

Conflicting priorities in policy management are only one element of the domestic violence-generated conflicts within police departments. Domestic violence has tended to worsen already strained ties between police commanders and their rank and file. Command officials are, by self selection and exposure, most likely to be exposed to "liberal" influences and thereby become agents for change. Many highly placed police officials like Bouza and Bannon have advanced degrees in social science and readily express support for victim rights. They have been trained in domestic violence management, or at least made aware of the research suggesting that domestic violence can be deterred by the police. Even without this attitudinal paradigm, police administrators are aware that political pressure would quickly mount should they not be seen as supporting effective police intervention. They are also aware of the risk of financially devastating lawsuits should their department respond improperly.

In sharp contrast, police rank and file are as a group, not as exposed to the influences cited above. To a large degree, layers of command and the protection of police unions insulate officers from political or legal pressure. Peer pressure in formation of attitudes remains very strong among officers. Attitudes of line officers have not necessarily changed, at least not to the same extent as administrators and official policies.

The importance of the cleft between police administrators and their officers is difficult to overstate. The rank and file are difficult to supervise as they are diffusely deployed. Officer discretion is considered

Attitudes of line officers have not necessarily changed, at least not to the same extent as administrators and official policies.

not only proper but essential to effective policing. Patrol officers are acknowledged to probably have more discretion than anyone else in the criminal justice system. As such, they have great ability to subvert un-shared department policies or goals. Simply put, the dichotomy in attitudes between police administration and police officers means that any program implementing a proactive policy is likely to face hard and uncertain implementation.

Conflict external to the department has become a new problem. The original focus upon reform was the visible problem with the police. This has been addressed by numerous state statutes and countless internal police department policies. However, the police are but one actor in a largely uncoordinated criminal justice "system." As such, large-scale arrests of domestic violence offenders are made without coordination with the mission and resources of other significant actors including prosecutors and the judiciary. Under that scenario, arrestees are merely processed "by the number" at the police station, with little if any aggressive follow-up occurring by the prosecutors. As a result, cases are ultimately dropped. When this occurs, it tends to inevitably increase police cynicism toward their role in domestic violence. Similarly, the victim's attitude hardens toward the police and the criminal justice system as they do not accord her sufficient protection.

Finally, we believe that there is a natural intrinsic conflict in the perceptions of the proper role of the police among the police, academics, battered women's advocates, and the victims of domestic violence. We posit that police, not surprisingly, tend to view this role as merely another competing demand for their limited output of services. As such, their hierarchy of goals in descending order of importance might be as follows:

Highest in importance: organizational imperatives

- no officers injured/killed
- the police role recognized favorably in the press (and in budget allocations)
- the activity not "dominate" police tasks as it is low status and not intrinsically interesting

Second in importance: the police self-defined mission is upheld and the public order is restored

- known crimes and criminals apprehended and convicted

Third and a weekly shared goal: victims of domestic violence are protected

- While we believe that most officers would clearly consider this a plus, they are aware that there are many classes of victims demanding police services, many of whom are not able to be helped.

Finally, many feminists and academics have stated that victims of domestic violence deserve to have their **"inherent" civil rights protected,** not just as individuals but because this is key to achieving a less violent, more egalitarian society. Police rarely if ever have the time, luxury or temperament to consider such long-range intangible goals.

In stark contrast, many academics and battered women's advocates would probably rank order these same goals as follows:

Of highest importance: the societal goal of achieving a more egalitarian, less violent society

- An important goal, but not to the same degree as the above, would be the protection of individual victims. Hence, mandatory arrest may be promoted even if a victim's desires are rejected.

To this group, maintenance of the police mission of restoring order is only of secondary importance, and police organizational issues receive very little legitimacy. In fact, many academics/advocates may even be broadly hostile to the police mandate as the police are perceived as being "agents" of oppression or of the "patriarchy." Other writers openly question police methods/organizations as being anti-minority, excessively militaristic, insensitive to crime victims, etc. Still others might change their opinion but frankly have not kept up with police literature, and thereby fail to recognize the extent of change in this rapidly evolving area.

The police are but one actor in a largely uncoordinated criminal justice "system." As such, large-scale arrests of domestic violence offenders are made without coordination with the mission and resources of other significant actors including prosecutors and the judiciary.

Many studies simply do not address, let alone express sympathetic understanding of, police officer preferences, the role of police discretion, or the political and budgetary imperatives facing the leadership of any struggling public bureaucracy.

As a result, many studies simply do not address, let alone express sympathetic understanding of, police officer preferences, the role of police discretion, or the political and budgetary imperatives facing the leadership of any struggling public bureaucracy.

Victims of domestic violence often have their own divergent priorities, different not only from the police but also, at times, from their normal benefactors and allies.

For the victim, her most important goal often is the immediate cessation of violence and the establishment of some deterrent to future abuse. Many women who are persecuted by former intimates will perceive that this requires arrest. Others, afraid of collateral effects, do not. Similarly, some victims believe an arrest is required to establish that she was the victim of a crime, and to punish the perpetrator. Other women might simply be satisfied that the police responded to her call and asked *her* if she wanted an arrest. This simple act may empower her in a manner that makes actual arrest unnecessary or even potentially counterproductive (see Ford in Buzawa and Buzawa, 1992).

In contrast, enhancing the societal goal of a more egalitarian, less violent society is probably not high in priority of most victims of domestic violence. Their immediate concerns simply outweigh such issues. Finally, as might be expected, little if any importance is placed on police organizational imperatives. In fact, in many cases, victims, due to past interactions, may be openly hostile to the police as an institution.

The importance of the foregoing analysis is that the dynamics of interaction between these groups make achieving consensus, policy formation, and implementation difficult. Under such circumstances, practices become less a function of a long-range planning process than a "tug of war" between several competing agendas. Unfortunately, in such a contest, the victim often loses.

Conclusion

"1930 will be a very good year."

U.S. Chamber of Commerce
(1929)

Despite our natural reluctance to engage in predictions, we perceive that the conflicts demonstrated above are likely to continue. Police policy elites, facing overwhelming budgetary crisis, must attempt to balance the growing demand for proactive policing with the competing ideology of community policing. Antipathy or at least suspicion toward the police as an institution remains widespread among many academics, feminists and advocates for battered women. For the reasons cited above, we expect that express conflict between police departments and victim advocates will continue the tension.

REFERENCES

Bandy, C.; Buchanan, D.R. and Pinto, C.   Police performance in resolving family disputes -- What makes the difference? *Psychological Reports, 58(3)*, 743-756.

Bannon, J. (1974).   *Social Conflict Assaults: Detroit, Michigan.* Unpublished report for the Detroit Police Department and the Police Foundation.

Bard, M. (1973).   *Training Police in Family Crisis Intervention.* Washington, D.C.: U.S. Government Printing Office.

Bard, M. and Zacker, J. (1974).   Assaultiveness and alcohol use in family disputes. *Criminology, 12*, 281-292.

Bayley, D.H. (1986).   The tactical choices of police patrol officers. *Journal of Criminal Justice, 14*, 329-348.

Bell, D. (1984).   The police responses to domestic violence: A replication study. *Police Studies, 7*, 136-143.

Berk, R.A.; Berk, S.F.; Newton, P.J. and Loseke, D.R. (1984).   Cops on call: Summoning the police to the scene of spousal violence. *Law and Society Review, 18(3)*, 479-498.

Berk, S.F. and Loseke, D.R. (1980-81).   "Handling" family violence: Situational determinants of police arrests in domestic disturbances. *Law and Society Review, 15(2)*, 317-346.

Binder, A. and Meeker, J. (1988).   Experiments as reforms. *Journal of Criminal Justice, 16*, 347-358.

Binder, A. and Meeker, J. (1992).   Arrest as a method to control spouse abuse. Chapter forthcoming in Buzawa, E. and Buzawa, C. (Eds.), *Domestic Violence: The Changing Criminal Justice Response.* Westport, Ct.: Greenwood Press, 1992.

Black, D. (1976).   *The Behavior of Law.* New York: Academic Press.

Black, D. (1980).   *The Manners and Customs of the Police.* New York: Academic Press.

Brosan, G.; Edwards, L.; Whiteman, E.; Spangler, R.J.; Vespa, J.; Mercer, E.; Shapiro, B. and Scherer, D. (1987).   *Maryland Spouse Report, 1986.* Maryland State Police Criminal Records Repository, Pickesville, MD 21208.

Buzawa, E. (1976).   Unpublished survey.

Buzawa, E. and Buzawa, C. (1990).   *Domestic Violence: The Criminal Justice Response.* Newbury Park, Ca.: Sage Publications.

Buzawa, E. and Buzawa, C., Eds. (1992).   *Domestic Violence: The Changing Criminal Justice Response.* Westport, Ct.: Greenwood Press. Forthcoming.

Buzawa, E.; Austin, T.; Bannon, J. and Jackson, J. (1992). The role of victim preference in the decision to arrest. Forthcoming in Buzawa, E. and Buzawa, C. (Eds.), *Domestic Violence: The Changing Criminal Justice Response*. Westport, Ct.: Greenwood Press.

Chapman and Pence (1988).

Cohn, E. and Sherman, L. (1987). Police policy on domestic violence, 1986: A national survey. Crime Control Institute, Washington, D.C.

Connecticut State Police (1990). Family violence reporting program: Law enforcement semiannual report, January 1, 1990 to June 30, 1990. Meriden, Ct.: Connecticut State Police.

Dobash, R. and Dobash, R. (1979). *Violence Against Wives: A Case Against the Patriarchy*. New York: Free Press

Dolan, R.; Hendricks, J. and Meagher, M. (1986). Police practices and attitudes toward domestic violence. *Journal of Police Science and Administration, 14(3)*, 187-192.

Dunford, F.; Huizanga, D. and Elliott, D.S. (1990). Role of arrest in domestic assault: The Omaha police experiment. *Criminology, 28(2)* May 1990, 183-206.

Dutton, D. (1987). Criminal justice response to wife assault. *Law and Human Behavior, 11(3)* September 1987, 167-264.

Dutton, D. (1988). *The Domestic Assault of Women: Psychological and Criminal Justice Perspectives*. Boston: Allyn & Bacon.

Elliott, D. (1989). Criminal justice procedures in family violence crimes. In L. Ohlin and M. Tonry (Eds.), *Crime and Justice: A Review of Research (pp. 427-480)*. London: University of Chicago Press.

Elliott, D. (1991), cited in R. Gelles, Constraints against family violence: How well do they work? Paper presented to the American Society of Criminology, San Francisco, November 1991.

Ellis, D. (1987). Policing wife abuse: The contribution made by "domestic disturbances" to deaths and injuries among police officers. *Journal of family violence, 2(4)* December 1987, 319-333.

FBI Law Enforcement Bulletin (1991). Domestic violence: When do police have a constitutional duty to protect. *FBI Law Enforcement Bulletin, 60(1)* January 1991, 27-32.

Ferraro, K. (1989). The legal response to women battering in the United States. In J. Hanmer, J. Radford and E. Stanko (Eds.), *Women, Policing and Male Violence* (pp. 155-184). London: Routledge & Keegan Paul.

Ford, D. (1983). Wife battery and criminal justice: A study of victim decision making. *Family Relations, 32*, 463-475.

Ford, D. (1987). The impact of police officers' attitudes toward victims on the disinclination to arrest wife batterers. Paper presented at the 3rd International Conference for Family Violence Researchers, Durham, NH.

Ford, D. and Regoli, M.J. (1992). The preventive impacts of policies for prosecuting wife batterers. Forthcoming in Buzawa, E. and Buzawa C. (Eds.) *Domestic Violence: The Changing Criminal Justice Response.* Westport, Ct.: Greenwood Press, 1992.

Garner, and Clemmer, E. (1986). Danger to police in domestic disturbances: A new look. In *National Institute of Justice: Research in Brief.* Washington, D.C.: U.S. Department of Justice.

Kantor, G.K. and Straus, M.A. (1987). The "drunken bum" theory of wife beating. *Social Problems, 34(3)*, 213-230.

Langan, P. and Innes, C. (1986). *Preventing Domestic Violence Against Women.* Bureau of Justice Statistics. Washington, D.C.: U.S. Department of Justice.

Lerman, L. (1984). Mediation of wife abuse cases: The adverse impact of informal dispute resolution of women. *Harvard Women's Law Journal, 7*, 65-67.

Liebman, D. and Schwartz, J. (1973). Police programs in domestic crisis intervention: A review. In J.R. Snibbe and H.M. Snibbe (Eds.), *The Urban Policeman in Transition.* Springfield, Ill.: Charles C. Thomas.

Loving, N. and Quirk, M. (1982). Spouse abuse: The need for new law enforcement responses. *FBI Law Enforcement Bulletin, 51(12)*, 10-16.

Manning, P. (1977). *Police Work: The Sociological Organization of Policing.* Cambridge: MIT Press.

Manning, P. (1988). *Symbolic Communication: Signifying Calls and the Police Response.* Cambridge: MIT Press.

Manning, P. (1991). Technological and material resource issues endemic to policing. Paper presented in the "Seminar Series on Executive Issues," Law Enforcement Management Institute, Lubbuck, Texas, July 1991.

Manning, P. (1992). Screening calls. Forthcoming in Buzawa, E. and Buzawa, D. (Eds.), *Domestic Violence: The Changing Criminal Justice Response.* Westport, Ct.: Greenwood Press, 1992.

Martin, Margaret (1991). Dual arrest: Arresting women victims of violence. Paper presented to the American Society of Criminology, San Francisco, November 1991.

Meeker, J. and Binder, A. Experiments as reforms: The impact of the "Minneapolis Experiment" on police policy. *Journal of Police Science and Administration, 17(2)* June, 147-153.

National Organization of Black Law Enforcement Executives (1990). *Law Reinforcement, Family Violence Training and Technical Assistance Project, October 1988 - July 1990, Final Report.* U.S. Department of Justice, Washington, D.C.

Parnas, R. (1967). The police response to the domestic disturbance. *Wisconsin Law Review, 2,* 914-960.

Pennsylvania Task Force (1989). *Domestic Violence: A Model Protocol for Police Response.* Pennsylvania Attorney General's Family Violence Task Force.

Pierce, G. and Deutsch, S. (1990). Do police actions and responses to domestic violence calls make a difference? A quasi-experimental analysis. *Journal of Quantitative Criminology.*

Pierce, G. and Spaar, S. (1992). Identifying households at risk of domestic violence. Forthcoming in Buzawa, E. and Buzawa, C. (Eds.), *Domestic Violence: The Changing Criminal Justice Response.* Westport, Ct.: Greenwood Press, 1992.

Pleck, E. (1989). Criminal approaches to family violence 1640-1980. In L. Ohlin and M. Tonry (Eds.), *Crime and Justice: A Review of Research, Vol. 11* (pp. 19-58). Chicago: University of Chicago Press.

Punch, M. (1985). Conduct unbecoming. London: MacMillan.

Radford, J. (1989). Women and policing: Contradictions old and new. In J. Hanmer, J. Radford and B. Stanko (Eds.), *Women, Policing and Male Violence* (pp. 13-45). London: Routledge and Keegan Paul.

Reiss, A.J. (1971). *The Police and the Public.* New Haven, Ct.: Yale University Press.

Saunders, D. and Size, P. (1986). Attitudes about women abuse among police officers, victims and victim advocates. *Journal of Interpersonal Violence, 1,* 24-42.

Scargzi, J. (1991). Attitudes of new police recruits concerning domestic violence: A pre and post test design. Paper presented to the American Society of Criminology, San Francisco, November 1991.

Sherman, L. and Berk, R. (1984). The specific deterrent effects of arrest for domestic assault. *American Sociological Review, 49,* 261-272.

Sherman, L. and Cohn, E. (1989). The impact of research on legal policy: The Minneapolis domestic violence experiment. *Law and Society Review, 23(1)*, 117-144.

Sherman, L. and Cohn, E. (1990). Effects of research on legal policy in the Minneapolis domestic violence experiment. From Douglas Besharov (Ed.), *Family Violence: Research and Public Policy Issues.* Lanham, MD: University Press of America, pp. 205-207.

Stanko, E. (1989). Missing the mark? Police battering. In J. Hanmer, J. Radford and B. Stanko (Eds.), *Women, Policing and Male Violence* (pp. 46-49). London: Routledge and Keegan Paul.

Stark, E. and Flitcraft, A.

Stith, S. (1987). Individual and family factors which predict police response to spouse abuse. Paper presented to the 3rd National Family Violence Research Conference, Durham, NH, July 1987.

Van Maanen, J. (1974). Working the street: A developmental view of police behavior. In H. Jacob (Ed.), *The Potential for Reform of Criminal Justice* (pp. 83-130). Beverly Hills, Ca.: Sage.

Van Maanen, J. (1978). Observations on the making of policemen. In P. Manning and J. Van Maanen (Eds.), *Policing: A View From the Street.* Santa Monica, Ca.: Goodyear Publishing.

Victim Services Agency (1988). *The Law Enforcement Response to Family Violence: A State by State Guide to Family Violence Legislation.* New York: Victim Services Agency.

Victim Services Agency (1989). *The Law Enforcement Response to Family Violence: The Training Challenge.* U.S. Department of Justice, Washington, D.C.

Walker, L. (1979). *Battered Women.* New York: Harper and Row.

Westley, W. (1970). *Violence and the Police: A Sociological Study of Law, Custom and Morality.* Cambridge: MIT Press.

Worden, R. and Pollitz, A. (1984). Police arrests in domestic disturbances: A further look. *Law and Society Review, 18*, 105-119.

Chapter 12

The Police
and
The Press

The Fourth Estate is society's permanent Inspector General in Residence. As society's ombudsman, the central role of the press is to rake up as much muck as it can manage, every day, and deliver it to the people. Anything impeding the media's flow of information actually interferes with the public's right to be informed. Thus, a chief at war with the media is, in reality, at war with the people he serves.

by Anthony V. Bouza

I magine a large corps of talented investigators, who can write engagingly, call into play unlimited resources, whose only raison d'etre is to discover, and comment publicly on, the problems besetting a society, and who have a huge and eagerly interested audience, and you've conjured up a free press. The Fourth Estate serves as a free society's permanent Inspector General in Residence. It is the community's ombudsman, restricted in its approach only by the limits of human inquisitiveness.

The police, as a mysterious repository of power and as the inheritors of many delicious secrets, become a natural target of an industry whose principal characteristic is curiosity. The things that cops delve into hold a permanent fascination for the public, and the media's role is to inform that public -- whether that action is convenient or not.

It isn't only what cops do that fascinates, but how they go about doing it. The people have an abiding curiosity about how power centers function. Power is inherently fascinating and frightening -- because it can be directed at anyone. Power has all the allure it needs to magnetize the media, and no one has more of it than the police.

The human animal is born with a deep interest in the world about him/her, and the press feeds the appetite for information. At its loftiest plane, it becomes a search for knowledge; at its lower levels, it lapses into voyeurism -- and the range of offerings in a free society touches both poles and everything in between.

Thomas Jefferson put it best:

> The basis of our government being the opinion of the people, the very first object should be to help that right; and were it left to me to decide whether we should have a government without newspapers, or newspapers without a government, I should not hesitate a moment to prefer the latter.

The Thirst for Information

When a dictatorship is toppled, as happened so dramatically and swiftly across Eastern Europe and Russia in the recent past, the thirst for information turns thousands into pamphleteers and causes hundreds of papers, magazines, radio and television programs to sprout. Nothing more eloquently illustrates the people's need to know than the rush to fill the informational vacuum created by dictatorships -- whose own approach to the retention of power is, first and foremost, to suppress the free flow of information. We've come to assess the extent of freedom by the latitude afforded the press.

A democracy's foremost adornment is a free press. It may also be its fiercest challenge and most vexing frustration. Free societies are characterized by such challenging ambiguities. And the press, because of its ability to influence the public's thinking, inevitably becomes a tremendous power source in its own right. This tempts its potential beneficiaries or targets to court its favor and, sometimes, tempts it to abuse its considerable power, in the nature of all human institutions. One of the first things learned by anyone who captures the public's - and, hence, the press's -- interest is the sheer awfulness of being held up to public ridicule or popular censure.

The police want to go their untrammeled way, performing beyond the glare of the media's searching inquiries; and the press wants to find out what's going on and report the results. Thus is a creative tension created that, in the daily welter of confused events, frequently blossoms into conflict.

Tensions

There can be other sources of tensions with the press, besides the usual ones of the police self-protectively withholding information or legitimately preserving the interests of justice by refusing to divulge critical facts.

A key one is the police acting as reporters to secure evidence of a crime or information on a critical event. Few events kicked up as much press fuss as cops posing as television newspeople arresting marijuana users, on school grounds, following on-camera interviews. There had been complaints of flagrant drug use on campus, and the cops resorted to this stratagem as the one effective method of nipping the problem in the bud. It worked, but the media was unforgiving over this subversion of public confidence in its operations. The press did not want the public suspecting that reporters might be cops in disguise.

The police should not be precluded from adopting any strategy that is not forbidden by law as they pursue legitimate police interests.

Obviously, such impersonations can be powerful tools that must be used with discretion and restraint, but the police should not be precluded from adopting any strategy that is not forbidden by law (such as practicing medicine or law without a license, which could constitute illegal impersonations) as they pursue legitimate police interests.

A prominent, scandalous crime can create a sort of press-feeding frenzy that can result in enormous tensions, as the police get badgered to release juicy tidbits that may work against the interests of justice. A crime involving a celebrity may expose the police to minuscule examinations of every facet of their operations and generate commentary on every single action.

The press can bring almost irresistible pressures on the police, which must, nevertheless, sometimes be resisted in the interest of promoting the long-term interests of justice.

And it must not be forgotten that the genius of our system lies in the existence of permanent tensions between many of its institutions that, left unchallenged and unexamined, will arrogate great power to themselves and be tempted to abuse it. Just as our executive, legislative and judicial branches check and balance each other's use of power, so does the press serve as a brake on the possible abuse of power by the police.

Such tensions are properly labeled *creative* and help to preserve an open, democratic society's freedom.

The Roles of the Police

As long as the police straightforwardly protect life and property, prevent crime, detect and arrest offenders, preserve the peace, and enforce the law, things move reasonably linearly -- though not without some routine static and occasional resentments. In such circumstances, the cops are doing their jobs and the press is reporting the results. Sometimes the cops do it well and take satisfaction in the recognition, and sometimes they stumble and bitterly resent being described as bumblers. In such circumstances, there is little room for role confusion, even if there might be space for umbrage. In dealing with the press, the police must possess the emotional maturity required by such complex situations as having to admit mistakes or acknowledge human fallibility. This is perhaps the most difficult lesson to learn and, as these things usually follow, certainly one of the most valuable.

In dealing with the press, the police must possess the emotional maturity required by such complex situations as having to admit mistakes or acknowledge human fallibility.

When the police are engaged in less explicit tasks, such as undertaking the control of a fractious underclass, the clash with espoused societal values is such as to promote secrecy, a sense of beleaguered isolation, and resentment over exposure of events that the public "will never understand."

When the cops are asked to raze shanty-towns, keep the homeless out of sight, clear away the downtowns, and clean up neighborhoods -- without being given the legal, moral or administrative tools necessary to the tasks -- they come into conflict with society's professions of legality, as expressed in the laws and public pronouncements. As the cops attempt to accomplish the implicit mission, usually expressed in exasperated terms about "cleaning up the town" and bringing "a little law and order to bear on the city's streets," they encounter a crucial dissonance between public postures and implicit directives.

Such assignments create role confusion and demoralize the police. When their actions are scrutinized and reported on, the resentment swells; yet it cannot be openly expressed. Cries of "politics" rend the air.

Since the overclass's message is hypocritically couched in such cautions as were employed by Henry II, when he openly wondered if no one would rid him of the priest (Thomas A. Beckett), without ever offering explicit directions about how this should be done, the cops feel free to do the dirty business in any way they see fit. Modern leaders have dubbed the stratagem as retaining "plausible deniability" -- which translates into "just get it done and don't bother me with the details, and don't count on my protection if you get caught."

The cops translate such "clean-up" assignments according to their views and convenience. The result is such events as the beating of Rodney King, Jr., by members of the Los Angeles Police Department, on March 3, 1991. What made that event unique was that it was filmed and widely shown. To cops everywhere, this was simply an example of the "asshole factor," in which they were merely keeping the obstreperous members of the underclass in their place, as per the instructions of the overclass. The cops understandably saw the ensuing furor and widespread condemnations as abandonment and hypocrisy.

Whenever society imposes "informal" tasks on their minions, through Chamber of Commerce-type calls to Mayors, Council Members and Police Chiefs -- faithfully transmitted to the troops -- to "take back the streets," "get the bums and panhandlers out of sight" and "keep the undesirables and derelicts under control," those charged with the duty to perform will accommodate their own prejudices as they carry out the assignments (see Dodenhoff's chapter). Since they're being asked to do something for which they have no legal mandate anyway, why not carry on in accordance with their own interpretation of what needs to be done and how it gets accomplished? And, of course, the cops are right -- the public isn't going to understand. Reporting on such activities can then be seen as being downright churlish.

What to Report -- and When

A serial rapist or killer strikes and the chief faces the dilemma of alerting the public or trying to avoid such unfavorable publicity. The chief will hope they can catch the predator swiftly. Failure to do so creates well-nigh intolerable pressures and incredible scrutiny. It's easy to commit a misstep in such settings. Every city has been plagued with such extreme examples as the "Son of Sam" killings in N.Y.C., or the abductions of boys in Atlanta, and every police chief is terrified of headlines that blare "Where Will He Strike Next?" and texts that report that "The Police Are Stymied."

Openly reporting the event to the press invites terrifying possibilities. Concealing information risks charges of "cover-up." The chief will hold that he didn't want to create panic or that they were working on promising leads or setting a trap and didn't want to alert the suspect. The reality, however, is often that the chief is trying to avoid the tensions attendant upon disclosure. No one wants a spooked public on his hands. The process is hallowed by the descriptive "covering your ass."

Disclosures of such police malfeasance as brutality or corruption will produce headlines. If the wrongdoings are discovered and prosecuted by the police administration, there is the hope that the police will be credited with alertness to internal problems, but the reports will still pack a sting. Wrongdoing discovered by outsiders not only stains the agency and its leaders and members, but it carries the imputation that the agency is neither introspective nor aware of the dangers within or, worse, that it is ineffective or uncaring in dealing with the problems within the ranks.

The Organizational Culture of the Police

The internal police culture is isolate, secretive, and terribly resistant to intrusions -- notwithstanding the profusion of books, films and television programs about cops and their lives and work (see Thibault's chapter). The shock of the Rodney King, Jr. incident lay in the public's confusion at an incomprehensible event and at the more disturbing disclosure that it may actually have been reflective of the organizational culture. That the event almost immediately centered on the police chief and his policies confirmed that the question was whether this was an aberration or of a piece with the agency's secret -- and tacitly understood -- approach to its mission.

The internal police culture is isolate, secretive, and terribly resistant to intrusions.

Police agencies are, internally, absolute monarchies, in which the chief is king (or, in such rare cases as Houston in 1991, queen). His every action -- and it is action, not words, that must be emphasized because that is what the troops focus on -- sends unmistakably clear messages to the organization. Every agency utters the same series of bromides about "equal enforcement of the laws" and the need to "protect and serve," but the actions of the chief are studied with the devotion of entrail diviners seeking signs of royal wishes.

Our affection for, and admiration of, such avenging angels as were depicted in the film "Dirty Harry," in which cops dispense perfect justice, without bothering much about the niceties of the law, in frank imitation of Brazil's notorious Death Squads, conceals the ugly reality of vigilante justice. We need heroes who are free to act without being handcuffed by technicalities such as the United States Constitution, the law, or such scrutiny as a free press might provide.

There is probably no agency in society that is in as forward, and as exposed, a position as the police.

In addition to what's taking place on the streets -- which frequently, as some startling home videos have revealed about Fort Worth, Texas; Long Beach, California; Tompkins Square Park in New York, and such other places as Los Angeles, show the police as dispensing summary justice to the underclass, according to their lights -- there are administrative questions centering on what's taking place in police board rooms, where policies are set and messages transmitted. There is the additional complexity of needing to see the citizens' complicity in these possible atrocities if we can hope to understand them and prevent future dysfunctions.

Is crime rising? Has some horrendous event resulted in criticism? Are there tensions with the police union? Is the Mayor unhappy over the handling of a demonstration? Are the cops staging a slowdown or suffering from "blue flu"? Is the press doing a series that embarrasses the police brass? These are typical of the questions and issues that provoke the sorts of stories that create enmity between the police and the press.

There is probably no agency in society that is in as forward, and as exposed, a position as the police. They are on the front line of America's battle of survival as it attempts to cope with tides of crime and violence that exceed war tolls and threaten to sweep all before them. The cities are disintegrating and the cops are charged with holding them together. It has been a losing battle, and it is one of the characteristics of human nature that we don't reward losers. The war in our ghettos and central cities is the modern equivalent of the Vietnam War, in terms of the popularity of the struggle and the fate, in terms of the public's esteem, of the combatants.

Power and Its Temptations

Disclosure is exquisitely painful, but suppression of information signals the death of freedom.

There is no human institution, anywhere, that will not be tempted to abuse its power if it isn't held to strict account over its use, and monitored carefully and consistently. Lord Acton had it right when he held that "power tends to corrupt and absolute power corrupts absolutely." He wisely withheld "tends to" when he referred to the possibility of total control.

The police have more power than any institution in our society. They guard it fiercely. The police "code of silence" is a well-known phrase in police literature. The systems of oversight and monitoring -- political figures, judicial bodies, prosecutorial officers, federal agencies, civil litigation, and such -- function unevenly.

The only agency permanently serving as a watchdog over police actions is the press.

Try to imagine the conduct of the Los Angeles Police Department that had the power to suppress any showing of the Rodney King, Jr. tape. Try to conceive the history of a N.Y.C. Police Department that didn't have to face the front-page disclosures of the corruptions that sparked the Knapp Commission inquiry of 1972. Try to conceive of the temptations attendant upon the suppression of any really negative report on the actions of the police, and you'll have a small idea of the temptation to suppress and of the cost, to a free people, of such suppressions.

Disclosure is exquisitely painful, but suppression of information signals the death of freedom.

The Chief

The chief is the commanding general. In addition to having been assigned to preside over a daily litany of defeats, he is usually notably unprepared for a task that would require unreasonable levels of diplomacy, intelligence, strategic sense, and political acuity.

The chief is usually an up-from-the-ranks survivor who has spent his adult life in one agency and devoted most of his energy to developing policing and investigative skills that are of no use to him as an executive. Policing is not a profession that admires intellectuality, nor is it one that develops, or rewards, managers. The top cop usually is just that -- the city's preeminent police officer -- and this is a hopelessly limiting, and rarely recognized, impediment to organizational progress or reform. The chief has frequently adopted the approach that features a simple view of the world: "We're the good guys and they're the bad guys; whatever we do is okay -- whatever they suffer is deserved." Such messages get transmogrified, in the street, into acts of brutality.

How we select chiefs insures a continuation of conflict with the press because the training, character, and intellectual factors absolutely required for success in such delicate endeavors as those dealing with the press are not only in short supply, generally, but not even considered in the scandalous approach to selection of chiefs in the overwhelming majority of the nation's cities.

Mayors, law enforcement's key executives -- because they choose the country's chiefs of police -- have never cottoned to the importance of this role and tend to make this, their most important personnel decision, on the basis of personal, arcane, and frequently irrelevant political factors. The results are inscribed on the face of every municipal crisis in the nation, which reflects mismanagement and official fecklessness much more deeply than the economic tragedies so frequently blamed for inadequate police service.

News

All of us are thin-skinned. The power of the press inspires fear and loathing. Few of us realize that news is whatever the people want to know, every day, and it is rarely a report of a bureaucrat's selfless devotion to truth, beauty, justice, and the American Way. News tends to have a negative bias. That the chief has led the agency for ten years, over rough shoals and dangerous moments, and that he has faithfully discharged his duties as a citizen and family member isn't news. That he has covered up some wrongdoing or inspired his troops to commit crimes is. It may, however, be fairly argued that the press might do more inspiring stories depicting the triumph of the human spirit, in its many guises, one of which surely is being a dedicated public official.

How we select chiefs insures a continuation of conflict with the press because the training, character, and intellectual factors absolutely required for success in such delicate endeavors as those dealing with the press are in short supply.

As society's ombudsman, the central role of the press is to rake up as much muck as it can manage, every day, and deliver it to the people. The press is a mere conduit of information to the public. The media serves the citizens' right to know. Once this is acknowledged, it follows that anything that impedes the media's flow of information actually interferes with the people's right to be informed. Thus, a chief at war with the media is, in reality, at war with the people he serves.

It is not an exaggeration to hold that most of the nation's police chiefs -- and their agencies -- see the press as the enemy, and wage a silent, pernicious war with the foe. It is mostly a muted and undeclared struggle, but it occasionally surfaces in outbursts whose sincerity is never questioned.

Behavior toward the press is going to be directed by the inner attitudes guiding the flow of action. Police executives have to be mercilessly introspective about their attitudes toward the press and establish how these affect the policies tacitly and explicitly adopted. Cosmetizing the news, concealing information, or engaging in hostilities with the media deprive a free people of the information vital to their effective functioning as informed citizens.

P.I.O.s

Indeed, one of the requirements for accreditation as a professional police organization is the appointment of a public information officer whose task is to "deal with the press." As a member of an industry that sprouted just to cosmetize the news -- known, innocently, as "public relations" -- the public information officer's duty is to apply rouge and lipstick to the department's countenance -- all the while professing to be facilitating the flow of information.

Some of the more sophisticated training programs -- especially for police chiefs and their top aides -- have included "media relations," which virtually assume the hostility of the press and brief the executives on how to survive press "attacks." I have rarely attended a conference of big city police chiefs that did not, inevitably, turn into a forum on the atrocities committed, against them or their departments, by a hostile and misunderstanding press.

These training programs would be of more value to the people, and, ultimately, to the chiefs, if they taught the executives to be more thick-skinned, to eschew taking news reports personally, to avoid wallowing in self-pity, to discover the charms of candor, and to understand the role of a free press in a democratic society.

News Activism

Nature abhors a vacuum.

The front pages and the evening television news are arenas in which the civic drama gets played out. Failure to include one's version, because of caution, timidity or inexperience, usually means having to suffer the opinions of those not similarly inhibited.

A typical scenario includes a black youth, involved in a crime, who is shot and killed by a white police officer.

The headlines and airwaves ring with sulphurous accusations of brutality, frequently followed by a chief's lame "no comment" or "the investigation is continuing." Such approaches create the impression of evasiveness or cover-up and abandon the field to those who, however irresponsibly, provide flashy sound bytes.

In those circumstances, the chief has to gather as much information as quickly as he can and fulfill his role as educator and spokesperson, filling the vacuum created by "no comment" with as much as he can reveal -- whatever its nature -- consistent with the law and the exigencies of the situation. If subsequent events prove this account flawed, the chief will be understanding of efforts to keep it informed and be resentful of self-protecting bureaucratic attempts to keep it in the dark or confused.

The chief functions in a complex world of unions, Mayors, councils, Chambers of Commerce, special interests, minorities and majorities of all shapes and descriptions, other criminal justice bodies, and a host of other groups and persons that may be brought together, or surface stridently, through the stimulus of specific events. The chief has to assume a visible activist role if he is to earn the public's confidence and support, which are essential to his effective functioning as a public executive. The police chief must, in short, become an existentialist, even if he can't pronounce the word.

Failure to assume the lead will have the chief reacting, defending, explaining and retreating -- usually long after the fact and following a good deal of probably avoidable damage.

Cooperative Efforts

The police need an informed, involved, cooperative public that can furnish valuable information and leads.

The police need an informed, involved, cooperative public that can furnish valuable information and leads. Programs such as *Crime Stoppers* -- where a crime is dramatized on television, in order to solicit viewer information and for which rewards are offered, confidentially -- is an excellent example of police, press, and people cooperating to solve formerly unsolvable crimes.

Public service announcements relating to police programs, such as techniques for self-protection or the securing of property, are another form of police-press partnership.

Community-orienting policing -- where the police work with neighborhoods to diagnose local problems, and prescribe and implement solutions -- relies on public awareness that can be enhanced through press exposure (see Murphy's chapter).

The police need the people's support, and this will only be elicited through trust. A shadowy, secretive, self-protective police agency will not inspire public confidence, nor will it elicit the sort of press cooperation so frequently essential to the police agency's success. The depth and extent of public trust will be principally influenced by the image created by the press.

Despite the daily criticisms and interminable complaints, there is every evidence that the American people trust its newspapers, radios, and television stations -- else how to explain their success and popularity. And the police will have to acknowledge this influence and work with the press to secure the public's help. Even recruitment programs, seeking qualified police candidates, can be made more effective through the use of free media advertising.

In the end, even such fabulously successful press manipulators as the FBI's J. Edgar Hoover came a cropper, following the tortured and frequently time-consuming musings of reporters, historians and writers. Today's literature is virtually unanimous in its condemnation of Hoover's approach to the uses of police power, as well as of the agency's relations with the press. In a free society, history will out.

Press Policy

Police departments shouldn't have public information officers. Every member of the agency should serve as a source for the public's right to know. The policy ought to be that information that might impede an ongoing investigation cannot be released, nor the identity of the victim of a sex crime or of a child perpetrator or victim. Information on searches and arrests should be confined to what is contained in the public record -- the court documents on which actions were predicated or which reflect the formal charges.

The surest guide is the law. Whatever is not forbidden, either by law or court order, ought to be released, unless articulable grounds can be found for withholding information. And by articulable grounds is not meant the pious mouthings of formulaic phrases devised by clever bureaucrats, but rather a formal and explicit statement containing specific reasons for failing to divulge, and which can be subsequently verified or refuted.

The emphasis has to be on release of information and on the permanent right of the citizen to be informed.

Conclusion

The police are a highly visible and terribly important agency of government, whose activities are of deep and legitimate concern to the citizens it serves. As the embodiment of the corps, the chief becomes the cynosure of press eyes. His actions, and the actions of his department, are news.

Adopting the views that the public has a right to be informed and that the chief has a duty to educate and alert the people he serves can be the foundation of a policy that results in positive relations between the chief and the people, and make his agency far more effective in its operations. The press will be a simple mirror of that relationship -- allowing for the imperfections that inevitably accompany every institution and its members.

As the embodiment of the corps, the chief becomes the cynosure of press eyes. His actions, and the actions of his department, are news.

Getting a good press really means operating an open, accessible system that acknowledges its responsibility for keeping the public informed on matters that affect its vital interests.

We all recognize that nothing is as subversive to a democracy as the interruption of the free flow of information. That this flow occasionally produces pain should be recognized as one of the unavoidable prices that freedom exacts.

> *And you shall know the truth, and the truth shall make you free.*
>
> John 8:32

Chapter 13

The Media and the Police: Contemporary Experiments in Cross-Education

Police service today exists in a "climate of criticism." Some of it is unwarranted: baseless bashing arising from the biases of individual media representatives who, like bad cops, are a discredit to their work. Some of it is constitutionally correct: the press in the posture of the watchdog holding police accountable.

by Patricia Kelly, Ph.D.

Cooperation -- not confrontation -- is the watchword for police/media interactions for the decade of the 1990s and, hopefully, beyond. Goodwill, increased understanding of the constraints of one another's working worlds, and a heightened awareness of ethical issues affecting access to information are the by-products of some bold educational experiments conceived and implemented by journalists and law enforcement specialists across our country.

In such cities as Louisville, Kentucky; Detroit, Michigan; Los Angeles, California and Boston, Massachusetts, police and press are meeting informally around tables and more formally in classroom settings to complain, criticize and, most importantly, work constructively to resolve the conflicts which have too long chilled their relationship. Such efforts provide useful models that can be duplicated or modified wherever police and press commit themselves to easing mutual tensions before they develop into no-win stand-offs at critical incident scenes.

"Today there are definitely more people saying let's get together, we do not have to be enemies," says Sgt. Carl Yates, a 20-year veteran of the Louisville, Kentucky Police Department and its official spokesman for the past 16 years.

In the case of the extremely popular media relations course designed by Yates himself and in other similar ventures worthy of examination, this "getting together" assumes the form of cross-education.

"I see recognition of a need for training in media relations now at all levels, not just at the chief's level, but at the patrol level and for middle management and front line supervisors," continues Yates. "And in some parts of the country, I have seen the media pushing as hard for this training as the police."

In the joint sessions that have proven most successful, police are not merely lecturing press, and media representatives are not merely talking at captive cop audiences. But reporters, news photographers, journalism educators, communications specialists, and law enforcement personnel are giving up the tug of war for the give and take. They are listening to one another, learning from one another, and clearly and decisively informing one another what each side can or cannot do to improve communication while protecting the integrity of their respective missions.

Perspectives from the Past

It was not always this way. Before we consider case studies of cross-educational undertakings that are working effectively, it is necessary to at least sketchily construct the historical context that helped produce them. A replay of half a century of police/media relations in this country reveals this irony: as the processes by which law enforcement and journalism professionals communicate have become increasingly sophisticated, the contacts between the two sides have become increasingly strained.

Time was when the description of covering the police beat, as offered by veteran Washington Post reporter Al Lewis, defined a typical cop-police reporter relationship. Lewis, who was known to his police contacts as "Uncle Al," and who began covering the Washington D.C. Police Department in 1935, reminisced about police/media interaction of the 1940s. "Back then," he said, "you'd never go to the scene of a crime without a bottle of booze in your pocket. It often came in handy. On a murder case, you'd hang around outside waiting for the homicide detectives to finish their initial inspection of the scene, and you'd strike up a conversation with one of the uniformed police officers who was the first one at the scene. After a while, you'd take the officer aside, offer him a swig or two from your bottle, and ask him for all the details. It nearly always worked."[1]

But such informality, ease of access, and rapport vanished, perhaps at least partially due to landmark legal developments that frequently caused police to take a stance with press that went beyond cautionary reticence to near paranoiac silence. Key among these were the landmark *Sheppard vs. Maxwell* decision (1966) and the American Bar Association's Reardon Report. In the former, the United States Supreme Court overturned the murder conviction of Dr. Sam Sheppard (found guilty of killing his wife) in an opinion that, like the A.B.A.'s report, addressed officers of the court and police officials, instructing them to carefully monitor and restrict their communication with the press during pre-trial and trial periods.[2]

Consequently, as so aptly put by James M. Ragsdale, editor of *The Standard Times* in New Bedford, Massachusetts, police and police reporters became "official, not friendly." Rules began to proliferate from both camps, and codes of conduct began to specifically govern how law enforcement personnel and journalists related to one another what information could be disseminated by police agencies, and how and when and to whom it could be released. As both sides, in Ragsdale's words, became "meticulously clean-scrubbed," they also became distant, even suspect of one another.[3]

Closeness was sacrificed to clarity of regulations. Police public information officers began to spring up to represent their agencies. No matter how well-meaning or how well-trained, these designees were often viewed with a jaundiced eye by journalists who felt that such spokesmen, whether sworn or civilian, were charged with dispensing the well-laundered, even sanitized version of police news.

The media's growing discontent with such officialdom and the police's growing recognition, albeit a reluctant one, that they need the press (and good press) have combined to form solid support for brining both sides together to define a new working relationship valid for our times.

There is a renewed awareness on the part of law enforcement agencies that: (1) the media prefers the immediacy of the on-site interview to the delays of the press release preparation, (2) reporters want direct access to the officers investigating the cases they are covering, and (3) if insufficient information is forthcoming from agencies or if that information is withheld beyond their deadlines, journalists will seek it elsewhere, sometimes from tainted sources who can jeopardize a police investigation.

An Educational Experiment

Such considerations recently prompted the public relations personnel of the Massachusetts State Police and a county district attorney's office to schedule a police/media relations instructional block for state police supervisors assigned to district attorneys' offices. The first of its kind in the history of those agencies, its purpose was to prepare the supervisors to prepare their own investigators to deal confidently and competently with the media. The development of such proficiency was judged to be especially important when the public information officers are not there to field the questions or distribute an official version of events.

The seminar, well received and now being planned for expanded time slots and audiences, brought police and press together for exchanges of educational benefit to both sides.

Print and television reporters invited to speak were clear in the conveyance of their message that they wanted as many facts as they could get as quickly as they could be gotten. They were adamant about their right to interview witnesses, referring to this process as part of their obligation to get a complete story. They claimed that if information is gathered from sources the police consider unreliable, it is frequently in reaction to the refusal of law enforcement officials to comment. They even attempted to cajole their police audience into helping the media circumvent the stranglehold that the Massachusetts Criminal Offenders Record Information Act (C.O.R.I.) traditionally had placed on accessing the criminal histories of the accused. One print reporter suggested that if police sources could not divulge this data, they might at least drop clues as to how it could be speedily obtained. "You can direct us to where the records are," he pleaded, referring to the strictures imposed by C.O.R.I., including ones which force journalists to face circuitous and tedious procedures to unlock the dispositions of individual criminal cases.

On the other hand, the other side of the issue was presented just as convincingly. An assistant district attorney was unequivocal in his assertions that investigators be scrupulous in keeping secret any information that could compromise the police function. He provided examples of how dissemination of facts or materials actually hamstrung prosecutors seeking convictions.

He cited the damage done to an investigation by a newspaper's publication of a suspect's photo in a homicide case before the witnesses could be contacted to view it. He talked of how the premature release by a medical examiner of the ruling that a fatal stab wound was not self-inflicted, and the furnishing of that fact by a reporter to the suspect, severely compromised the subsequent police interview of that person. He pointedly told them why they needed to be circumspect about their media interactions. "The less you are quoted, the better it is," he said. "You, as an investigator, have to be the best witness for your investigation. The bottom line is that there is a trial down the road, and you do not want to become the media's witness in that trial." He urged them to react to the press with a judicious and measured response in the earliest stages of a criminal investigation. "The biggest danger," he cautioned, "exists in the initial hours, when too much information is released at the scene."

Such is the set of conflicting messages that strikes to the heart of the duel that keeps police and press divided.

Asked to address at this same seminar the subject of the importance of good police/media relations, I played a philosophical position somewhere near the middle. I spoke of how provision of information and protection of the integrity of an investigation are not mutually exclusive terms. I shared defensive communications strategies -- such as tips on how to counter entrapping questions -- to increase the officers' abilities to remain in control of what they want to say and how they want to say it, in the heat of a reactionary interview, in the unrelenting focus of the television camera. We talked about how to deal with the news media when the coverage target is the police agency itself: the public relations nightmare which can occur when law enforcement personnel are accused of wrongdoing. That discussion centered on minimizing the damage by remaining forthright in dealing with the press.

I reinforced what the officers readily acknowledged: that police today exist in a "climate of criticism."[4] Some of it is unwarranted: baseless bashing arising from the biases of individual media representatives who, like bad cops, are discredits to their professions. Some of it is constitutionally correct: the press in the posture of the watchdog, holding police, like all other public servants, accountable. I therefore recommended that police be more proactive in their media relations. Since the media is the lens through which the public perceives its police, it is important that efforts are made to get the law enforcement side of the story out, especially with the threat of negative coverage.

Few points made by the presenters went unchallenged by the police audience. The result was dialogue. It is impossible to assess, on the basis of this one educational experiment, whether any attitudes or behaviors would be modified. But it was apparent -- in the spirited debate, in the probing nature of questions posed -- that there was attentive listening and informational exchange in an atmosphere of mutual regard. There was also unanimous agreement among participants that such cross-education exercises are valuable, and a recognition that although police and press will and should never be in courtship, a more peaceful and productive coexistence is possible. "Remember," wrote one officer in his wrap-up evaluation, "that they [the press] are the eyes and ears of the people for whom we work. Since they are people and professionals, treat them with consideration and respect." And on a more pragmatic ending note: "If you treat them like dogs, they can bite you."

Since the media is the lens through which the public perceives its police, it is important that efforts are made to get the law enforcement side of the story out, especially with the threat of negative coverage.

Cross-Training Sheds Light

Melissa M. Faulkner, director of communications for the Center for Urban Studies, Wayne State University, Detroit, Michigan, uses the term "enlightenment" to describe the typical reaction of police officers and media personnel who have been brought together in similar media relations training sessions she has designed.

Having taught both at police academies in her home state of Michigan and at sites across the country under the aegis of the Northwestern University Traffic Institute School of Policing and Staff Command, Faulkner believes that the presence of journalists as educators in such classes is not icing on the cake, but an ingredient essential to the learning process.

"They help police officers to understand such concepts as 'what is news,' and it is important for an officer to hear a media representative respond to such common police complaints as 'I was quoted out of context,'" maintains Faulkner, whose specialties are technical writing, public speaking, and media skills development. "For example, it is effective when a reporter will advise them to go first and directly to the reporter who quoted them, and then, if there is no satisfaction obtained, go to the reporter's editor."

In a pilot study of police perceptions of the media which Faulkner conducted in 1989, she found that many respondents supported a media orientation program for their agencies and the involvement of media representatives in training. She ranks the concept of cross-education as critical if "police and media are going to keep the channels of communication open."

"For police to be able to communicate with the media more effectively, they need to know what kind of information media are looking for [presumably what the public wants to know] and how to deliver that information," she says. "That is why it is essential for media representatives to be involved in training for police -- to show a good-faith effort in this two-way communication situation and to address directly questions that police have about the nuances of the job."

Further, she finds that this "training forum" affords a common meeting ground set apart from the day-to-day crime settings that are the customary intersection points for police and police-beat reporters.[5]

The Louisville Experience

Just such a forum, featuring hands-on hard work, fast-paced imaginative exercises, information-filled field trips, and issues-probing panels, is provided by the police/media relations course developed 11 years ago by Sgt. Carl Yates of the Louisville, Kentucky Police Department. Forty hours of in-service training is required annually of police officers in that state who qualify, and this five-day program is among the ones offered under those guidelines. Through the years, the curriculum has become finely tuned; it is tightly organized and infused with renewed life from a willing pool of media professionals who give of their time and talent.

Sgt. Yates finds that after media representatives say "Yes, we will come out and talk," they also discover that "they are learning themselves about police from what they hear in the classroom." He cites the example of journalists being jolted at the level of upset registered by police participants about the media's application of the word "alleged" in crime coverage stories. In fact, local press reconsidered its use of this term after officers convincingly complained that it was inserted in contexts which cast an unwarranted criticism of police credibility. It was shown that the same story sense could be conveyed, explains Yates, "by simply saying that police charged a person with a crime."

"That is only one minor example of what the media finds out about the police in these sessions," he adds. "Even though they may ride with police, they do not often find out enough about the human side of the officers, and after a class a reporter might say, 'Gee, I had no idea that police feel so strongly about this or that.'"

Journalism professionals assume major responsibilities for the instructional component of Yates' classes. The first day's program features a get-acquainted segment with a guest speaker, followed by a student interviewing practicum, orientation sessions on media relations, an examination of the role of the public information officer, and a review of specific press policy guidelines. Rounding out the opener is a panel discussion, with participants from the radio, television, and print media.

According to Yates, some pragmatic tips come from that panel: "A radio person might tell our officers that they need very little information, but they need it quickly, and a TV representative might say we don't go live that often, but we have very, very tight deadlines, a couple a day, and we need to push for those, because time is important and expensive."

Perceptions are communicated by both sides. "An officer might say, 'I feel very uncomfortable talking with a radio reporter,'" relates Yates. "That officer will explain that he does not know when he is talking on-the-record or off-the-record. Or another might say, 'Gee, the thing I hate the most about newspapers is that they are indelible.' Usually, this first session will be the time that an officer who harbors some problems he had with the media will use to get that problem off his chest. So we prepare the panel that the police audience might be upset and vent it on them, but they always say, 'fine, we are not thin-skinned.'"

Subjects covered on Tuesday include principles of communication, exploration of the roles of the police reporter and the functions of the investigative reporter, preparation of the press release, and the logistics of conducting the press conference. That day ends with a close look at how editorials and opinion pieces are generated. (This subject of media commentary, especially as it involves police and law enforcement-related topics, was also a key concern of the Massachusetts State Police officers participating in the police/media class detailed earlier in this discussion. They wanted to know who wrote the editorials, and whether reporters' opinions were factored in the process.)

Wednesday is field-trip day. The morning is consumed giving officers first-hand viewing of electronic media operations; they spend an afternoon at a newspaper. Interactive learning experiences are emphasized. "We do not insult officers by giving them just a so-termed tour," says Yates. Specific assignments are implemented within the field-trip framework. For example, police participants are given a local and a national story to focus upon early in that day, and they watch closely how it is developed, played by the radio, television, and print reporters they visit.

They go behind the scenes at a television station to view the assembling and airing of a news broadcast. Small group sessions with newspaper personnel are scheduled. In round-robin formations, officers will sit with print reporters and editors at computer terminals, learning about such assignments and editing techniques as who devises the headlines, why, and how.

They also are invited to listen in on the newsroom's daily news conference, during which the various editors will lobby for inclusion of certain stories in that day's edition. These exercises are designed to provide an insight into news judgments, and the realities of time and space limitations. The managing editor and key staff people will then stay and entertain questions from the officers.

Cross-education is a key to a comfortable co-existence.

During the visits with the electronic media, some law enforcement participants find themselves challenged by an occurrence that seems impromptu, but is actually the product of some planning on the part of Yates and cooperating media personnel. "Early in the day on Tuesday, they are given some information on a high speed chase and are told to familiarize themselves with it," he says. "Then, while on tour, one of them will be singled out and subjected to an ambush interview on this incident by a radio or broadcast journalist. It is amazing how some will handle it so smoothly, and then there will be some scenarios that have us falling out of our seats laughing."

Having fun is certainly not frowned upon in this course, and the exercise which combines work and constructive play is the one which ends the week on Friday afternoon. But Thursday's intervening curriculum is a bridge to this finale, and it is one of assessments and analyses. There is a review of the field trip, followed by a presentation from attorneys on the fair trial versus free press issues, with legal representatives drawn from both law enforcement and media.

The next segment addresses police/media relations specifically keyed to crisis and hostage situations. The day winds down with the showing of the videotapes taken during the student practicum of the first day and those surprise reactionary interviews of the field visits, with tips being shared for effective interviewing strategies tailored for demands of print and broadcast.

Sgt. Yates characterizes Friday's events, both preconceived and extemporaneous, as the pinnacle of the course, as far as its participants are concerned. "It is a day when no one ever looks at his watch," he says. "They really, really enjoy this."

"This" is somewhat scripted play of role reversal, during which the police receive a graphic lesson -- sometimes much to their chagrin -- of what it is like to be on the side of information accessing, rather than dissemination.

"The scenario involves a controversial situation that occurs on the jurisdictional line which has two police agencies responding," he recounts. The class is divided up into teams to cover it. Each police agency has a press conference on opposite sides of the town, so the teams have to split up for their coverage. They are assigned to write and "air" on tape a two-minute TV script and to write a story for print with a headline.

The spirit of competition runs real, and it runs high as rival teams vie for the most complete, compelling and accurate version of events. Sometimes the coverage is factual; sometimes, well, it is compounded of fact and fiction. A panel of media experts grades the officers on their performances.

Frequently, the teams will argue with the press evaluators, vehement in their insistence that they did not invent information or a quotation. "Then we look back at the videotape of the press conference to find out that yes, it is true, that this person never did say that," says Yates.

Often the cops-become-reporters will complain that they did not have enough time to complete their assigned tasks. In short, among other things, summarizes the Louisville sergeant, police learn "they can make the same kind of mistakes they accuse the media of making, and they learn it is not easy to get all the information in under pressure of deadline."

Educational plans such as the one created by Sgt. Yates afford the police and the media views from windows into one another's world; and in the case of at least the Louisville experience, such apertures remain open after the close of the course. In addition to the regular scheduling of this study unit, bimonthly meetings are held between police and media to, in Yates' words, "help reinforce, monitor, question, and continually evaluate our progress as it affects the ability of the police and the news media to do their job on a day-to-day basis." In fact, the 40-hour course itself grew out of such meetings, originally called because of the tension existing between police and press in that jurisdiction.

"The reason the police took the first step and asked the news media if they would be interested in attending weekly, early morning, and informal meetings was the fact that our relationship with the media was strained," says Yates. "We meet them more than halfway and sit down over coffee on a regular basis to talk things out. We had no idea that such a meager beginning would have such a positive and long-lasting impact on future police/media relationships."[6]

A central goal of the effort is to prevent problems from festering between these meetings, and to keep open channels through which they can be attended to immediately. Individual officers who have criticism or correction are encouraged to first contact the reporter who covered the story in question, and if no resolution is negotiated at that level, to then contact the reporter's editor. If that later outreach fails, Yates recommends a sit-down with the reporter, editor, and appropriate officials from the law enforcement agency.

"Many times these concerns," elaborates Yates, "are resolved and are never mentioned at our regular bimonthly meetings. After all, that's what this effort is all about -- learning to resolve our differences through understanding. If we are successful, then our bimonthly meetings do not turn into bitch sessions over unresolved problems that have been neglected."

Yates also keeps the media closely informed of potential changes in police policy that could affect them. Their input is requested. "If it is a policy that will not work on a practical level, then why must it?" he asks. "We are not asking the media's permission. We are asking their opinion."[7]

The Standard Gravure Shootings: The Policies Worked

There is tangible proof -- unfortunately demonstrated in the most tragic of circumstances -- that dedication to improvement in police/press interactions has paid off in Louisville.

On September 14, 1989, Joe Wesbecker, 47, a worker on disability leave from the Standard Gravure Printing Company, armed with an AK-47 assault rifle, entered that plant and shot 21 co-workers, leaving nine dead before he took his own life.

Yates lists the "firsts" recorded in the wake of the terrible spree. It was the first time Louisville police, emergency medical crews, local hospitals, police chaplains, and local media ever responded to an incident of this magnitude. It would measure the mettle of all.

"Police/media relations will never be more tested than in an incident of major news importance, especially with the added attention from national and even international news," says Yates.

Clear and collaborative press policies were in place. They were adhered to even in the heat of the moment, and the needs of local reporters were not made subservient to those of the visiting networks. A media information post was set up in a courtyard next to the printing plant, in fulfillment of Louisville police/press guidelines that allow for two perimeter lines at all scenes -- the outer for the general public, the inner for the news media. "We don't do this because the media has any more 'right' of access than does the public, but because in the spirit of cooperative understanding, we recognize that they have more of a 'reason' to be there," contends Yates.

Yates, as is his custom, played his role as he interprets the function of the public information officer: being a facilitator, interviewing the on-scene commander, then making himself the interviewee, providing the information that could be released, refusing to dwell on the data that could not, explaining why such data had to be withheld, and putting reporters in touch with specific investigators.

Because the perpetrator was dead, and police had no one to prosecute, certain customary restrictions also did not apply. For example, media representatives were allowed to view all the guns and ammunition Wesbecker carried and were permitted to attend and report on the test firing of those weapons on the police range.

The media, in turn, helped the Louisville police to document the event in a training and information video. TV stations contributed aired news tapes which were combined with police videotapes and edited with the assistance of broadcast professionals. Yates drafted a script, and a TV anchor did the voice-over. The video has subsequently served as a powerful instructional aid for many audiences.[8]

This, then, was a crisis which offered verification that police and media could cooperate to serve the public, guided by policies carefully crafted in calm, that worked like well-oiled machinery in the turbulence of the emergency scene.

In Detroit, a Different Scenario

Not so in the case of the crash of Northwest Airlines Flight 255 at Detroit Metropolitan Airport in August of 1987. The clash of police and press at that disaster scene -- in fact the basic issue itself of media access to that site -- dramatically demonstrated to both law enforcement officials and journalists that confusion and confrontation benefit no one, and that preventive measures were in order.

"This was a traumatic event for police officers; it was a traumatic event for media," recalls Steve Haines, staff photographer for *The Detroit News*. "Communication between police and press was very, very poor. For two days we were not allowed on the scene. While the media was kept back, we watched Red Cross officials touring. It was asinine."

Haines, who had served as chair of the National Press Photographers Association Police-Press Committee, adds that "we got information by hook or by crook or by any means;" and although the police and airport officials were "infuriated" when the information was inaccurate, he ties its unreliability to the lack of a central dissemination source.

"At one point," he recounts, "a TV station was invited to the scene to use the lights so investigators could see, and they were told not to shoot the scene, but they did, and some had this footage and some did not."

Chaos and ill will were generated, and Haines, his editor, and the paper's picture editor decided to discuss their concerns with airport personnel.

"When they found out we did not want to cut their throats, but we just wanted better access, a disaster plan was written up," says Haines. "It is true that if they are not funneled to the right area, some media personnel will get in the way and a real danger will be posed, and police do not need to be hassled when they are too busy to deal with us. What we wanted was to get close enough to the scene to see, hear, and make an account."

Out of the communications snafu of the Detroit disaster came the constructive project of forming police-press committees in that state. Haines now chairs the Police-Press Committee of Michigan, which has been the impetus for bringing media and emergency services personnel together in both wide-ranging round-the-table discussions and in the more structured conference format. In general, Haines feels, police are somewhat more interested than the press in improving the relationship. He believes such guardedness is tied to ethical perceptions of the reportorial function.

"There is an attitude on the part of media that they might have to give up something," he says. "They feel that they have to be adversary, that they have to be a watchdog; and if you are a friend, you cannot be a watchdog. You have to bring some stories to light; and if you are too close, you cannot do your job."

But Haines is also "amazed" at how much information both sides are willing to swap once they do face each other at these meetings, and mutual apprehensions begin to dissipate. He hears common themes of concern: "The press talks about wanting to be able to get hold of police sources who are accountable. The gag-order mentality of some patrolmen is driving them nuts. You know, they are saying, 'you covered that accident, officer; why can't you tell us this or that about the car?'"

The Michigan committee, the majority of whose membership are law enforcement personnel (Haines pegs the percentage at "about 85"), publishes a newsletter which accepts articles from across the country dealing with police/media relations and associated topics. A recent issue, for example, contained excerpts from a transcript of a police/press panel held on the East Coast. During that program, police and press photographers from the state of New Hampshire debated the controversial publication of shots depicting suffering victims. How traumatic is it for loved ones to view them? How traumatic is it, in fact, for the firefighter or the police officer to view them and relive the emotions of the event? Can the socially redeeming qualities of the picture -- that is, its potential to deter similar tragedies -- compensate for such pain? These were some of the concerns aired in the context of developing the subjects of First Amendment rights and access problems.[9]

Photojournalists are, in fact, a constituency very, very interested in police/media relations because of the vulnerability they feel as often the first responding media representatives to newsworthy scenes where the emotional climate is volatile. In a 1989 survey of National Press Photographers Association members (526 queried, 266 responding), 64.9 percent reported experiencing hostile encounters in that year, and 91.2 percent claimed the same during the course of their careers.[10]

An article in which this study is amplified, as well as five other studies on police/media relations subjects, were collected into a white paper which was published in 1991 under the auspices of the National Press Photographers Association and The Gannett Foundation. "We have gotten excellent feedback on this effort," says Haines, from police departments in such places as Tennessee, Virginia, Maryland, and Los Angeles.

In Los Angeles, These Efforts Are Echoed

Los Angeles is another area where photojournalists are spearheading efforts to defuse police/press tension and draft access guidelines that will permit both sides to perform their functions with minimal interference and maximum regard for the safety of all involved.

Joe Messinger, president of Press Photographers Association of Greater Los Angeles, says a subcommittee on media access and information is compiling a media guidebook which will not repeat policy already defined by the California Police Chiefs Association, but will contain guidelines on topics not yet covered.

The formation of that subcommittee came in response to what Messinger terms "the injustices I was seeing around me."

"My friends were being arrested while trying to do their jobs," he says. They were spending vast amounts of money to defend themselves. One free-lance photographer lost her home to attorney's fees. Others were staffers working for less than courageous employers who wouldn't step in unless the case was a civil suit in which the employer was also named."

"Ninety-eight percent of law enforcement people are pretty much on [the media's] side."

Messinger hopes the guidebook, which will have the input of emergency services personnel, will "prevent future incidents of denial of access, unlawful confiscation of film and equipment, and unlawful declaration of an area as a crime scene in order to deny access to news media."

He is also not without criticism of the action of those he tags as "the unthoughtful among our own ranks." "They are," he continues, "the photographers who climb cliffs on rescues and end up needing rescue themselves, thereby interfering with the operation. They are the helicopter pilot who, in jockeying for a camera position, gets too close to a brush fire and fans the flames toward firefighters."[11]

Although Messinger and his fellow committee members, who include photographers and a reserve Deputy Sheriff, decry what they perceive as unfair treatment by law enforcement officials, he is quick to assert that the offenders represent a very small sample of the police population.

"Ninety-eight percent of law enforcement people are pretty much on our [the media's] side," he contends. "That is, they know we do a service. The one or two percent of the problem causers are either older cops with a chip on their shoulder, maybe having been hurt by the media in the past, or certain energetic younger guys." He relates an anecdote in which the stonewalling figure was a police officer who was trying so hard to be the good soldier, he turned literalism into lunacy: "A firefighter told me of going to the scene of a fire and being informed by an officer that he could not go beyond that checkpoint because 'no one is allowed beyond that point.' The firefighter had to persist and say, 'Look at those engines behind me; what do you think we have come for?'"

The College Classroom:
Let's Start on the Ground Floor

Police-press committees such as those headed by Haines in Detroit and Messinger in Los Angeles, and police-media courses such as those being taught by Sgt. Yates in Louisville and Faulkner across the country, join law enforcement and journalism professionals to troubleshoot problems and to write new prescriptions for healthier interactions. But can educational programs be conceived at more elementary levels that will keep the fires from being fanned, which will prevent that officer at that checkpoint from taking that posture, or that photographer on that cliff from engaging in foolhardy maneuvers?

Based on the reception of courses I have designed primarily targeted to the undergraduate population of Northeastern University, Boston, Massachusetts, I believe this to be true. Under the sponsorship of modest in-house grants, I have created two seminars, inter-disciplinary in focus, modeled on the cross-education design. The major objective of the one entitled "Police and the Media" is to bring criminal justice majors and journalism majors together in the same classroom to shape their perspectives, to give each a realistic picture of the working world of the other: the respective ethics, goals, limitations, frustrations and stressors. Detective-Lieutenant Richard E. Kelly of Massachusetts State Police (co-founder of that agency's Psychological Services Division), who co-teaches the course with me, says he sees it as helping "seed the fields of law enforcement and journalism with newcomers who will not allow myths and imaginary conflicts to put wedges in police-media relationships."

Among the instructional objectives of "Police and the Media" are: (1) challenging the pervasive image of police as unreasoning strangleholders of information and journalists as self-serving raiders on their fortress, (2) exploring the negative stereotypical views that police officers and journalists tend to hold of one another's profession, and (3) examining the areas in which both groups are justifiably likely to remain adversarial, and those in which they might work harmoniously for the public benefit.

Cross-education projects, akin to the ones employed by Sgt. Yates in Louisville, encourage the students to be both observers and participants in the professional settings of law enforcement and journalism. Journalism majors spend on-the-job time with police officers, watching them, riding with them, interviewing them. Criminal justice majors do the same with police beat reporters. Results are analyzed and presented in reports that are shared with the class at large. There is a videotaped role-playing project, in which journalism majors play police officers, and criminal justice majors act as reporters: the former assigned to control a critical incident, the latter asked to cover it.[12]

Cross-education projects encourage the students to be both observers and participants in the professional settings of law enforcement and journalism.

At the seminar's end, students have reconsidered the presumptions that fed their prejudicial views. They are, consequently, less likely to perpetuate them in their respective careers. In fact, both Lt. Kelly and myself have been contacted by some of them after graduation and have been told they have applied these "lessons" in police/media relations in their reporting and policing duties.

The other course devised, titled "Reporting Techniques in Law Enforcement," is not intended to convert attitudes, but to squarely and directly apply skills employed by journalists to law enforcement settings. The curriculum is keyed to criminal justice majors and to journalism majors interested in training for a police-related public information function. Again, the participation of law enforcement professionals is necessary for the course's validity, and to increase its credibility, especially to students enrolled who are working police officers.

The informing concept is simple: communication skills and techniques essential to reporters are equally as essential to law enforcement officials when they are, in fact, operating as "reporters" themselves. Because research (which includes samples gathered from agencies in several states) indicates there is significant variance in report-writing approaches, a representative organizational scheme was selected. And the instruction focused primarily on the basics of clear communication, central no matter what the format. Police officers from two different agencies, who have taught report writing in their respective academies, agreed to donate their time as consultants. They guest lectured, aided in creating scenarios as practical exercises, assisted in grading, and were available to me for checking out practicums I scripted to assure that proper law enforcement procedures were followed.

Students who had been or were currently employed by law enforcement agencies cited as most useful lectures and hands-on projects which improved the clarity, concision, and precision with which they wrote. They also earmarked organization of data as the single most difficult communications task. They found the application of the traditional journalistic inverted pyramid -- priority presentation of the most important information -- a technique helpful to them both in gathering facts at an emergency scene and packaging them for formal expression.

Also relevant, they decided, were some typical patterns used by journalists to interview subjects. A lecture was presented defining directive and non-directive interviewing, the former consisting of very specific questions, designed to elicit very specific answers, the latter encouraging a more open-ended, conversational approach geared to promote the interviewee to open up. In a videotaped, role-playing project then assigned the class, students acting as police officers, without being cued, appropriately applied these interview modes to fit the occasion. For example, in the case of a domestic violence call, the officers used the non-directive approach and used it well, making the victim feel less victimized and more in control. Conversely, at an accident scene, witnesses received directive interviewing, again perhaps the most effective way for the officer to impose order at the scene and gather the definitive information needed for the official report.

Also as part of the interviewing segment, a veteran police officer, an expert interviewer in cases of child abuse and sexual crimes against children, shared her experiences and her strategies for gathering information from child victims and witnesses. The criminal justice majors learned, just as journalism majors learn, that effective questioning is not a slap-dash, one-mode approach. It is, rather, a constellation of techniques which, when executed with sensitivity for the subject, can maximize information gathering and serve well the respective police and reportorial functions.

This is early-on cross-education, where police and journalists can step into one another's setting for benefits that can be mined down-the-road. "Cross-education is as important today as it was a decade ago," says Melissa Faulkner. "You need to have a continuous dialogue. If that could be accomplished before both get to their professional environment, you would see changes in the attitudes of both groups. Police would not have the hard and set stance, and both sides would better understand. Police/media courses should be part of the curriculum for both prospective police and journalists, a required course for both sides."

If law enforcement and media professionals such as Faulkner, Yates, Haines and Messinger continue to be dedicated to their missions and inspire imitation among their counterparts, the future of police/media relations in this country will be far more promising than its past. And such potential is there.

Faulkner is scheduling the appearance of journalists in her police training sessions whenever she has willing press representatives.

Haines is urging professional journalists to get into cadet training classes, and police professionals to participate in training journalists. His police/press groups want to work with community colleges and universities to incorporate police/media relations training into curriculum. Sgt. Yates is considering offering a Media II course in Louisville, designing it for college credit, increasing the complexity and sophistication of techniques taught. (In fact, for several years, such multi-level courses have been part of the offerings at the Institute of Police Technology and Management, University of North Florida, attracting both civilian and sworn public information officers nationally and from Canada.)

Indeed, these programs and plans are most encouraging signs that police and press professionals at the training forefront will not let their efforts stagnate in an early stage of success. There is still much work to be done if police and press are to remain in a relationship so appropriately defined by Faulkner's term of "enlightenment."

Cross-education is a key to comfortable coexistence. It can lead law enforcement officials and journalists to that meeting ground in the middle of the road where prudent balances and compromises can be struck. It can help assure that cooperation, not confrontation, remains the watchword for police/media interactions for the decade of the 1990s and, yes, hopefully beyond.

NOTES

1.   Kiernan, Michael. "Covering the Police Beat," in Kelly, Patricia A. (Ed.): *Police and the Media: Bridging Troubled Waters*. Springfield, Ill.: Charles C. Thomas, 1987, p. 74.

2.   Gilmor, Donald M. "Crime Reporting: From Delirium to Dialogue" in Kelly, Patricia A. (Ed.), *Police and the Media: Bridging Troubled Waters*. Springfield, Ill.: Charles C. Thomas, 1987, p. 197.

3.   Ragsdale, James M. "On the Police/Press Connection," in Kelly, Patricia A. (Ed.), *Police and the Media: Bridging Troubled Waters*. Springfield, Ill.: Charles C. Thomas, 1987, p. 229.

4.   Palmer, Thomas. "Truth Elusive When Mood is Explosive," *The Boston Globe*, December 2, 1991, p. A24.

5.   Faulkner, Melissa M. "In-Service Training: Current Trends," in *Police/Media Relations and Victim's Rights*. National Press Photographers Association and The Gannett Foundation, 1991, pp. 34-35.

6.   Yates, Carl. "The Standard Gravure Shooting, the Relationship in Action," in *Police/Media Relations and Victim's Rights*. National Press Photographers Association and The Gannett Foundation, 1991, p. 9.

7.   Ibid., p. 11.

8.   Ibid., p. 12.

9.   Haines, Steve. "Issues of Access Pose Dilemma for Police and the Media," in *PPC Monitor*, Vol. I, p. 1.

10. Sherer, Michael D. "Working Rights of the Press," in *Police Media Relations and Victim's Rights*. National Press Photographers Association and The Gannett Foundation, 1991, p. 15.

11. Messinger, Joe. "Media Access and Information," in *PPC Monitor*, Vol. I, pp. 2-3.

12. Kelly, Patricia A. "College Course Helps Dispel Perceptions about Police-Media Relations," in *PPC Monitor*, Vol. I, p. 4.

Chapter 14

The Police Family: A Contemporary View of an Old Problem

The secret to solving problems in the police family revolves around communication and consideration, but genuine commitment still plays the most important role.

by Keene Howard

E ven as the concept of the "traditional" family has changed over the past two decades, the issues surrounding the police family have more dramatically changed. As our social structure places greater demands on the family unit, the problems associated with the police officer and his family are magnified. The problems are the same and yet different of those years ago. But, as we continue into the '90s, we must address these issues in a more contemporary manner.

In order to realistically approach the dynamics of this unique family, the existing differences between this family unit and all others must be established. This chapter will identify specific qualities which contribute to this uniqueness, clarify some of the causes, and offer specific and realistic solutions.

As the spouse of a veteran police officer, I will approach this subject from a somewhat personal standpoint. Through the years of our marriage, our family has made the transition from shift work to the detective bureau to community services to narcotics and back to uniform. With each of his changes, we too had to adjust. Our level of fear and frustration fluctuated almost yearly, depending upon his assignment. However, a common thread ran consistently, regardless of the hours worked, the element of danger, or the rank. That common thread is the pride we feel about the work he does. I know that persons outside the police family have a difficult time understanding the life-style which we live. But he would not change his career choice, nor would I. Police officers contribute more to the daily lives of every individual in society than any other single profession.

The "Police Personality"

Those who have become professional law enforcement officials are truly a rare breed. It is difficult to distinguish between those who had what it takes to be a cop and those who became cop and developed what it takes to be one. Regardless, the police personality is obvious the minute one is encountered (see Thibault's chapter). The general qualities possessed by this individual can sometimes be a source of conflict in the family.

Early in our marriage, we discovered that our professional lives would not be entirely compatible at home. As a teacher of 18 years, I was geared toward "instructing" others as to what to do and how to do it. As a police officer, his mode of operation was "telling" others not only what to do and how to do it, but when to do it ... NOW! This behavior has been indicated by many who have studied police families as a primary source of conflict in the home.

The police personality is obvious the minute one is encountered.

As I stood one evening, pointing my finger with instructions, he quickly noted that he was not a high school student who required total direction for his every move. And, within weeks after our marriage, he was found guilty of treating me like a suspect.

The solution to this problem was a relatively easy one: communication and consideration. Reminding the police officer that he is at home with those who love and trust his judgment is often all that is needed to correct this demanding attitude. Arguing doesn't work. They are too good at it and usually win!

Another quality of the typical police officer is, what I call, "the discover the problem -- solve the problem -- and leave the problem" syndrome. With the exception of long-term investigations, most police officers deal with short-term problems at work. In other words, they answer a call, ask questions, survey the scene, make a decision to arrest or not, and leave -- problem solved! Very few (if any) family situations can be handled so quickly and efficiently. Especially when dealing with children, we, as parents, deal in long-term problems and solutions.

Life is a process, not a case to be closed. Encouraging my police spouse toward a more patient approach has been helpful and effective. Occasionally, he needs to be reminded that there is no "due date" on decisions at home. He often expresses a sense of relief at the thought of such a luxury.

Family discussions about serious matters can be difficult if the police spouse cannot come out of the "interrogation mode." I often control my eye movements so as not to give him the advantage of knowing whether or not my story is completely accurate. The instinctive suspicious nature of the police officer can be especially difficult. I can vaguely remember a time in my life when I trusted people. After living with my husband for several years, I now know that everyone surely has at least one misdemeanor offense on their record, most people use drugs, and all of my friends drive on expired tags, speed regularly, and never attempt to stop on a yellow light. Gentle reminders that everyone is innocent until proven guilty, even in court, has been a lighthearted way to pull my husband out of the dark room with the blinding light and into our hearts filled with confidence and love.

Life is a process, not a case to be closed.

I can truthfully understand the existence of each of the qualities. Police officers work diligently to perfect each of them in the professional sense of the word. It is necessary in order for them to be effective. If families, especially spouses, can recognize the need for the demanding and suspicious qualities at work, understanding their potential existence at home will be easier. Again, communication is the key. We, as spouses, need to be the first to recognize the differences in our mates and defend their right to be different -- not deny it. It is impossible for the spouse to know what he is doing that we don't like, if we don't find a caring way of telling him. After all, allowing for flaws in others is a great way to explain those in ourselves.

"Pick up the Badge; There is a Heart There"

One of the qualities which most police officers who I know possess is one which often gets in their way. This is the persistent need to remain unemotional. Because of the sensitive nature of the work, most officers find it more easily tolerated if they do not become emotionally involved with each situation. Therefore, they learn a behavior which is difficult to turn on and off.

In a marriage, regardless of the profession of the spouses, sharing and being open is essential. Spouses often complain that their police husbands are unable to show emotion which, in their own eyes, might label them weak. Just recently, a retiring officer who we know left the department after 25 years. During his retirement reception, he shared several very touching stories which left many of his friends and co-workers with a tear in their eye. And, consequently, he shed a tear. With his family, later that evening, he said with frustration that he should have never shown such emotion. "Cops don't cry," he said.

> *I encouraged each officer to pick up his or her badge and look under it. The discovery was to have been that there is a heart under there which is bigger and more giving than in most individuals.*

Very recently in my career, I was actively involved with our police department in the training of officers from across the country to teach a drug abuse prevention curriculum, "Project D.A.R.E." One of the most impressive characteristics of almost every officer we trained was not only the ability but, more importantly, the need to share and show emotion. Many officers did not come to the training with this attribute evident. But, within a short time, they became so involved in the reality of their own personal desire to help children, they could not contain their feelings. During one particular session for which I was responsible, I encouraged each officer to pick up his or her badge and look under it. The discovery was to have been that there is a heart under there which is bigger and more giving than in most individuals. Why else would someone choose to do what they do?

I have found that officers in general are sensitive, caring individuals who have chosen a service profession in order to help people. The problem remains, however, that society has imposed an image of the "tough cop," which prevents this superior quality to be evident. Therefore, the spouse must take responsibility for emotional release. We cannot allow this image to create a static resistance to our love and support. Men especially need the constant reminder that "Cops can cry, and good ones do!" Their ability to encounter their own emotions will provide for more give-and-take at home as well as with their friends.

"Waiting ... Wondering"

The wife of a police officer must deal with the everyday challenge of surviving the endless anxieties and doubts which accompany this honorable yet often thankless job. She knows only too well that the job must many times be her husband's top priority, because it is in allowing this priority to exist that he will, as well. For, in the isolated world of the police officer and his family, survival truly is the name of the game. However, it is usually the officer alone who the community worries about surviving. And surely enough, he is the one who puts his life on the line every minute of every day at work. But while he is protecting and serving the community, there is usually a family waiting, wondering, and surviving. I have learned to deal with many of the built-in problems by simply trusting that every day when he leaves, he will also come home. I learned early on that I must believe in his ability to protect, not only our community but himself as well.

This particular problem exists in every police family I know. It doesn't matter if the assignment is regular patrol, internal affairs, or undercover narcotics investigation -- the mortality of a police officer is constantly on the minds of those who love him. We have found several solutions to short-term fears with which I must deal. If my husband is involved in an especially dangerous situation, he always calls me as soon as the opportunity avails itself. Just a short reminder that he is all right is usually all I need to renew my confidence. This seems like such a small thing, but most spouses will agree that it eliminates so much concern and means so much.

When the job does not exactly end when it is supposed to, those of us waiting at home many times are left eating an already cold dinner. And when a "call-out" takes our officers away from birthday parties, anniversary dinners, and other special events, we again are left holding on to the promise that they'll be home soon. These things just go with the work. We all realize this and try to understand. But, there are compromises which can make this medicine a little easier to take. For example, when these interruptions occur, we make a genuine effort for a prearranged time of "pay back." Short weekend trips alone or a favorite family activity can replace some of the time our officers must devote to others.

"My Dad is a Cop!"

Helping our children understand the scope of their father's work can be another difficult task. They, as do other children, see policemen depicted on television and in movies. More often than not, these portrayals contradict the man they call their dad. Depending upon their age, some children find this very confusing and hard to handle.

Young children are often exempt from many of the fears. They do, however, learn to be quiet during the day when daddy is sleeping, and wish that he were home at night to tuck them in. They are proud of the car and all of its lights. They brag about his job to their young friends, and promise he'll show them his gun.

As they grow older, the unusual hours can become frustrating. When everyone else's dad works normal hours, they must deal with shift work and unpredictable hours. Their dad often has to miss school events and ball games. In addition to that, their friends' parents sometimes say negative things about the police. Again, this is confusing and frustrating.

During the teenage years, having a policeman for a father can be difficult. Inwardly, the children probably remain proud of his career. But their peers may taunt them about the impending restrictions of "living with the law," and pride may turn into something else. Many teens feel constant pressure to never do anything wrong that might embarrass their dad. And, as we know, many resist.

In order to help our children understand and accept their role in this family, we must reinforce the value and importance of their father's work. In their presence, we should demonstrate trust, confidence, and support for our spouse and his commitment to doing what is right. We can teach a respect for law by our own example.

We need to provide opportunities for the children to share their concerns, fears, and frustrations. We should not protect them from the reality of the work, nor should we protect our spouses from dealing with their fears. Allowing them to express what they are feeling will enable them to share positively as they grow older.

"Police Families Together"

Several years ago, I approached our police chaplain about my own insecurities of being the wife of a police officer. Given the statistics about police marriages and divorce, illness and early death of officers, and other rather intimidating evidence, I felt that a support group of some kind would be productive. With his help, and the help of other interested officers, we formed a group called "Police Families Together." Our goal was to provide opportunity for any interested families to get together at various times for general sharing and interaction. We met in each others' homes when convenient and in large facilities when necessary.

Some of the most successful activities involved special holidays. We had a Christmas dinner with Santa for the kids. We went caroling to shut-ins and bought gifts for those less fortunate. All of this was a type of therapy for many of us. Again, the giving quality of the officers was evident, and they were sharing it with their peers.

A necessary but regrettable responsibility which we accepted was that of active support for families of deceased officers. We have provided food, child care, and shoulders to cry on for families whose officers have died.

Once a year, we tried to have an enrichment retreat for officers and their spouses. Our chaplain led the weekend activities. For those who wanted it, there were spiritual opportunities. Others needed only to be away from home with their spouse. But for everyone, it was a wonderful chance to talk about the one thing which we all had in common ... the life of a police officer.

We are a part of a unique family unit which has survived countless problems.

I don't believe that we, as police families, should isolate ourselves from others. I encourage my husband to develop interests away from work and friends away from the department. But anyone who lives with a policeman knows the brotherhood which exists; and as their spouse, we need to accept it. The wife of an officer once complained about her husband's "circle of cop friends" and her dislike for their constant companionship. She made the comment that just because her husband worked with Joe, she certainly didn't have to like Joe's wife and she didn't want to spend every free evening with them. This is true. But we can and should sacrifice occasionally to allow our officers to spend time away from the job with those with whom they enjoy spending their time. The more we involve ourselves with them and their work, the easier it will be to understand and accept our role in all this.

"Protect and Serve ... Each Other"

Those of us who married police officers had an idea of what we were getting into. Those who were married and their spouse then became an officer did not know. Regardless, we are a part of a unique family unit which has survived countless problems for hundreds of years. Some of our conflicts today are the same as those of families before us -- and some of our problems are common only to our times. We live in a society today which offers more resistance to authority than ever before.

We have higher crime rates, increased drug use, and an evidence of a greater lack of respect for law and justice than previously. The "bad guys" have bigger guns than do our officers, and there are more of them.

Police marriages must be based on genuine commitment to succeed. After all, if we do not believe we can make it, we probably will not.

All of these things create a world which is less than peaceful and our spouse is sent out every day to maintain and restore peace. He is supposed to protect and serve our communities with an unconscious bravery. And he is to do it with ultimate respect and consideration for mankind. It is almost more than anyone can do.

Since we are partners to this unique individual called a policeman, we must learn to protect and serve, as well. Ours is a different responsibility, though. We must work diligently for a marriage partnership different from most we know. We can and should nurture our own individuality, also. Many of us are professionals in our own right. We have careers which are demanding and time-consuming. But there are times -- many times -- when we must concede to the priority of our spouse's responsibilities. We cannot let our egos get in the way of his safety or our marriage. We must be willing to compromise in order for consistency to prevail.

Police marriages must be based on a genuine commitment to succeed. After all, if we do not believe we can make it, we probably will not. We must also develop a relentless trust in our partner and the potential for uncompromising relationship. There can be no unspoken fears or uncried tears. We must allow ourselves every opportunity to sustain the uncommon demands of our marriage. We are a part of an exact profession which contributes more to every community's existence than any other. Police families must grow together as they learn to protect and serve ... each other.

Chapter 15

Critical Issues in Campus Policing

Campus police are placed in curious positions because administrators must balance conflicting institutional and social demands of providing safety and security to an environment which exists for free and open inquiry.

Continued impetus for the development of professional campus law enforcement services lies with increased public awareness of campus crime.

What is the role of campus law enforcement?

by R. Bruce McBride

C rime on campus has become an important national issue because of media reports on a number of highly publicized murders which occurred between 1986 and 1990. Concurrently, there has been a rise in the number of civil lawsuits filed by student victims and their parents against institutions for failure to provide and maintain reasonable security measures. These incidents and lawsuits have prompted discussion about campus personal safety and legislative mandates for colleges and universities to publicize security policies and crime statistics. However, the professional literature on personal safety topics focuses primarily on underlying social and legal causes of campus crime, educational programs for crime prevention, victim assistance, and the need for crime statistics.[1] Scant attention has been directed to the role of campus law enforcement departments, who have the primary responsibility for policing and securing the campus environment. This chapter will review the historical development of campus law enforcement since the turn of the century. Based on three service models that exist at this time, the critical issues in campus law enforcement administration are presented on the basis that campus departments operate in a unique organizational culture and environment.

Overview

In the United States, there are over 5,500 institutions of higher education including public and privately-owned universities, colleges, agricultural and technical schools, community colleges, and two-year and technical schools.[2] For this discussion, the term "campus law enforcement" includes three models of service.

Campus Police -- campus personnel who have the same law enforcement powers as municipal and state police officers. Campus police departments provide the same range of law enforcement services as compared to municipal departments. This model is found in the majority of public colleges and universities in the United States. Their jurisdiction, however, may be limited to the campus and building properties owned by the college or university.

Public Safety -- the merger of law enforcement, security, environmental health and parking services. The term "public safety" is very inclusive. For many large public institutions, separate organizational entities for police, environmental safety, fire safety, and parking are found under the umbrella title "division" or "department" of public safety, with a chief or director in charge of each unit. In other institutions, the "department of public safety" performs all these functions but personnel generally do not have law enforcement powers of arrest, execution of warrants, or issuance of state authorized traffic summonses, among others. Depending on campus policies and state legislation, campus public safety officers often are not armed.

Security -- perform mainly watch and guard services, with criminal investigations turned over to state and local police because department personnel do not have law enforcement powers. The security model is found largely in private institutions where security officers serve as employees of the institution or are contracted through private watch and guard agencies.

Development of Campus Law Enforcement

The development of modern campus law enforcement services can be divided into three periods: post-World War II, which witnessed an explosion in institutional growth in both private and public sectors; the late 1960s and early 1970s, which marked increased concern for violence on campus and the decline of "in loco parentis" rules and regulations; and 1980 to 1990, a period marked by increased professionalism of campus police and public safety, and legislative and public concern over campus crime.

The Post-World War II Era: 1945-1965

As discussed by Powell, the first campus to use law enforcement officers was Yale University in 1894.[3] The decision to hire New Haven police officers for campus patrol came about after a series of riots between students and townspeople. Many faculty opposed this development for they perceived that the officers would tell their police colleagues of internal campus business. Two officers -- William Weiser and James Donnelly -- were eventually hired by Yale, but they retained their municipal powers of arrest and eventually were hired by the University. Recalling his experiences as the first campus chief, and foretelling many current mission statements for campus departments, Chief Weiser noted the need for promoting good relations with students in order to win their respect and friendship.[4]

Before World War II, most campuses employed private watchmen or off-duty police officers to keep out outsiders and insure that rules were not broken regarding drinking, curfews, and campus policies. After 1945, national policies regarding economic recovery and the need to provide greater access to higher education resulted in dramatic increases in enrollments and physical plant development, especially for public colleges and universities. As a result, campuses developed more formal security services which performed watch, guard, and fire safety functions. Most typically, security reported to the physical plant or facilities director. Harkening to duties performed during the 19th Century, these security officers were generally concerned with parking problems and the reporting of students who broke campus rules to the Dean of students. The give-and-take interchanges between these watchmen and students gave rise to the "campus cop" -- a popular stereotype as an elderly father figure who, hopefully, would look the other way when it came to student pranks.

Campus Activist Period: 1965 to 1980

During this period, campuses became the centers of social protests against the Vietnam war, antiquated campus governance rules, racial and gender discrimination, and local social issues. Quite often, local and state police were summoned by administrators to end sit-ins, building takeovers, and violent protests. Observers of higher education began discussing the problem of "campus crime" associated with violent protests, increases in sexual assault, and violent felony crimes committed by both students and non-students. At the same time, there was the demise of "in loco parentis" rules and procedures dealing with all aspects of student conduct. Through a series of national and state court decisions, students were accorded the same legal rights and privileges as adults, such including due process in campus disciplinary proceedings. As Kaplan observes, students were no longer second-class citizens under the law. They became recognized under the federal Constitution as "persons" with adult rights and responsibilities.[5]

Observers generally agree that University administrators realized that a campus-sponsored force was needed to address campus crime problems rather than relying on outside police forces.[6] Quite often, when and after outside police responded to an incident, there were complaints of brutality against protestors and curious onlookers. These developments gave rise to established formal police or security bureaucracies and prepared formal policies to deal with campus crime problems. The trappings of these early campus law enforcement organizations included official law enforcement powers, some basic training in police procedures, formal recruitment and selection procedures, building or refurbishing station houses, and purchasing patrol cars, uniforms, and associated police equipment. Although many departments used the title "campus police," they often did not have official law enforcement powers of arrest and detention, and did not have to carry firearms. During this period, the presence of armed police personnel was often viewed by the students and faculty as the antithesis of an environment dedicated to open inquiry and research. Nevertheless, to deal with increased incidents of building takeovers, demonstrations, and disruptions to classroom and research activities, legislatures and boards of trustees adopted formal codes of student conduct to both ensure open academic inquiry and maintain public order. Formal hearing procedures and sanctions, ranging from letters of reprimand to banishment from campus grounds with possible arrest, were developed for students, faculty and visitors.

It was at this time that campus chiefs and directors formed various network groups or were invited to join local and regional police associations for information sharing and training. Soon a national network developed which led to the creation of The International Association of Campus Law Enforcement Administrators in 1958, which is recognized today as the leading association for campus law enforcement administrative concerns. Regional and state associations of campus law enforcement administrators were also created such as the Northeast

College and University Security Association, begun in 1953. Noting the number and concerns of campus law enforcement departments, The International Chiefs of Police, which represents the interests of municipal and state police in this country, allowed campus directors and chiefs to join as full members in the 1980s.

1980 to Present

Campus law enforcement departments continue to professionalize through one of the three campus law enforcement models presented earlier. Aspects of this development include increased personnel selection standards and training, refined operational policies, clarification of law enforcement authority, higher wages and benefits, and a greater participation in the educational environment. Campus police chiefs or directors of public safety today generally report to a senior administrator such as a vice president for administration or student affairs. Many campus police departments often mirror and compete with state and local law enforcement agencies in terms of resources and personnel. In many municipalities, campus police departments provide services for neighborhoods within proximity of campus boundaries. For private colleges and universities, the same dynamics occur with the exception of security officers who have no official law enforcement authority. In many states, however, enabling legislation allows private institutions to create police departments. In others, large private institutions have begun legislative lobbying efforts to obtain peace officer powers for their personnel. Overall, the private security or contract guard model of the post-World War II era is today most often associated with small private institutions and private university hospitals.

While it is unclear whether campus crime has actually increased, there is an ongoing debate on campus safety because of numerous serious violent felony crimes which gained national media attention.

This continued impetus for the development of professional campus law enforcement services lies with increased public awareness of campus crime and continued campus unrest. While it is unclear whether campus crime has actually increased, there is an ongoing debate on campus safety because of numerous serious violent felony crimes which gained national media attention. One such incident resulting in legislative policymaking was the murder of Jeanne Clery at Lehigh University in 1986. Based on allegations of poor security measures in campus residence halls, her parents -- Constance and Howard Clery -- sued the University for failure to maintain security standards. Through monies obtained in an out-of-court settlement, the Clerys formed Security on

Campus, Inc. to serve as a national clearinghouse for campus security problems and to lobby for state and national mandates for security measures. This group was responsible for the passage of several state statutes mandating the reporting of crime statistics and campus security policies to potential students and employees. The group played a pivotal role in the passage of Title II -- The Student Right-to-Know and Campus Security Act, requiring all colleges and universities to immediately report serious incidents of crime to all members of the community, and by September 1992 to make available to students and employees statistics on certain categories of crimes and campus policies regarding security measures and procedures.[7]

Beyond these legislatively mandated security policies, all campuses continue to address current social problems. In his discussion on the campus environment, Boyer speaks of the decline in civility on campus marked by greater incidents of hate crimes against African, Latino and Asian American students, and foreign students and staff.[8] The majority of campus law enforcement departments today have written protocols for responding to these bias crimes. Many campuses must deal with other problems found outside campus boundaries such as gang warfare, homeless persons, and the rise of drug use. Alcohol abuse remains the chief problem in terms of personal abuse and a contributing factor in personal assault and property crimes. Today, most institutions have placed increased restrictions and prohibitions on campus-sponsored events serving alcohol. Increased scrutiny is being placed on fraternities and sororities for injuries and deaths resulting from alcohol abuse and social activities.

Campus administrators continue to be faced with crime and related safety problems caused by the internal and external organizational environment.

Thus, campus administrators continue to be faced with crime and related safety problems caused by the internal and external organizational environment. The topic continues to receive national attention through the media and in state and federal legislative hearings. One national newspaper ran a week-long series reporting crime statistics provided by colleges and universities, individual victim case studies, and a report card rating individual campuses on the basis of crime statistics and number of campus law enforcement personnel.[9] Based in part on the Right-to-Know and Campus Security Act, institutions today must report serious incidents and situations to the campus community within a reasonable time period. Many have initiated crime watch bulletins or police blotter sections in the campus newspaper. In higher education circles, campus crime and personal safety topics continue to remain standard agenda items for state and national professional associations related to college attorneys, student affairs personnel, and administrative staff. Each year, a National Conference on Campus Violence is sponsored by Towson State University on various topics such as crime prevention programs, campus disciplinary procedures, bias crime, and sexual assault.

Organizational Climate Framework

At first glance, there appear to be close operational and organizational structural similarities between municipal and campus law enforcement agencies. There are, however, a number of unique differences, the first being the demographics of a campus environment. The majority of people on a campus are between the ages of 18 and 25 years, and are therefore the primary purposes of research and study for either two to four years, depending on the degree program, and from only September to May. By day and evening hours, this population is augmented by adults who serve in various administrative, teaching and staff functions. For institutions with large campus residence populations, the only visible adults are either residence hall or campus law enforcement staff.

A striking aspect of the campus environment is the organizational culture with traditions that can be traced to the colonial period. Up until the post-World War II era, most American colleges and universities were church sponsored and available only to that segment of the population that had the financial means to pay tuition and fees. These "communities of scholars" were administrated by the faculty, with the campus president often being the first among equals from the faculty ranks. Decisions regarding curriculum, tuition, academic standards, and most aspects of campus life were based on the faculty committee structures, with major decisions arrived at by consensus and spirited debate. As outlined by Delworth, a gradual growth in the number of professional administrative titles, such as dean, registrar, residence life director and other titles, occurred after 1930.[10] Today, while colleges and universities often structurally reflect private and public bureaucracies, the traditions of "the academic community" still remain for the vast majority of institutions. Decisions on most aspects of campus life are based on campus governance deliberations among faculty, students, and administrators. Procedurally, nothing is simply. As department chair of a criminal justice department, the writer spent countless hours in committee debates over the granting of tenure, budgets, and curriculum development.

In a college or university educational environment, one purpose is to question and challenge the status quo -- thus, it is no wonder that the authority and decisions on even the most mundane topics are questioned. Campus law enforcement departments are placed in a curious position because administrators must constantly balance the conflicting institutional and social demands of providing safety and security to an environment which exists for free and open inquiry. Not surprisingly, there remains the continuing debate among campus administrators and students between the use of stringent arrest policies versus the use of internal institutional sanctions to deal with law violators. As discussed by Bordner and Petersen in their early work on campus policing, campus law enforcement remains the operational arm of the administration, and certain laws are enforced less aggressively based on campus policies.[11] It is reasonable to state that all campus law enforcement departments today operate within this same framework. Minor offenses are often referred to campus judicial boards rather than to the criminal justice system for disposition. If the campus judicial board has good practices and procedures, referred cases are handled efficiently and effectively with the objective of protecting the campus community. Because of the current concern for campus crime, felony and misdemeanor complaints will often go through both campus judicial and the criminal court proceedings.

Most campus law enforcement departments generally reflect the community service model postulated by Wilson and later refined in the 1970s by many municipal departments with community or team police programs.

The Community Service Law Enforcement Model

Most typically, a campus police department provides the same range of services as its municipal counterpart: responding and investigating crimes, enforcing state and local (campus) ordinances, providing traffic control and enforcement, and responding to a wide range of non-criminal calls. But because of the unique campus environment, most campus law enforcement departments generally reflect the community service model postulated by Wilson and later refined in the 1970s by many municipal departments with community or team police programs.[12]

In the community service model, the operational philosophy of the department is to provide a wide range of services to the community which include responding to non-criminal calls, increasing crime and safety awareness through a variety of public and media presentations, and having officers interact with the community in all kinds of social and formal situations.[13]

In the 1970s, this community service operational philosophy was adopted by the vast majority of campus law enforcement departments and still continues today. A review of campus law enforcement mission statements would indicate a desire for officers to be part of the campus educational program, to provide crime prevention services, and to offer a wide range of non-police services. Using this as a basis, many institutions, such as the State University of New York, adopted the campus public safety officer concept, which merged security, law enforcement, parking, environmental health and safety, and fire safety operations and services under one organizational entity.

In this decade, campus law enforcement agencies continue to refine these concepts under the titles of "community policing" or "problem-oriented policing."[14] Applying these concepts to campus organizations, underlying factors related to an institution's crime and security problems are solved in consultation with other campus constituencies such as residential life and student affairs. Importantly, patrol officers are given greater individual discretion in addressing problems in the zones or posts where they are assigned. In addition to their normal duties, patrol officers are assigned certain areas of the campus to work with student and faculty groups on crime problems. In a sense, their patrol zones become their turf. Campuses using this problem-oriented approach with specific zone assignment of patrol personnel include Michigan State University and Vanderbilt University.

Continuing Administrative Concerns

Based on this historical and organizational development of campus law enforcement agencies, there are a number of continuing administrative issues that are faced by campus department managers. All departments have one thing in common -- the lack of money. As campus departments do not directly generate income in the form of tuition or research dollars, campus law enforcement administrators compete with other ancillary

supply and service managers for resources. Needless to say, before the
1970s, most departments had low budget and support priority and were
inadequately funded, equipped and staffed. Beginning in the 1970s,
campuses that developed either police or public safety models increased
funding for personnel, office space, and law enforcement related
equipment. In budgeting for campus law enforcement operations, most
institutions historically were reactive rather than proactive, which
means that concerns for staffing, patrol deployment, equipment and
security procedures become of great importance and investment only
after an incident or an expensive tort action.

Current legislative and media concern for campus crime has not
contributed to law enforcement expenditures, mainly because of the
current economic recession and its negative impact on all areas of
campus life resulting in increased tuitions, postponed maintenance
projects, and decreases in services. Campus law enforcement managers
share a similar fiscal paradox with their municipal counterparts --
provide more services with little chances of increased funding. All
institutions, however, are now forced to reassess their campus law
enforcement and residence and student life procedures and policies. At
the same time, campus law enforcement managers are forced to review
their fiscal and operational situations through strategic planning,
performance assessment of patrol personnel and security equipment,
and risk assessment. In addition to these budgetary matters, the
following topics are of continuing concern.

Campus law enforcement managers share a similar fiscal paradox with their municipal counterparts -- provide more services with little chances of increased funding.

Personnel Turnover

A common challenge facing many campus law enforcement administrators lies with recruiting and retaining qualified personnel. Adapting
a concept from Territo's work on police personnel selection, many
departments are faced with the problem of negative personnel retention.[15]
This occurs when over half of patrol personnel leave the department
within two to four years after appointment. This means that the
department must devote a great deal of administrative resources for
recruitment and training processes to staff line positions. As many
officers transfer to municipal and state agencies, remaining personnel in
the campus department develop a poor self-image because their peers
have gone on to municipal or state police where career opportunities are
perceived to be better.

The reasons for negative turnover can vary according to the type of campus law enforcement model. Younger officers working for campuses with security and public safety model programs often view the campus law enforcement employment as a temporary experience before joining the "real police." Campus departments that have adopted the police model also have retention programs for a variety of reasons; the chief items often are noncompetitive wage and benefit scales packages and lack of a planned career ladder.

At first glance, while improved wage and salary benefits appear to be the easy fix for turnover, there are more fundamental issues which must be addressed by campus administrators. Regardless of the service model used, campus law enforcement departments suffer from a "keystone cop" or "campus cop" legacy, discussed earlier in this chapter. For example, in their study of the "DTU Campus Police," Bordner and Petersen found that most officers viewed campus law enforcement employment as a temporary experience before joining the real police. From an occupational subculture standpoint, campus officers in the study viewed themselves as second-class officers in comparison to their municipal peers because they dealt mostly with student service calls. Commenting on the perceptions of the department by the campus community, respondents often bemoaned the fact that they had to constantly explain that they were not "security guards" just simply issuing parking tickets. Aside from these perceptual problems, campus police work was reported to be "dead end" because of the lack of career mobility, challenging tasks, and not being able to do real police work.[16] Until the early 1980s, the majority of campus chiefs and directors were retired from non-campus law enforcement agencies, thus sending a message that one must serve with the "real police" for managerial promotion.

Most officers view campus law enforcement employment as a temporary experience before joining the real police.

The concept of "real police work" in campuses using the security or public safety models today includes the dilemma of responding to serious calls unarmed or without law enforcement powers, or having the campus community failing to acknowledge official authority when officers are indeed legally authorized by the state. A common story often recounted among campus departments is the crime victim or arrestee who wants to talk to the "real police" and not campus security. For departments with the police model, many non-campus law enforcement agencies fail to recognize the official powers of campus departments because their powers are derived from state education laws and not the criminal procedure law.

While recent academic studies on the campus police or law enforcement as a profession are lacking, many administrators informally report that the occupational dynamics reported by Bordner and Petersen still remain, regardless of the service model employed, and despite the revisions in recruitment standards which often include college education, physical agility testing, psychological testing, and a series of oral interviews. The reality is that not all law enforcement candidates will be content to be confined to a campus where the chief mission is to provide services to a student and faculty population. Thus, the campus law enforcement executive must recruit and select community service oriented candidates who also hail from the same state or regional law enforcement labor pool. Pre-employment processes that have been successful to achieve this objective include intensive orientation sessions on campus law enforcement employment, student internship and work programs for persons interested in the field, and group interviews involving campus situations where the candidate makes decisions and takes appropriate action in a campus setting.

Selection of a community service minded person for campus law enforcement is only half of the challenge. Personnel factors that must be addressed by campus agencies to retain qualified staff include employee recognition, training, career ladder paths, and job description designs that provide the "best fit" between the organization's needs and the employee's personal goals. Additionally, searches for managerial positions should be competitive and give preferential treatment for campus law enforcement personnel.

Training

As discussed by Thibault, police training in general has come a long way since the turn of the century when it consisted of recruits being matched with veteran officers to learn the job.[17] Today, most states have regulations for minimum standards which directly impact those campus law enforcement agencies with police or peace officer personnel. Nationally, campus police and public safety departments train their officers in local or regional police training academies. One problem with this multi-agency training is that personnel are not classroom trained or socialized for the campus environment. For example, there is general agreement among campus law enforcement administrators that different methods are used to deal with crime situations in the campus environment. Current programs used to address campus-specific training needs include post-academy training, field training, and specialized in-service training programs for graduates of basic police training courses.

Campuses with security model programs often provide little training except for on-the-job orientation. Administrators at these institutions bemoan the lack of available training programs for the campus environment or the lack of resources. However, as all law enforcement administrators know, officers who do not know how to handle situations because of ignorance are criticized by other campus administrators, the campus community, and often the press. Lack of morale, surges of unnecessary grievances, poor community relations, and liability payments related to tort actions filed by citizens are all negative by-products of little or no training for campus security officers. One training delivery method that can address this problem is regional consortium arrangements among private colleges and universities to pool resources and offer basic and supervisory training for their security officers.[18]

Campus law enforcement agencies share a similar problem with many police agencies in the United States with regard to in-service training. The greatest allocation of training resources in this country is given to entry-level or recruit training with little attention given to planned in-service and specialized training courses over the span of an officer's career. Thibault recommends the phase approach to training whereby courses such as recruit, intermediate, specialized and executive development are offered for officers in a planned fashion during their career.[19]

Ethno-racial Tension and Bias Crime

Educators and social critics historically have recommended a wide range of reforms aimed at providing greater access to higher education for African, Latino, Asian and Native-American students to address long-standing national economic and social problems. Observers and futurists continue to predict that college admissions for the traditional white school age population of 18 to 23 years will decline.[20] As all colleges and universities today seek to attract a diverse student population, the number of these traditionally "under-represented students" has increased. At the same time, the ethnic and racial tension found in cities, towns and villages is also present on campus in residence halls, classrooms, and in interactions with campus law enforcement personnel.

The historical tension between law enforcement personnel and non-white citizens is aptly discussed in the literature on police occupational subculture and police-community relations. What all these observations and studies conclude is that African, Latino, Asian, and other ethnic persons do not receive the same level of courtesy and respect shown to white citizens, that they are more likely to be involved in violent confrontations with police over even routine matters, and that the delivery of services to their communities is comparatively low in terms of efficiency.[21] Not surprisingly, the negative perceptions of campus law enforcement by students mirrors their experiences and perceptions with police either at home or off-campus. As with municipal and state police, there has been an increase in the number of complaints lodged against campus law enforcement personnel for false arrest, discourtesy, and unfair treatment.

As with municipal and state police, there has been an increase in the number of complaints lodged against campus law enforcement personnel for false arrest, discourtesy, and unfair treatment.

Another factor in racial and ethnic relationships with campus law enforcement lies with department and individual officer attitudes and responses toward bias and ethno-racial crimes. For this discussion, bias or ethno-racial crimes are offenses which occur against a person on the basis of his or her race, color, ethnicity, sexual orientation or religion. The majority of these incidents are based on race or sexual orientation and involve harassing letters or notes, phone calls, and sometimes public statements made by persons unknown to the victim. As reported this year by *Campus Security Report*, these incidents included physical assaults of African-American and white student victims for racial reasons, and the distribution of general hate letters and posters which target African-American and Jewish students. Campuses have responded with a number of educational programs and "crisis protocols" to deal with these incidents. Student conduct codes have also been revised to include penalties for bias behavior. As noted in the report, campus anti-harassment rules and regulations often become embroiled in questions about violating First Amendment rights.[22]

The obvious question regarding this issue of ethno-racial tension on campuses is the response and involvement by campus law enforcement departments. In recent years, during both the response and investigation of ethno-racial and bias crime incidents, campus law enforcement personnel, who are most often white males, are accused of siding with whites in disputes. They are also accused of using their police powers, such as arrest and the use of physical force, against African-American and Latino students and staff more quickly in comparison with white students and staff. During the past three years, complaining about brutality and insensitivity in these situations occurred at Southern Illinois University, SUNY at New Paltz, University of New Mexico, and many other institutions.

Many campus law enforcement administrators have taken a proactive stance to counter allegations of this nature. For example, in the SUNY New Paltz incident, seven African-American students and a white female student were arrested for disorderly conduct and resisting arrest after campus and town police responded to a loud radio being played in a dining hall during dinner. The reasons the students were playing the radio as a protest action were based on a number of previous incidents and allegations of unfair treatment of African-American summer students by a campus police administrator, dining hall staff, and other campus staff. Although the arrested students eventually were found guilty of the charges two years after the event, the incident became politicized and resulted in a University-wide Chancellor's review and grand jury proceedings against the eight students.

In response, campus and University-wide public safety staff developed a bias crime and incident response protocol which included increased training for law enforcement staff, the use of student life mediators in disputes, and prompt notification of senior personnel. In many situations, the basic causes for these disputes have nothing to do with campus law enforcement personnel. Most campus law enforcement departments have taken similar steps which include cultural diversity training for all campus first-line personnel, emergency notification procedures, first-response procedures for patrol personnel, and increased formal and informal interactions with students and officers for post-incident reviews.[23]

As the majority of campus law enforcement personnel are white males, campuses have publicly made concerted affirmative action efforts to increase the number of African, Latino and Native-American officers as one means of reducing daily ethno-racial tension on campus. While research in this area is mixed as to whether these programs achieve this objective, campus departments appear to share the same problems with municipal police in recruiting and selecting these persons. Varying by campus and type of service model used, these include all the reasons discussed earlier in the personnel turnover problem coupled by the historical reality that "the police," in general, are viewed as an instrument by non-white persons as a social instrument of oppression.[24]

Campus Unrest

This term, which was coined by the President's Commission in its study of campus violence and shootings at Kent State and Jackson State in the early 1970s, was applied to a wide variety of situations which include demonstrations, building take-overs, picketing, bombings, and criminal acts that occurred in response to racial injustice and the Southeast Asia war.[25] When used today, campus unrest, or the more common term "campus protest," applies to student and faculty actions which disrupt the normal business of the institution in the form of demonstrations, building take-overs, and the building of shantytowns. Incidents of this nature are generally nonviolent, and their effect on the institution varies by the dynamics of the issue, the personalities of the main actors involved, the extent of media attention, and final resolution of the issue among administrators and protestors. During this past year, campus protest situations occurred throughout the United States for a variety of reasons. These included the non-appointment of certain faculty, United States foreign policy, research on laboratory animals, pro-life versus pro-choice regarding family planning and abortions, the use of force and arrests by campus police against certain groups, sexual assault policies and incidents, increases in tuition and fees, and multi-cultural diversity in the curriculum. At large university centers, protests over these and other issues are a frequent occurrence and daily part of campus life.

Based on many experiences in the 1970s, campus law enforcement administrators use passive response methods to deal with situations, including non-deployment of uniform officers, mediation by student affairs personnel, and strict guidelines on the use of force if police action is taken. Generally, campus and outside law enforcement personnel are used only as a last resort in cases where the protest activity becomes violent. Nevertheless, the planning and monitoring of protest situations consume personnel budgets for overtime and distract departments from daily patrol and crime prevention programs. Returning to the discussion on campus law enforcement personnel selection and management, these incidents require a well-trained department who can positively interact with campus faculty and students.

Of equal concern to administrators at large campuses are those events which invite large amounts of people such as sporting events, concerts, speeches by controversial public figures, and VIP visits. As outlined by Hartsock and Herdt, a great deal of planning must go into policing these activities which include traffic control, securing for VIPs, rowdy behavior, use of alcohol and drugs by attendees, protest actions by political groups, interactions and coordination with other law enforcement agencies, and so on.[26]

Conclusion

National and state legislation regarding the reporting of campus security policies and crime statistics has not, for the most part, resulted in campus law enforcement departments receiving greater allocations of fiscal resources, staff, and equipment.

Although campus law enforcement departments share many commonalities with municipal and state police, they are functionally unique because of the campus environment. Attention has been focused on campus law enforcement operations because of legislative and media concern for campus crime incidents and campus safety. The majority of departments were conceived during the late 1960s and early 1970s based on campus unrest over United States foreign policy, racial discrimination, campus governance, and local social issues. The profession of the police and public safety service model is a recent development based, in part, on the institutional need for safety and security of staff, students and visitors, and the reluctance of outside police forces to become involved in daily campus life.

Recent national and state legislation regarding the reporting of campus security policies and crime statistics has not, for the most part, resulted in campus law enforcement departments receiving greater allocations of fiscal resources, staff, and equipment. In fact, the present economic recession has forced campus managers to assess basic department components such as services, staffing, and security technology. These legislative developments, however, have forced all institutions to critically review their department and operational policies in connection with residence hall and student life activities, and to conduct campus crime prevention planning and educational programs for all members of the campus community. Colleges and universities with the security services model have the additional task of collecting and reporting campus crimes. Up to now, few security departments voluntarily reported offenses to the Uniform Crime Report or to state crime statistic agencies.

Based on the three service models presented, critical management issues were presented which included personnel turnover, funding, training, ethno-racial violence, and campus protests. Many of these issues are related to the sense of second-class status delegated to campus law enforcement departments and personnel by the campus community and the police occupational subculture. As suggested throughout this discussion, there is a need for academic inquiry into all areas of campus policing which would assist in discussing and addressing these management issues.

Of the three service models presented, campus police departments continue to professionalize and refine their law enforcement operations mainly in the community service or problem-oriented police philosophy conceived in the 1970s. Administrators of these departments report new and innovative ideas in such areas as security technology, campus community-police relationships, student patrols, patrol tactics, and responding to special crime problems. Additionally, many departments have completed or are planning for state or national law enforcement accreditation, which involves a self-evaluation and external review of policies and practices under the aegis of state police commissions or the Commission for the Accreditation of Law Enforcement Agencies, Inc.[27]

Departments with the public safety model, meanwhile, are assessing their present operations regarding the merger of law enforcement, security, parking, environmental health and safety, and fire safety. This, in part, is because of the specialization in qualifications and training that have occurred in the areas of environmental health and safety and fire safety with regard to Occupational Safety and Health Act compliance, state and local fire code compliance, state right-to-know laws regarding hazardous materials in the workplace, and the training of first-response personnel in hazardous materials situations. For the most part, there are few, if any, public safety personnel who perform all the above tasks under one job description. Many public safety departments entitled public safety are actually police departments or security departments that have adopted the title but not the operational tenets of the model.

Campus security departments face extraordinary challenges especially with regard to personnel selection and training. In many states, security organizations have come under criticism for the lack of hiring and training standards and questionable operations practices. In addition to providing crime statistics, campus security departments face the additional dilemma of responding to the law enforcement needs of the campus community. In New York, for example, several large private institutions with security department operations are considering law enforcement powers for their officers in order to provide a prompt response for crimes on campus. This is not to suggest that all campuses should consider replacing their security personnel with sworn officers. The security service model is very appropriate for those campuses that have the availability of a police response both for crimes in progress and criminal investigation follow-up.

NOTES

1. Smith, Michael C. *Coping With Crime on Campus.* New York: Collier Macmillan, 1988, pp. 93-117. Sherrill, Jan M. and Siegel, Dorothy G. (Eds.), *Responding to Violence on Campus.* San Francisco: Jossey-Bass, 1989, pp. 17-97.
2. State University of New York, Office of Institutional Research: "Comparative Data Base on Post-Secondary Institutions in the United States," December 1991.
3. Powell, John W. *Campus Security and Law Enforcement.* Boston: Butterworths, 1981, pp. 3-4.
4. Ibid., p. 4.
5. Kaplan, William A. *The Law of Higher Education.* San Francisco: Jossey-Bass, 1978, p. 175.
6. International Association of Campus Law Enforcement Administrators. *The Campus Law Enforcement Administrator: A Definition of Role in Higher Education Administration*, 1982, p. 5.
7. Student Right-to-Know and Campus Security Act, Public Law 101-542, 1990.
8. Boyer, Ernest. "Address on Campus Climate." SUNY Albany: School of Education, November 1990.
9. *USA Today*, Vol. 9, December 7, 1990, pp. 6a-7a.
10. Fenske, Robert H. "Historical Foundations of Student Services," in Ursala Delworth, Gary Hanson and Associates, *Student Services: A Handbook for the Profession*, 2nd ed. San Francisco: Jossey-Bass, 1990, pp. 5-24.
11. Bordner, Diane C. and Petersen, David M. *Campus Policing: the Nature of University Police Work.* Lanham, MD: University Press, 1983, pp. 206-214.
12. Wilson, James Q. *Varieties of Police Behavior.* Cambridge: Harvard University Press, 1968, pp. 200-226.
13. Thibault, Edward A.; Lynch, Lawrence M.; and McBride, R. Bruce. *Proactive Police Management*, 2nd ed. Englewood Cliffs: Prentice-Hall, 1990, p. 212.
14. Goldstein, Herman. "Improving Policing: A Problem-Oriented Approach," *Crime and Delinquency*, Vol. 25, 1979, pp. 236-258. Spelman, William and Eck, John E. "The Police and Delivery of Local Government Services: A Problem-Oriented Approach," *Police Practice in the '90s.* James Fyfe (Ed.). Washington: International City Management Association, 1989, pp. 55-72.

15. Territo, Leonard; Swanson, C.R. Jr.; and Chamelin, Neil C. *The Police Personnel Selection Process.* Indianapolis, IN: Bobbs-Merrill, 1977, pp. 8-9.

16. Bordner and Petersen, pp. 66-75.

17. Thibault, et al., pp. 318-324.

18. Renesslaer Polytechnic Institute, Department of Public Safety. "Basic Campus Public Safety Program Offered by Capital District Consortium." Troy, New York, August 1991.

19. Thibault, et al., pp. 334-342.

20. Morales, Thomas and Wallace, Jeffrey J. "Towards the Cultivation of Pluralism: A Report Prepared by the University Task Force on the Cultivation of Pluralism." Albany: SUNY Central Administration, 1990, pp. 1-2.

21. McBride, R. Bruce. "Perceptions of Discrimination Within Occupational Socialization Processes As Held By Newly Appointed Police Officers in Selected New York State Police Departments." Unpublished dissertation, SUNY at Albany, 1986, pp. 18-21.

22. "Racism and Race Incidents on Campus: An Update," *Campus Security Report*, Vol. 3, No. 3, March 1991, pp. 5-10.

23. Kern, Douglas. "A Four-Step Response Model to Bias Crime." Unpublished paper, Albany, New York: SUNY Public Safety, 1990.

24. McBride, p. 38.

25. "President's Commission on Campus Unrest," *Campus Unrest.* Washington: Government Printing Office, 1970, p. 19.

26. Hartsock, J.R. and Herdt, Peter J. "Police and Security Planning for Special Events at the Ohio State University," *Campus Law Enforcement Journal*, Vol. 19, No. 2, March-April 1989, pp. 18-20.

27. Behan, C. "The Accreditation Process," *Police Practice in the '90s.* James Fyfe (Ed.) Washington: International City Management Association, 1989, pp. 124-134.

Chapter 16

Criminal Investigation Trends

Most strategies to fight crime have failed because they have defined crime as a police problem rather than a community problem.

How can police integrate crime prevention initiatives with investigative crime control activities of traditional policing?

Is law enforcement willing to challenge conventional wisdom in the vital area of criminal investigation? If detectives can no longer be solely responsible for investigating and closing criminal cases, then who is?

by: **Elizabeth M. Watson**
William A. Young

During the past several years, police practitioners have taken critical, internal looks at their own operations and have asked themselves, "How can we better serve our communities?" This introspection has fueled a change process that has become known in various forms as community-based policing. It is characterized, perhaps primarily, by the fact that it views crime politically, rather than as a series of discreet incidents. Instead of responding to criminal incidents in a piecemeal fashion, there is a growing trend toward problem-solving as a more effective and long-lasting approach to fighting crime and restoring order. For example, analysis of calls for service in various cities has shown that there are relatively few locations which generate a disproportionate demand for police service. There are at least two ways to deal with that problem: 1) hire more police to improve the capacity of the department to continue responding to the ever-increasing demand, or 2) enlist the aid of the entire community in working with the police to help solve the underlying problems in those areas. The latter approach is more closely aligned to the community policing philosophy, and it requires significant operational modifications in departments which ascribe to it.

Community policing is not "soft policing," nor is it a panacea by which all of society's problems can be addressed and resolved. Instead, community policing merely reaffirms the obvious, namely that policing is a complex responsibility, and police officers are much more than agents of law enforcement. Indeed, as important as it is to apprehend criminals, it must be acknowledged that overcrowded prisons spill their surplus back into the community, and the devastating cycle continues and grows.

Dealing with the frustration of what some have called "the revolving doors of the criminal justice system," some agencies have endeavored to modify their approach to fighting crime. This chapter will discuss the change implications of community-based policing as it relates to police investigations and investigators.

Historical Perspective

To properly consider future trends pertaining to criminal investigators, it is necessary to look back and consider the evolution of criminal investigations since the turn of the century in order to understand why change is currently necessary.[1]

Detectives around the turn of the century (1900-1930) enjoyed considerable autonomy. "The political machines which ran the cities often ran the police departments. Detectives not only mixed with the criminal element but sometimes regulated criminal enterprise for the benefit of the local politicians and themselves."[2] Police officers and detectives were more loyal to politicians than to their departments and the community. Corruption was widespread, managers were amateurish, and most police organizations were politically vulnerable.[3] Major reforms led to the creation of Civil Service Systems to take politics and corruption out of police work by the end of the "Roaring Twenties."[4]

During the Professional Era (1930-1970), the central mission was crime control. Centralized organizational structures were predominant. Responsibilities became highly specialized. There was a heavy emphasis on technology, and organizations were semi-military in nature. Discipline of officers became a major issue during this era, and anti-corruption/ politics initiatives began. Police departments became more technically sophisticated in investigating crime.

One of the first empirical studies of criminal investigations came from the professional era. In 1965, the President's Commission on Law Enforcement and Administration of Justice Report contained findings from a study conducted by the Institute of Defense Analysis in conjunction with the Los Angeles Police Department. The Commissions Task Force Report indicated that 25 percent of all crimes reported to the police resulted "in arrest or other clearances."[5] Of those cleared, 75 percent were cleared by arrest, 90 percent made by patrol officers. The most important factor in clearance was determined to be whether or not a suspect was named in the initial report. If the suspect was neither known to the victim nor arrested at the scene of the crime, the chances of his being arrested were slim.[6]

During the 1970s, policing became more reactive to issues, more highly specialized and programmatic. We saw an increase in directed activities and the development of specialization.

A 1970 study by the New York City Rand Institute found that a substantial amount of detectives' time was wasted on the investigation of cases that could not be solved. The conclusion was that cases should be selected for follow-up investigation based on the likelihood of possible solution.[7]

In 1972, the Stanford Research Institute (SRI) received a grant from the National Institute of Law Enforcement and Criminal Justice to develop criteria from an analysis of burglary cases for six police agencies in Alameda County, California. The study determined the predictability of solving burglary cases. The model correctly predicts 67 to 90 percent of the outcomes.

During the 1970s, policing became more reactive to issues, more highly specialized and programmatic. The Rand Institute found that a substantial amount of detectives' time was wasted on the investigation of cases that could not be solved.

According to Greenberg and Wasserman:[8]

> All criminal cases do not have an equal potential for solution; a large number of cases solve themselves when particular investigative elements are present; in the absence of these elements, certain cases should be screened out of the investigative process. These conclusions lie in direct contrast to traditional investigative strategy which supports active investigations, to varying degrees, of almost all criminal cases.

In 1975, the Rand Corporation's Study of the Criminal Investigative Process sought to describe "Investigative Organizations and Practices" including how detectives spent their time and how crimes were solved.[9]

The Rand Study found that:

- Substantially more than half of all serious crimes receive no more than superficial attention from investigators.

- An investigator's time is largely consumed in reviewing reports, documenting files, and attempting to locate and interview victims on cases that experience shows will not be solved.

- The single most important determinant of whether or not a case will be solved is the information the victim supplies to the immediate responding patrol officer.

- Of those that are ultimately cleared but in which the perpetrator is not identified at the time of the initial report, almost all are cleared as a result of routine police procedures requiring no imaginative exercise of investigative experience and skill.

Some of the suggestions recommended by the Rand Study to improve investigative productivity were:

- Reduce follow-up investigation on all cases except those involving the most serious offenses.

- Assign generalist-investigators (who would handle the obvious leads in routine cases) to the local operations commander.

- Assign serious-offense investigations to closely supervised teams, rather than to individual investigators.

- Increase the use of information processing systems in lieu of investigators.

- Initiate programs designed to impress on citizens the crucial role they play in crime solution.

A response to remedy the "investigative inefficiencies" outlined in the Rand and SRI Reports resulted in the development of a national program to help law enforcement agencies more effectively manage criminal investigations. Although representatives from the agencies involved in *Managing the Criminal Investigation* process indicated the program was successful, analysis of findings were less encouraging. While the initial test of MCI failed to produce more than it promised, it did provide a milestone for future development.[10] Greenberg and Wasserman indicate that the implementation of MCI be viewed as an ongoing process. They suggest several "Conditions for Success" in implementing MCI:

- Commitment from top management
- Training
- Call screening system
- Data system and analysis
- Cost considerations

An important component of MCI included expanding the responsibilities of patrol officers in the investigative process. This change from tradition required patrol officers to perform more comprehensive "initial investigations." It also included latitude to seek "early case closures" through following leads obtained during the initial investigation throughout the arrest, or telling the victim that further investigation was unlikely in the event of no meaningful evidence.

The 1970s ended with detectives feeling threatened because of management's interest in better accounting for detectives' time and activities.

The 1970s ended with detectives feeling threatened because of management's interest in better accounting for detectives' time and activities. There was clearly a need to develop a case screening process, and to expand the police officer's role to perform some follow-up investigations.

The 1980s saw many police agencies attempting to develop processes, to deal with increasing problems in our neighborhoods, and to rethink the method of service delivery to accomplish this mission. Police officers' roles were expanded, and community interaction was promoted.

Herman Goldstein introduced "Problem-Oriented Policing," identifying those locations and/or individuals who generate a high volume of calls for service or repetitive calls and developing proactive strategies to eliminate problems.[11]

In 1987, Rossman identified things departments can do to improve the quality of investigations. They are:[12]

- An emphasis by an agency's top manager that improving the quality of investigations be established as a high priority goal.

- Using measure of investigative quality in selection, assignment, rotation system, work load management, paperwork reduction, and improved report preparation.

- Improved feedback from the prosecutor and the courts.

- The transmission of the police management's commitment to quality investigation throughout the department.

At the present time, the police profession continues to struggle to identify alternative methods of service delivery. Agencies more and more are turning to community policing as opposed to conventional policing models used the past few decades. Major cities are altering organizational systems to support this change. Performance evaluation, training, and communication systems, as well as the roles of the police officer and criminal investigator, are changing.

Why We Need to Change the Way We Conduct Criminal Investigations

Interestingly, during this same period of time, from the late 1970s into the 1980s, there was much similar scrutiny on the efficiency and effectiveness of uniformed patrol operations. Two studies completed by the Kansas City Police Department on preventive patrol and response to citizen calls for service called into serious question the random and reactive nature of these well established patrol strategies. A further examination of this issue was launched by the National Institute of Justice in 1980 in the form of the Differential Police Response (DPR) to citizen calls for service. This field test confirmed what earlier research had suggested: rapid police response to all citizen calls for service was only critical in a very small percentage of these calls. Otherwise, rapid response alone had no measurable impact upon the successful resolution of the call.

The implications of this operational patrol reality to the investigative functions become very clear:

- Patrol officers responded to the scene of a crime not to conduct a true preliminary investigation, but rather to simply document on an offense report what happened, and then clear the call in order to quickly respond to another call.

- Once the case reached the investigative unit, there were often times complaints about the quality of the alleged preliminary investigation which result in many investigators starting over on the case.

At the same time, increased volume of cases requiring investigation has placed investigative resources under increasing pressure. According to Peter Doone, Chief Inspector with the New Zealand Police:

Traditional deployment of detectives within departments has been to establish a large centralized unit responsible for investigating a comparatively small number of the most serious crimes.

> The result has been a system of prioritizing both patrol and investigative functions to the stage where response time for low priority calls for service are measured in hours and sometimes days, while the chances of a burglary or car theft offense without obvious leads receiving significant investigative attention are remote. A system developed and implemented in the 1950s and 1960s is cracking under the strain of the crime problems of the 1980s.

Chief Inspector Doone suggests that there is an increasing polarity between the patrol and investigative functions within a police department. Doone says that patrol officers and their managers are frequently critical of the performance of detectives whom they see as elitist, secretive and ineffective in solving crime. Perceptions of detective working predominantly day shift, generally free from supervision and showing few obvious signs of productive activity, exacerbate these feelings.[13]

The detective function has been poorly directed and managed.

Traditional deployment of detectives within departments has been to establish a large centralized unit responsible for investigating a comparatively small number of the most serious crimes and some specialized classes of crime city-wide.[14]

Some decentralized units deployed at divisional stations investigate the less important crimes. Day-to-day contact with patrol officers is limited. This structure and development independent of patrol has not assisted attempts to penetrate the commonly perceived mystique of detective work. According to Greenberg and Wasserman:[15]

> Quite simply, the findings suggest that the value of the patrol officer in the initial investigation has been underestimated: the value of the detective in follow-up activities has been overestimated; and the role of each can be redefined in a way that can improve the allocation of resources devoted to investigation activities.

Research pertaining to criminal investigations is clear: much investigative effort has been put into cases which have inherently low probability of being solved. Research further suggests that the detective function has been poorly directed and managed.

Research has shown that unless leads to the identity of the perpetrator are available at the time the crime is reported, the chances of solving it are slim. This is not always the case. Police managers can cite sufficient cases where despite the lack of leads at the offset, an effectively led team investigation can and does result in the identification and apprehension of the offender.[16]

J.E. Eck (1987), in an unpublished paper addressing Canadian Police Chiefs, stated:[17]

> Generally we find in our detective branch some of our most talented people. I can't think of a single police agency in which someone is promoted to the detective branch because they've been very good at something. So if detective units are not performing, it's not due to lack of talent or trained personnel. It's probably because of a lack of something else. How do we capture that talent? How do we get them to something more worthwhile if indeed research is correct?

Future police department organizational models must be structured and managed so that all units have a common and well integrated commitment to effective crime fighting and problem solving in collaboration with the community. Given the present levels of crime and violence in many of our communities, the police can ill afford to maintain the compartmentalized strategy for responding to and investigating crime and other problems afflicting these communities.

Implications for Change

A review of the history of investigations and related research thus far reveals several implications and/or ideas that should be evaluated when considering future trends pertaining to the criminal investigative function. They are:

- Expanded community interaction and involvement.

- Direct focus on *resolving* crime and other problems.

- Changes in internal police operational roles to ensure collective and shared responsibility for crime fighting.

- Improved management of criminal investigations to include better case screening, identification, and utilization of solvability factors as a basis for follow-up case assignment, and to expand analyses of crime trends and patterns.

- Improved liaison with the courts and prosecutors as a means of developing training for investigators, and to ensure quality control of the investigators' work product.

- Development of crime analysis systems, not only to identify crime trends and patterns, but also to identify and track "habitual offenders" who contribute disproportionately to the crime problem.

- Integrating investigators, centralized and decentralized, with patrol officers.

- Expanding the role of patrol officers in the criminal investigative process.

Given the present levels of crime and violence, the police can ill afford to maintain the compartmentalized strategy for responding to and investigating crime.

Some cities presently are making attempts to integrate criminal investigators more directly into the community and to improve the operational linkage with patrolmen.

The Houston Police Department, in 1987, opened the first of several decentralized Command Stations. A decision was made to decentralize criminal investigations along with other functions. At this same time, Houston also implemented "Neighborhood Oriented Policing." The Houston "NOP" philosophy promotes community interaction, problem identification, and planning and organizing resources to solve and prevent crime and social problems.

Over a three-year period, the Westside Criminal Investigators evolved from crime specialist to area generalist. The Westside Investigators have geographical areas of responsibilities. Those areas coincide with patrol officers' beats and neighborhood assignments. It is intended that the patrol officers, detectives, patrol sergeants, and crime analysts will develop into teams of interactive service units.[18] It is believed that working as team members with the same area of responsibility and concern for crime problems in that area, patrol officers and detectives interacting with concerned citizens will have a positive impact on the resolution of community problems.

Random patrol and random investigation causes random results.

Merging Patrol and Investigative Operations

Investigative operations of most departments still remain centralized. They also tend to focus on specific time frames (shifts) rather than defined areas. The common denominator of both investigation and patrol operations is that they react to incidents, either calls for service or investigations after the fact. Random patrol and random investigation causes random results.

Patrol and investigative operations tend to work largely as separate entities under different management systems. Instead of consolidating resources and approaching policing as one issue, each has selected a part of the whole and has attempted to deal with it independently.

One of the most critical intra-agency relationships in a police department is that of the investigative and patrol functions. To operate efficiently, each function should be highly dependent on the other. Yet this is often one of the most strained points of exchange within law enforcement agencies.[19]

The patrol officer functions in an uncertain hostile atmosphere with the ambitious, often unpopular mandate to maintain order. The detective, however, usually enjoys higher pay, more interesting work and more freedom, and has a better sense of what is expected of him. When one reflects upon these differences, it does not seem strange that conflicts may arise between operational units.[20]

Traditionally, patrol units have been given responsibility only for preliminary investigations or complete responsibility for investigation of "minor" offenses. At some point prior to the conclusion, responsibility for investigation of serious crimes is handed off to the investigative specialist. The patrol officer feels he is left with only routine and mundane investigations, while the detective investigates the interesting or spectacular cases. The patrol officer relegated to the role of "report taker" may see little personal incentive to conduct a thorough and meticulous preliminary investigation or to forward any information not specifically required by procedure for the ultimate closure and will receive no credit for a subsequent arrest made by the detective bureau.[21]

A lack of common identity may result in a "we versus they" relationship between the groups. This relationship clearly is not conducive to close cooperation and exchange of information needed for combined crime reduction efforts.

According to Joseph J. Staft:

> A means of establishing strong personal and operational relationships between patrol and investigative personnel is the adoption of a team policing model. The term "team policing" means combining the patrol and investigative functions within one geographically based organizational unit.[22]

Both entities are vitally important in our criminal justice system. The challenge for police managers is to identify new organizational models to accomplish the integration of patrol and investigative function in a decentralized mode, working with citizens in neighborhoods to solve and prevent crime problems.

There are several ways to improve the communications between patrol and investigative operations. The simplest way is to develop rules and

Successful criminal investigations in the future will not simply depend upon the efficiencies of uniformed patrol and criminal investigations.

programs, or the development of a formal hierarchy with specific avenues for communication. The weakness of these systems is that information channels become overloaded. To prevent overloading of hierarchical channels, lateral information channels must be developed. The simplest form of lateral relations is direct contact between two people who share a problem.[23] This means simply permitting direct contact and dialogue between officers assigned to patrol and those assigned to investigations. All too often, when investigative and patrol units are separated, investigators fail to solicit information actively and patrol officers fail to volunteer it. Thus, no communication takes place. To obtain greater capability for exchanging information between patrol officers and investigators, they can be assigned to the same organizational unit by creating task forces or permanent teams.[24] A task force or team under the direction of a single supervisor is a reasonable consideration for the patrol and investigative functions.

Peter Doone suggests that when thinking of ways to integrate the investigative function with community and problem-solving concepts, two things need to be considered:

- The tension between centralized management and control of resources versus a decentralized structure.

- The tension between investigators, their places in the organization and what they stand for versus balance of the police organization and the community they work within.

He concludes that it is a reasonable consensus that a decentralized mode of operation utilizing community policing and problem-solving strategies offers a substantially better way of providing police services.

The challenges facing policing in the future on how to substantively improve the criminal investigative function go well beyond simply decentralizing a number of investigators. Indeed, there is a whole new strategy of policing emerging in this country -- *Community Oriented Policing* -- that is forcing a comprehensive reexamination of all internal systems, policies and practices that relate to the total delivery of all police services in the community. What is clearly happening in this ongoing transformation process is the realization that the *police organization*, not just individual units, must focus on how to improve its crime-fighting capacity. Every unit within the organization, whether operational or staff support, must have a stake in the crime-fighting action. Successful criminal investigations in the future, therefore, will not simply depend upon the efficiencies of uniformed patrol *and* criminal investigations.

Looking into this future, there are some clear issues which will require attention as police departments revise or construct crime-fighting models:

> *There should be complete parity between uniformed*
> *patrol officers and criminal investigators; one cannot*
> *be viewed as more important than the other.*

Traditionally, patrol officers have felt neglected and ignored by the police organization. Indeed, career success as perceived by many police officers is defined by getting out of patrol as soon as possible in one's career and getting into a specialized unit. None of these specialized units has been more glamorized than criminal investigations. Being a detective and working in plain-clothes has been a highly desirable "plum" in policing. With the advent of Community Oriented Policing, the pendulum has begun the swing back toward patrol, and in most cases with great emphasis and attention. In many departments, detectives feel either threatened or like they are not a part of the ongoing implementation of Community Oriented Policing. If meaningful improvements are to be made in policing in general, and criminal investigations in particular, the pendulum cannot be allowed to swing so far back that criminal investigators become the "victims" of the organization. Good street patrol officers and good detectives are equally valuable to any police department.

> *Sophisticated and well targeted operational crime*
> *analysis must be readily available to patrol officers*
> *and investigators.*

In many departments, detectives feel either threatened or like they are not a part of the ongoing implementation of Community Oriented Policing. Good street patrol officers and good detectives are <u>equally</u> valuable to any police department.

The timely, accurate and complete analysis of all major crime types can be a vital resource in the fight against crime at the patrol level. This analysis has two components: technical and operational. Technical crime analysis if that which can be provided through computers and programming. The challenge here is to automatically convert crime information into a form that is readily usable on the street by patrol officers and investigators so that they are better able to understand the scope of the crime problems in their specific area of responsibility.

Working together with patrol officers, decentralized investigators concentrate on fighting <u>all</u> crime within specific geographic boundaries.

Operational crime analysis, on the other hand, results from interpreting the data to determine emerging trends and patterns of criminal activity for the purpose of enhancing the investigation as well as preventing or deterring their occurrence.

Establishment of crime-fighting teams is required to ensure a well-integrated and single-focused strategy to combat crime and other problems in neighborhoods.

An integrated strategy to more effectively fight crime is not a new and innovative idea in policing. There have been many attempts in the past to implement such strategies (i.e. team policing). These efforts have failed, in part, due to the ultimate rejection of this strategy by the many vested interests within police organizations. Additionally, however, they may have failed because they defined crime as a police problem, rather than as a community problem. Based on that fundamental error, resulting crime-fighting strategies were rarely devoid of community commitment or assistance. Community Oriented Policing represents a solution to this obstacle (see Murphy's chapter). Since crime is a community problem, the resources of the entire community must be mobilized to combat it. Government is only one part of the community, and the police department is just one part of government. In this crime-fighting model, all of the resources of the community are focused on crime control. Community Oriented Policing *systematically* rather than *programmatically* alters the police role and response toward crime. Furthermore, the internal value system that drives this new strategy demands a collaboration within the organization, and between the organization and external resources, that focuses on achieving meaningful results rather than simply documenting high levels of activity.

There is a need to distinguish between the rule of the centralized criminal investigator from that of the decentralized investigator.

The movement toward decentralizing selected criminal investigative functions and resources is widespread throughout police departments in the country. There is more to effective decentralization that just re-aligning people and organizational boxes, however. The decentralized investigators must fit in with and complement the patrol officers in daily operations. They become area specialists and crime generalists. In other words, working together with patrol officers, decentralized investigators concentrate on fighting *all* crime within specific geographic boundaries.

The centralized investigators, on the other hand, should focus their efforts on specific crime types (i.e. robbery, burglary). As crime specific experts, they are best suited to perform *operational* crime analysis on a city-wide basis. Their responsibility is to share information with decentralized investigative teams, and to help coordinate responses to identified crime problems that span geographic boundaries. Additionally, they represent a solid resource in the development of strategic plans aimed at preventing and deterring certain types of crime in the future.

> *There must be changes in the way police receive, manage, and respond to citizen requests for services generated through 911.*

As was alluded to earlier in this chapter, there has been extensive research and experimentation on police response to citizen calls for service. Departments throughout the United States have for some time been trying to reduce the calls dispatched to uniformed patrol units through means such as telephone reporting units and delayed dispatches of low priority calls. There are a series of reasons why it is now time to become more aggressive in identifying a multitude of alternative responses to a high percentage of such calls that would be *acceptable* to the community. Although this issue is not the subject of this discussion, it is relevant to the issue of building strong criminal investigative teams in the future consisting of patrol officers and investigators. There are many such "services" that could be offered to the community on a proactive basis in return for their support to off-load certain calls for service from patrol units. One thing is for certain: ways must be found to significantly intensify the role of uniformed police officers in the crime-fighting loop.

Hopefully, this chapter will stimulate further discussion and debate within the police profession concerning how we can improve the criminal investigative process in the future. It is not meant to offer all of the potential solutions, because there are many in this business with good ideas. One purpose, however, has been to suggest that we must now be willing to challenge conventional wisdom in the vital area of criminal investigation. As has been stated here, it no longer can be solely the detective's job to investigate and close criminal cases. It must become the entire organization's commitment and responsibility.

It no longer can be solely the detective's job to investigate and close criminal cases. It must become the entire organization's commitment and responsibility.

Conclusion

As the expectations of citizens change, so must the police agencies that serve the citizen. When change becomes necessary, it is important to allow our minds to grow and not to be inhibited or constrained by conventional thinking. The traditional approach to police work, with its focus on rapid response, increased arrests, and higher clearance rates, has failed to control the nation's growing crime problem. It is important to point out here that these traditional approaches, in and of themselves, are not bad or wrong; they are merely insufficient. Community/problem oriented policing expands the rules of police officers, supervisors, managers and, yes, detectives. More importantly, perhaps, it defines the police response as part of a larger community response to the crime problem.

Police managers seriously attempting to adopt a community-oriented crime strategy are finding it necessary to promote increased community interaction and problem resolution as part of daily operations at every level of the organization. Many such managers are reorganizing, dencentralizing, and changing role responsibilities at both the operational and managerial levels.

When we take a look at the history of the criminal investigator, and if we agree with available research and learn from the experiences of those cities experimenting with change in this area, then there are several future implications to consider. First, the police officer's role should be expanded to allow for more direct investigation in the initial follow-up investigations and early case closure process. Second, some investigators should be decentralized and assigned geographical areas of responsibility that coincide with areas assigned to patrol officers. Third, detectives should be assigned proactive as well as reactive responsibilities. Just as a patrol officer responds to calls for service and identifies and resolves problems, the detective should investigate crimes and work with line officers and citizens to identify and resolve community problems. The idea is not only to arrest violators but to prevent crime from happening in the first place. Fourth, rather than attempt to investigate every case, only those cases that survive a thorough screening and assignment process should be investigated. In larger cities, this screening can be facilitated through automation. Fifth, crime trends should be analyzed by centralized crime experts, and comprehensive crime-fighting strategies should be implemented by decentralized teams of police officers,

Traditional approaches, in and of themselves, are not bad or wrong; they are merely insufficient.

investigators and citizens, using all of the resources that can be brought to bear on the problem.

If current trends continue, the future criminal investigator will have opportunities that exceed those of merely struggling to keep pace with an ever-increasing case load. Investigators will have an array of options to pursue. Some may choose to become crime specialists, focusing their energies on analyzing crime trends and developing strategies to deal with them. Some may choose, instead, to be area specialists, committed to fighting all kinds of crime in a given geographical area.

NOTES

1. Kelling, George L. *Police and Communities: The Quiet Revolution.* Washington, D.C.: U.S. Department of Justice, National Institute of Justice, Vol. 1, 1988.
2. Eck, John E. "Solving Crimes: The Investigation of Burglary and Robbery," *Investigative Operations Neighborhood Oriented Policing.* Washington, D.C.: Police Executive Research Forum. Houston: Houston Police Print Shop, 1989, p. 48.
3. Koby, Thomas G. "History of Policing" (lecture). Houston: Police Sergeants Inservice Training, 1990.
4. Marchiafava, Louis J. "The Houston Police: 1878-1948." Houston: William March, Rice University. Quoted in Bieck, W.H. and Oettmeier, T.N., *Integrating Investigative Operations Through Neighborhood Oriented Policing.* Houston: Houston Police Print Shop, 1989, p. 49.
5. Silver, Isidore. *The Challenge of Crime in a Free Society: A Report by the President's Commission on Law Enforcement and Administration.* New York, NY: An Avon Book, 1968. Quoted in Bieck, W.H. and Oettmeier, T.N., *Integrating Investigative Operations Through Neighborhood Oriented Policing.* Houston: Houston Police Print Shop, 1989, p. 60.
6. Ibid., p. 60.
7. Eck, John E. "Managing Case Assignments: The Burglary Investigation Decision Model." Washington, D.C.: Police Executive Research Forum, 1979. Quoted in Bieck, W.H. and Oettmeier, T.N., *Integrating Investigative Operations Through Neighborhood Oriented Policing.* Houston: Houston Police Print Shop, 1989, p. 61.
8. Wasserman, Robert and Greenberg, Ilene. *Managing Criminal Investigation.* Washington, D.C.: U.S. Department of Justice, LEAA, National Institute of Law Enforcement and Criminal Justice, 1979.
9. Greenwood, Peter W. and Petersilia, Joan. "The Criminal Investigation Process," *Summary and Policy Implications*, Vol. 1. Santa Monica, California: Ran Corporation, 1975.
10. Ibid., Wasserman and Greenberg.
11. Goldstein, Herman. "Improving Policing: A Problem Oriented Approach," *Crime and Delinquency*, Vol. 25, No. 2, 1979.
12. Rossman, Henry H. "Improving the Quality of Police Investigations" (unpublished article), 1987.

13. Doone, Peter. *Potential Impacts of Community Policing on Criminal Investigation Strategies.* Wellington: Victoria University, Study Series, 1989.
14. Ibid.
15. Ibid.
16. Ibid., Wasserman and Greenberg.
17. Ibid., Doone.
18. Eck, John E. "Address to Canadian Police Chiefs" (unpublished paper). Canada, 1987.
19. Ibid., Bieck and Oettmeier, 1989.
20. Ibid., Doone.
21. Staft, Joseph J. *Effects of Organizational Design on Communications Between Patrol and Investigative Functions*, Part I. Cincinnati, Ohio: 19).
22. Ibid.
23. Ibid.
24. Galbraith, Jay. *Designing Complex Organizations.* Reading, Mass.: Addison-Wesley Publishing Co., 1973.

Subject Index

APPENDIX I

About the Contributors

Geoffrey P. Alpert,

professor of criminal justice at the University of South Carolina, holds a B.A. and M.A. from the University of Oregon and a Ph. D. from Washington State University. Dr. Alpert is a research professor at the Institute of Public Affairs, University of South Carolina, a former Principal Investigator in the Police Pursuit Project sponsored by the U.S. Department of Transportation, and has served as Research Director, Police Pursuit Project, Dade Association of Chiefs of Police, Dade County Florida.

He has published numerous professional articles and books in law enforcement and criminal justice. His latest book, is *Police Pursuit Driving* (Greenwood Press). He is the author, with Lori Fredell of *Police Use of Deadly Force: Firearms and Vehicles* to be published in 1992 (Waveland Press). Dr. Alpert is a nationally recognized expert on pursuit driving issues and has served as an expert witness in landmark civil and criminal actions. He most recently conducted a study for the Dallas Police Department on the use of Deadly Force.

Cornelius J. Behan

is a native New Yorker and served 31 years with the New York City Police Department. He rose through the ranks until assuming responsibility for all patrol forces. During his career, he was commander of detectives, the Public Morals Bureau. Planning and the 17th Division in Queens County, the Police Academy, Brooklyn South Area and Chief of Personnel. As chief of Patrol he commanded 21 thousand sworn officers and 5 thousand civilians.

In 1977, by unanimous vote of the county council, he was appointed Chief of the Baltimore County Police Department in Maryland, the 25th largest in the county. He is responsible for modernizing the department, creating the Computer Crime Unit, Legal and Psychological Services Unit, The Police Foundation, and introducing community policing and management development.

Chief Behan received his baccalaureate degree from John Jay College of Criminal Justice where he has been honored as a distinguished alumnus. He has authored numerous articles and received many honors and awards, and is the past president of the National Executive Institute, Maryland Chiefs of Police Association, and the Police Executive Research Forum.

John W. Bizzack

is a twenty-two year police veteran and is presently a Captain with the Lexington, Kentucky, Division of Police. He has served at all levels and areas of police service and holds degrees in criminal justice and business administration and is presently involved in doctoral study. He is also certified to teach a variety of subjects related to law enforcement.

He has written various articles about law enforcement issues and is the author of three books: *Police Management for the 1990s: A Pracitioner's Road Map* (Thomas), *No Nonsense Leadership* (Autumn House) and *Criminal Investigation: Managing for Results* (Autumn House). He has a wide range of experience in criminal investigation, police management, law enforcement accreditation and community involvement activities. He has served on numerous federal, state and local panels and task forces concerned with the improvement of policing and other social issues. He is the recipient of various awards, commendations and letters of merit from his and other agencies as well as from the private sector.

Anthony V. Bouza

is a native of Spain, emigrating to the U.S. as a youth. His police career has spanned nearly four decades. He rose through the ranks of the New York City Police Department to command all Bronx forces. He served as Deputy Chief for the New York City Transit Police and Adjunct Professor at John Jay College of Law Enforcement before he was appointed Chief of Police in Minneapolis, Minnesota in 1980.

He earned his B.B.A. and M.P.A. from Baruch School at City University of New York. Chief Bouza served as Chief of Police in Minneapolis until 1988. Since then he has authored two book: *The Police Mystique* and *Bronx Beat*, written columns for The Tribune, served as a consultant and expert witness. He has also served as Gaming Commissioner for the State of Minnesota and President of the Center to Prevent Handgun Violence, Washington D.C. Chief Bouza is the author of various published and unpublished articles and papers relating to various issues in policing. His other books include Police Administration, Organization and Performance and Police Intelligence. He continues to be an effective advocate and spokesperson for reform measures.

Eve & Carl Buzawa

have co-written two books concerning domestic violence issues. Their first book, *Domestic Violence: The Criminal Justice Response* was published in 1990 (Sage Publications). *Domestic Violence: The Changing Criminal Justice Response* is scheduled for release in 1992 (Greenwood Press).

Eve Buzuwa received her B.A. from the University of Rochester and her Masters and doctorate from Michigan State University. She has written extensively in the area of domestic violence and policing and is a Professor in the Department of Criminal Justice at the University of Massachusetts - Lowell.

Carl Buzuwas received his B.A. from the University of Rochester, his Masters from the University of Michigan and a J.C. from Harvard Law School. He is in private practice.

Peter C. Dodenhoff

has been the editor of Law Enforcement News since it was founded in 1975 by John Jay College of Criminal Justice. He has written articles on a wide range of law enforcement and criminal justice topics, and has conduced in-depth interviews with scores of leading police professionals, public officials, academicians and others. He holds a B.A. in criminal justice from John Jay College.

G. Patrick Gallagher

is currently the Director of the Institute for Liability Management and Vice President with Gallagher Bassett Services, Inc. He has become a nationally recognized expert in managing law enforcement liability through his extensive experience in providing services to review and develop policies, provide expert witness services, conduct a wide range of supervisory and management training and perform management studies and liability assessments.

In prior positions, he was Director of Police Standards and Training for the state of Florida, Director of Police Foundation's Police Executive Institute, and Director of Public Safety for South Bend, Indiana.

He has authored numerous articles addressing the management of police liability and has co-authored a text on comparing policing titled: *Behind the Uniform*. Additionally, he writes a monthly column for the British Police Review.

Kenne Howard,

from Lexington, Kentucky, has been a teacher for the past 18 years. She earned her Bachelor's Degree from the University of Kentucky in 1973. She also holds a Master's Degree in Secondary Education and is currently completing additional graduate hours in Administration and Supervision in Education, also at the University of Kentucky.

During her career, she has taught at the elementary and secondary levels, coordinated and written curriculum, and provided numerous workshops for parents, educators and police officers.

In 1990, she was named the National D.A.R.E. (Drug Abuse Resistance Education) Educator of the Year, by the National D.A.R.E. Officer's Association. She is married to a police lieutenant from the Lexington, KY police department.

Patricia A. Kelly

has a doctorate in English from Brown University and is an associate professor of journalism at Northeastern University in Boston., where she has been honored for excellence in teaching. She has developed two inter-disciplinary courses for journalism and criminal justice majors, and her articles describing those experiments have been published in education and media outlets.

Dr. Kelly has received first-place awards from United Press International and form New England and Massachusetts press associations for her police reporting and feature writing for daily newspapers. She has taught seminars on police-media relations and writing skills for IPTM (Institute of Police Technology and Management), University of North Florida and has consulted on media issues with law enforcement agencies in Massachusetts and New York. She is editor of *Police and the Media: Bridging Troubled Waters* (Thomas).

Richard Leo

holds a Master's Degree in Sociology from the University of Chicago. A Jacob K. Javits Fellowship recipient, he is currently a second year graduate and law student in the Jurisprudence and Social Policy Program at the University of California, Berkeley.

He has begun research for his doctoral dissertation, which will be an empirically-grounded sociological analysis of police interrogation in America.

Patrick V. Murphy

is director, Police Policy Board, The U.S. Conference of Mayors and chairman, Murphy, Mayo and Associates. He was president, for 12 years, of the Police Foundation, a private institute which produced important research on police use of deadly force, women on patrol, managing criminal investigation and the Kansas City Preventive Patrol Experiment which found undirected motorized patrol to have an insignificant effect on crime prevention. This study was responsible for stimulating the strong trend toward community oriented policing.

He was chief police executive in New York, Detroit, Washington and Syracuse as well as the first administrator of the U.S. Law Enforcement Assistance Administration (LEAA). He reformed the control structure of the New York Police Department at the time of the Knapp Commission into one of strict accountability at every level. He revised the use of firearms policy in three cities.

He has written extensively on policing and served on innumerable blue-ribbon panels throughout the world on improving the administration of justice. He holds a B.A. from St. John's University and an M.P.A. from the City College of New York.

R. Bruce McBride

is Executive Director for Public Safety for the State University of New York. In this capacity, he is responsible for the coordination of law enforcement and personal safety operations at SUNY's 28 campuses.

Before his appointment in 1987, Dr. McBride was professor of criminal justice at the SUNY College of Technology, Utica/Rome and Utica College at Syracuse University. While at Utica./Rome, he served a department chair for four years.

Dr. McBride began his law enforcement career as a campus security officers at SUNY Oswego in 1972. He was a police officer and investigator for the Baldwinsville Police Department. In this post he was appointed the public relations officer and began a program on criminal justice education in his district's school system.

He is the co-author of *Proactive Police Management* and *Criminal Justice Internships* and various articles on police and campus police management. He received his Bachelor's, Master's and Doctorate degrees in Educational Administration and Policy Studies from SUNY Albany. He is also an instructor and advisor for the Bureau of Municipal Police for its executive management course and police physical standards committee.

Timothy N. Oettmeier

is an 18 year veteran with the Houston Police Department. He has served in positions of patrol, dispatch, and training. Additionally, he has served an executive assistant to Assistant Chiefs of Police and the Chief of Police.

As a Lieutenant, he is presently assigned to the Houston Police Academy as its Director. He has attained a Bachelor of Science Degree, majoring in psychology, from the University of Houston (1975); a Master of Arts degree, majoring in Criminology and Corrections, from Sam Houston State University (1978); and a Doctor of Philosophy degree, majoring in Criminal Justice, from

Sam Houston State University (1982). Dr. Oettmeier has also published several articles and written numerous reports on police management and operational issues.

Lawrence W. Sherman

is an experimental criminologist: an inventor and tester of strategies for crime control. His best-known work in the Minneapolis domestic violence experiment, which was the first controlled experiment in the effects of arrest on crime. That experiment helped influence almost half of the U.S. cities overs

100,000, which changed to a domestic violence arrest policy within two years after the Minneapolis results supporting that policy were announced.

The President and founder of the Crime Control Institute in Washington, D.C., and a professor of criminology at the University of Maryland at College Park, Sherman has directed 15 field experiments with close to $8 million in federal funds, obtained primarily under peer review competitions.

The author of over eighty books and professional journal articles, Sherman began his career with the New York City Police Department as a Sloan Foundation Urban Fellow in the Lindsay administration. From 1979 to 1985 he served as Director of Research and Vice President of the Police Foundation, which was created by the Ford Foundation in 1970. He earned a Ph.D. in sociology at Yale University in 1976, a Diploma in Criminology from Cambridge University in 1973, an M.A. from the University of Chicago in 1970, and a B.A. from Denison University in 1970. He is marreied to Eva Fass Sherman, a Washington attorney with whom he edits the Security Law Newsletter, a monthly legal reporter for the private security field.

Jerome H. Skolnick

is Clairs Clements Dean's Professor of Law (Jurisprudence and Social Policy) at the University of California, Berkeley, in which he has held various professional positions since 1962. For ten years he was Director, Center for the Study of Law and Society.

He is the author of numerous books, articles and edited books, including *Justice Without Trial; The Politics of Protest; Society and Legal Order* (w. Richard D. Schwartz); *America's Problems* (w. Elliot Currie); *Crisis in American Institutions* (w. Elliot Currie); *Criminal Justice* (w. John Kaplan); *Police in America* (w. Thomas Grey); *House of Cards: Legalization and Control of Casino Gambling; Crime and Justice* (w. Martin Forst and Jane L. Scheiber) and most recently, (with David Bayley) *The New Blue Line: and Community Policing*.

He has taught at Yale Law School, Harvard Law School, NYU Law School, U.C. San Diego, and the University of Chicago, where he also held an appointment as Senior Social Scientist, American Bar Association.

Dr. Skolnick holds a Ph.D. in Sociology from Yale University. He has been the recipient of numerous grants, honors and awards in recognition of his research and scholarship. He has also been elected to and served on the Boards of the American Sociological Association and the Law and Society Association

William C. Smith

is Director of the Legal Services Division and former Assistant General Counsel for the South Carolina Criminal Justice Academy. He earned his B.S. from Georgetown University and his J.D. from the School of Law of the University of South Carolina.

He was the author of the legal chapter for the IADLEST Law Enforcement Driver Training Reference Guide and the legal advisor to the task force which created it. He has served as lecturer and consultant for numerous law enforcement academies and organizations on topics of police civil liabilities of emergency

vehicles operations, issues in law enforcement decertification, and numerous other procedural and substantive legal issues. He is also the Judge Advocate and legal advisor for the National Association of Professional law Enforcement Emergency Vehicle Response Training (ALERT), a non-profit corporation devoted to improvement of emergency vehicle operations training. He is an advisor to several private industry concerns on legal issues affecting pursuit simulator development.

He is also the author of numerous papers and articles on a wide range of legal issues affecting law enforcement operations: the most recent of which are *Defensability of Law Enforcement Training* (October 1990, Criminal Law Bulletin), and *Beyond City Limits* and *Into the Wood(s): A Brief Look at the Policy Impact of City of Canton v. Harris and Wood V. Ostrander* (1991 American Journal of Police.

Edward R. Thibault

received his Ph.D. from the Maxwell School of Syracuse University in 1971. with a dissertation which was published under the title "The Anomic Cop". He has a M.A. in Political Science and in Social Studies from S.U.N.Y. at Bufalo.

For the past twenty years, Professor Thibault has been on the faculty of S.U.N.Y. at Oswego and has taught course in criminal justice and sociology. He created the B.A. in Public Justice degree in 1972 and was director of this program for six years.

He has published in the Journal of Probation and Parole, the Journal of Police Sciences and Administration , The Police Chief and Crime and Delinquency. *Proactive Police Management* (Prentice-Hall, w. Lawrence M. Lynch and R.Bruce McBride) is in its second edition. This work is used extensively throughout the U.S. in higher education and police training and become something of an academic bestseller.

He has organized thirteen regional and state-wide criminal justice meetings for faculty in higher education. He has been president of the New York State Criminal Justice Educators Association, and Northeastern Association of Criminal Justice Sciences.

His major areas of expertise are police culture, juvenile justice, institutional and community corrections and violence between inmates.

Elizabeth M. Watson

joined the Houston Police Department in 1972. She earned the ranks of detective, lieutenant, captain and deputy chief before being appointed Chief of Police in January 1990.
She is now an Assistant Chief in Houston

Asst. Chief Watson implemented the Neighborhood Oriented Policing program in her department while serving as deputy chief from 1978 to 1990. Her plan became the model for the citywide Neighborhood Oriented Policing initiative.

Apart from the Houston Police Department, she is a member of a number of police and management associations. She serves on the executive committee of the I.A.C.P. and is on the editorial board of the American Journal of Police, advisory board of the Southwestern Law Enforcement Institution and the University of Houston-Downtown Criminal Justice Center.

In addition, Asst. Chief Watson works with several organizations outside the area of law enforcement. She is a member-at-large of the board of directors of the San Jacinto Area Girl Scouts and she serves on the University of Texas Health Science Center's Committee for the Prevention of Injury and Violence.

Asst. Chief Watson is an honors graduate of Texas Tech University with a degree in Psychology. Her husband is a sergeant with the Houston Police Department.

William A. Young Jr.,

joined the Houston Police Department in 1971. He rose through the ranks of the department and was promoted to Assistant Chief in 1991.

Assistant Chief Young, as a patrol captain, was responsible for first implementing and managing efforts of the Neighborhood Oriented Policing concept in 1987. These initiatives included the decentralization of criminal investigation. In 1988 he received the Manager of the Year award for this work.

During his career, he has worked extensively in the criminal investigation area, in both management and operational functions. Assistant Chief Yourg has a A.A. degree in Criminal Justice and a B.S. in Public Administration. he is also a graduate of the FBI National Academy and the Texas Law Enforcement Management Institute. He is currently involved in graduate studies.